Conducting Educational Research

Second Edition

Sara Miller McCune founded SAGE Publishing in 1965 to support the dissemination of usable knowledge and educate a global community. SAGE publishes more than 1000 journals and over 600 new books each year, spanning a wide range of subject areas. Our growing selection of library products includes archives, data, case studies and video. SAGE remains majority owned by our founder and after her lifetime will become owned by a charitable trust that secures the company's continued independence.

Los Angeles | London | New Delhi | Singapore | Washington DC | Melbourne

Conducting Educational Research

Guide to Completing a Thesis, Dissertation, or Action Research Project

Second Edition

DANIEL J. BOUDAH

East Carolina University

Los Angeles | London | New Delhi
Singapore | Washington DC | Melbourne

FOR INFORMATION:

SAGE Publications, Inc.
2455 Teller Road
Thousand Oaks, California 91320
E-mail: order@sagepub.com

SAGE Publications India Pvt. Ltd.
B 1/I 1 Mohan Cooperative Industrial Area
Mathura Road, New Delhi 110 044
India

SAGE Publications Ltd.
1 Oliver's Yard
55 City Road
London EC1Y 1SP
United Kingdom

SAGE Publications Asia-Pacific Pte. Ltd.
18 Cross Street #10-10/11/12
China Square Central
Singapore 048423

This book includes screenshots of Microsoft Excel 2003 to illustrate the methods and procedures described in the book. Microsoft Excel is a product of the Microsoft Corporation.

Printed in the United States of America

Library of Congress Cataloging-in-Publication Data

Names: Boudah, Daniel J., author.

Title: Conducting educational research : guide to completing a major project / Daniel J. Boudah.

Description: [Second edition] | Los Angeles : SAGE, [2019] | Includes bibliographical references and index.

Identifiers: LCCN 2019007660 | ISBN 9781544351698 (pbk. : alk. paper)

Subjects: LCSH: Education—Research—Methodology.

Classification: LCC LB1028 .B624 2019 | DDC 370.72—dc23
LC record available at https://lccn.loc.gov/2019007660

Acquisitions Editor: Steve Scoble
Editorial Assistant: Elizabeth You
Production Editor: Gagan Mahindra
Copy Editor: Lynne Curry
Typesetter: C&M Digitals
Proofreader: Eleni Maria Georgiou
Indexer: Wendy Allex
Cover Designer: Anupama Krishnan
Marketing Manager: Jillian Ragusa

SUSTAINABLE FORESTRY INITIATIVE
Certified Chain of Custody
At Least 10% Certified Forest Content
www.sfiprogram.org
SFI-01028

19 20 21 22 23 10 9 8 7 6 5 4 3 2 1

• Brief Contents •

• Detailed Contents •

• Preface •

Research is a broad term that usually means the systematic and rigorous process of posing a focused question, developing a hypothesis, testing the hypothesis or focus by collecting and analyzing relevant data, and drawing conclusions. Research methods vary, but the goal of research is almost always the same: to answer a question. The questions may range from "Does A cause B?" to "What is A like?" Educational research answers questions important to students, teachers, administrators, related service providers, and other stakeholders.

In an effort to encourage research-based practice and data-based decision-making, university-based teacher education programs, as well as some school-based professional development efforts, often require novice and experienced educators to conduct some form of research. For example, in university programs today, individuals who are working toward Master of Education, Master of Teaching, Master of Science in Administration, Doctor of Education, and similar degrees are required to complete a research project or thesis that involves identifying a relevant question, reviewing the literature base for information, developing a research or project plan, collecting and analyzing data, drawing conclusions, and reporting outcomes.

Purposes

Thus, this book is designed for two purposes. First, this book was written to enable university students (primarily graduate students) to engage thoughtfully in conducting educational research. Second, this book was written to help educators engage in research on "problems of practice" that leads to data-based decision-making. There are already a number of textbooks on the topic of research in education, and though many are very thorough and helpful, they may be too comprehensive to give direct assistance to students as a "field guide" *during* the process of conducting a thesis or major research project. There are also many "action research" books available, and while much of the current action research in the field of education may be of some value, it may not be sufficiently rigorous or allow educators to address many of the complexities that they face every day in schools. This book, therefore, will enable individuals in education or related fields to conduct relevant research in a systematic and rigorous way, research that will yield reliable and trustworthy outcomes that can inform practice or system issues.

Consider this a guide to be used *during* the research process rather than to introduce students to research for the first time. After a student or educator has completed at least an introductory research course, become somewhat familiar with statistics, and is ready to begin a major project or thesis, this book begins. The chapters are organized to provide guidance through the entire research process, prompting researchers to stop and apply their understandings at each step of the process. Scaffolding is, therefore, provided in the form of questions, outlines, tables, and other supports for researchers to complete from the beginning of a project to its completion, particularly to link research questions to designs, then designs to data sources, and data sources to appropriate analyses. Understanding these parts of the research process and their relationship to one another typically makes the difference in whether a novice researcher can conduct thoughtful research in education-related settings.

This book will assist education students and professionals in the step-by-step implementation of a research project or thesis, or to address a "problem of practice" in or related to a school or clinical setting. It is organized and written to provide guidance for the following tasks:

- Developing a research question
- Searching and analyzing existing literature for the current state of knowledge on a topic in question
- Developing a research plan/proposal
- Designing and conducting research, including data collection
- Analyzing and interpreting data
- Sharing the conclusions with others

The research types and designs addressed in this text are included in the table below.

Type of Research	Research Design
Experimental/Quasi-experimental	Group (posttest only, pretest-posttest, comparison group, time-series)
	Single subject (ABA, multiple baseline)
Descriptive	Qualitative (case study, grounded theory)
	Survey
	Correlational
Mixed Methods	Includes one or more designs from Experimental/Quasi-experimental and/or Descriptive types of research

Pedagogical Elements

A number of pedagogical elements are included in this book to facilitate the research process.

- Each chapter begins with an outline and chapter objectives and ends with a summary and discussion questions. Bolded words in the text are included in the Glossary.

- The "Technology in Research" boxes provide concise information on a sampling of topics to help researchers take advantage of current related technologies and online resources.

- The "In Their Own Words" vignettes contain tips and suggestions from recent graduate students and professionals who have completed projects.

- A critical element at the end of each chapter is "Your Research Project in Action." This portion of each chapter prompts students to apply what they have learned to their current research projects through a series of guiding questions or prompts. For example, in Chapter 5 on experimental and quasi-experimental designs, "Your Research Project in Action" requires students to address variables to be used, access to participants, timing of intervention, duration and location of intervention, and data sources. Practical, detailed guidance is essential to successful research, and this section helps provide a crucial linkage between knowing something *about* research and understanding how to *carry out* research in education.

Changes in the Second Edition

Several key additions and updates are included in the second edition of this book.

Key additions:

- Sections on Mixed Methods research, one on designing and conducting and one on analyzing and interpreting, found in Chapters 7 and 11

- Section on analyzing and interpreting Single Subject Design research, found in Chapter 9

Key updates:

- Extensive new references

- Technology in Research boxes

- In Their Own Words boxes

- Appendix on the use of Microsoft Excel

In summary, this book will guide you through the entire research process, from developing and focusing research questions; to searching and analyzing the existing literature; to selecting the most appropriate research design, measurement, and method(s) of analysis; to interpretation and communication of outcomes. The intended audience is educators, including teachers, administrators, counselors, clinicians, psychologists, and other education-related service providers in master's-level university programs or experienced educators in school or clinical settings. It may well be that those individuals are one and the same; that is, experienced educators working on master's degrees while continuing to work in a school or clinical setting full-time. Feedback from users of the first edition of this text has proven very useful and provided excellent validation for the organization and presentation of information for the intended audience. Therefore, I am confident that the text will be of great value to you.

• Acknowledgments •

This book would not have been possible without the early efforts and contributions of Dr. Peggy Weiss of George Mason University. Thank you, Peggy.

In addition, I want to thank my wife, Pamela. Thank you for your patience, support, and ideas regarding the usefulness of this book.

I am grateful to the editors and staff at SAGE for your encouragement and invaluable assistance throughout the production process.

Thank you, also, to the following reviewers for your thoughtful and valuable feedback on the second edition.

David L. Brown, Texas A&M University-Commerce

Earl E. Thomas, Saint Xavier University-Chicago

Eric Shyman, St. Joseph's College, New York

Janine S. Fisk, University of Wisconsin, Eau Claire

Jinyan Huang, Niagara University

Liangyue Lu, Grambling State University

Melody Whiddon Willoughby, Florida International University

Susan De La Paz, University of Maryland

Terrie T. Poehl, Northwestern State University of Louisiana

Finally, and most importantly:

Not to us, O Lord, not to us

But to your name be the glory,

Because of your love and faithfulness.

(Psalm 115:1)

1

Research in Education

Chapter Objectives

In this chapter, the reader will

- understand the need for thoughtful, systematic research in education.

- be able to describe the research-to-practice gap.

- identify how research can be used at both the policy, school, and classroom levels.

- distinguish between experimental and descriptive research.

- define important designs related to experimental and descriptive research.

- describe quantitative and qualitative research methods.

- identify the steps of the research process.

The field of education is full of debates on many topics. As Chester Finn (2000) once said,

Phonics or whole language? Calculators or no calculators? Tracked or mixed-ability classrooms? Should teachers lecture or "facilitate"? Ought education be content-centered or child-centered? Do high-stakes exams produce real gains or merely promote "teaching to the test"? Which is the most effective reform: Reducing class size? Expanding pre-school? Inducing competition through vouchers? Paying teachers for performance?

And on and on and on. Within each debate, moreover, we regularly hear each faction citing boatloads of "studies" that supposedly support its position. Just think how often "research shows" is used to introduce a statement that winds up being chiefly about ideology, hunch or preference. (para 1–2)

Conducting Research in Education: Art or Science?

Ideology, hunch, or preference often seems to drive the debates and decisions in education. One reason is that people often disagree about the professionalism of education. Is teaching truly a profession like medicine, where knowledge is built by studying certain phenomena and determining the most effective and efficient ways to deal with them, or is teaching more of a creative vehicle for individuals doing what they think is right? Different groups answer this question in different ways, usually incorporating varying degrees of science and art.

If arguing that teaching is art or craft, then a body of educational knowledge potentially would be developed by individuals through idiosyncratic means. Unfortunately, this concept of teaching creates limits for the profession. That is, if knowledge of teaching and effective practices were only transmitted by individual trial and error and not through data-based inquiry, then it would be very difficult to call teaching a "profession" in the same way we typically talk about law, medicine, engineering, and others. Merriam-Webster defines *profession* as "a calling requiring specialized knowledge and often long and intensive academic preparation" *(Merriam-Webster's Dictionary,* 2018). Thus, for a profession to have specialized knowledge, the facts and ideas related to that field must be validly and reliably documented, generalized, and shared—something that is impossible on any scale using only individual trial and error. That is why science and data-based inquiry are so important to the field of education.

Science is an approach to the development of a consistent, documented system of knowledge, based on rigorous, systematic observations that lead to hypotheses or theories that are then tested and refined in an iterative process (Vaughn & Damman, 2001). To identify effective practices for teaching students, for instance, scientific inquiry or research is essential.

Research, then, is a broad term that usually means the systematic and rigorous process of posing a targeted question, developing a **hypothesis** or focus, testing the hypothesis or focus by collecting and analyzing relevant data, and drawing conclusions. Research methods vary, but the goal of research is almost always the same: to answer a question or group of related questions. The questions may range from "Does A cause B?" to "What is A like?" Researchers answer these questions by using a systematic process of identifying relevant phenomena and evaluating them. Educational research answers questions important to students, teachers, administrators, parents, and other stakeholders. Table 1.1 lists several examples of the uses of educational research.

TABLE 1.1 ● Example Uses of Research in Education

Level	Purpose	Research Question
Policy	To develop curriculum guidelines	What components are necessary for effective reading instruction at all grade levels?
	To guide systemic changes	What components of modified block scheduling are most effective for a middle school?
	To address grant proposal criteria	What components are necessary for effective reading instruction?
Classroom	To identify problems	Is Johnny's behavior out of the ordinary?
	To monitor progress	Has Johnny's behavior improved since I moved him away from his best buddy?
	To change instruction or practice	Johnny's behavior has not improved since I moved him. Will it change if I offer an incentive?

The Current Research-to-Practice Gap

More than two decades ago, Carnine (1997) described three main reasons why many educators do not rely on research to inform practice. First, some educational research lacks trustworthiness because of a lack of quality in design and implementation. Second, research often lacks usability; results are not always written clearly, and methods sometimes are not adequately described. Third, it is often quite difficult for practitioners to obtain research information quickly and efficiently. Several years later, Landrum, Cook, Tankersley, and Fitzgerald (2002) asked a group of teachers to rate the trustworthiness, usability, and accessibility of research information from colleagues, workshops or in-services, college courses, and professional journals. As if to underscore at least some of Carnine's reasons, teachers rated information from colleagues and workshops significantly higher on trustworthiness, usability, and accessibility than college courses and professional journals. More recently, and perhaps not surprisingly, Gukert, Mastropieri, and Scruggs (2016) found that the adoption of evidence-based practices among teachers resulted in adapting and modifying practices to meet individual needs rather than implementation with fidelity to practices in original research. Therein lies the gap between what researchers advocate and the actual practices of some educators.

The research-to-practice gap continues to exist in all areas related to education, from early childhood education (Grifenhagen, Barnes, Collins, & Dickinson, 2017) to special education (Guldberg, 2017), counselor education (Lee, Dewell, & Holmes, 2014), educational administration (Cho, 2016), and residential care (Thompson et al., 2017) as well as within specific disciplines including business education (Glenn, 2015).

How should the research-to-practice gap be bridged? There have been many responses to this question. One was from Boudah, Logan, and Greenwood (2001), who analyzed the results of five research-to-practice projects funded by the US Department of Education. They concluded that successful research-to- practice work required the following:

- An up-front commitment by researchers and school educators, as well as an ongoing, honest relationship
- Intensive work by researchers and teachers
- Extensive, sustained effort
- Building-level (although not necessarily district-level) administrative support
- The involvement of key individuals
- Financial resources and teacher recognition (p. 296)

All of these components add more time and hard work to an already long school day. The overriding purpose, however, is to improve outcomes for students and contribute to professional growth.

Congress has tried to reduce or bridge the research-to-practice gap through legislation. The reauthorization of both the Elementary and Secondary Education Act—better known initially as the No Child Left Behind Act and, more recently, as the Every Student Succeeds Act (ESSA)—and the Individuals with Disabilities Education Act requires that schools be held accountable for student progress and the use of instructional methods derived from scientifically based research. Therefore, it is imperative that education professionals know what research-based instruction is, how to determine if a practice is research-based, how to implement it in schools, and how to document its effectiveness.

The connectedness of research with practice is vital for sustaining and improving specific educational practices. Therefore, the primary purpose of this book is to help you understand, conduct, and share research. The secondary purpose is to aid in the development of practitioners who conduct and use scientific inquiry to better the field of education, whether they be administrators, teachers, guidance counselors, or other educational service providers.

Examples of Research at the Policy and Classroom Levels

Some very practical examples do exist regarding the impact that relevant research can have on instruction at both the policy and classroom levels. For example, in 2000 the National Reading Panel (NICHD) issued a report, *Teaching Children to Read*, which identified the effective components of early reading instruction. The Panel reviewed *100,000 studies* of reading to determine that

- phonemic awareness can be taught and learned.

- systematic and explicit phonics instruction is more effective than non-systematic or no phonics instruction.

- repeated and monitored oral reading improves reading fluency and overall reading achievement.

- children learn the meanings of most words indirectly, through everyday experiences with oral and written language.

- text comprehension can be improved by instruction that helps readers use specific comprehension strategies.

Thus, programs that do not include the elements of phonemic awareness, phonics instruction, oral reading, vocabulary instruction, and reading comprehension instruction were largely dismissed as ineffective. Combined in a coherent program, these effective components have improved the reading performance of all types of students. These elements have become a critical part of the evaluation of reading programs at many levels, including those that have received grants through the Department of Education.

Careful review of research has given educators many tools for effectively addressing many of the challenges they face in schools. However, it is often difficult for teachers and other educators to give up programs or practices they feel comfortable with, even if the practices do not have the elements identified by the National Reading Panel or the *What Works Clearinghouse* (https://ies.ed.gov/ncee/wwc/PracticeGuides), another government-sponsored outlet for vetted educational practices. This is why thoughtful evaluation of practices and decisions about instructional techniques are needed. This is also why educators and other stakeholders must collect data about student performance as part of professional practice. When evidence indicates students are not improving, educators need to find better alternatives.

Examples at the Classroom Level

Research, then, is not just for the upper levels of education policy making; it can and should be part of everyday classroom events. For example, teachers may begin with statements such as these:

- Johnny is defiant.

- Madeleine can't read at grade level.

- Esmerelda just doesn't "get it" in my class.

The reality is that these statements do not provide anyone with much information. What does it mean to say Johnny is defiant? How often is he defiant? What does he do?

Are there certain times and situations in which Johnny is defiant? Does Johnny's behavior occur in other classrooms or situations? The same is true for the statements about Madeleine and Esmerelda. How would anyone make a decision about instructional solutions based on these statements?

Defining problems and conducting classroom-based or high-quality "action research" allows teachers and others to (a) make data-based decisions, (b) monitor student progress, (c) change instruction, and (d) reflect on practice (Crockett, 2004). In addition, school-based educators can implement a systematic process for carrying out Response to Intervention (RTI) (e.g., Deshler, Mellard, Tollefson, & Byrd, 2005), or what is also now referred to as Multi-Tiered System of Supports (McIntosh & Goodman, 2016).

Making Data-Based Decisions. The statements about Johnny, Madeleine, and Esmerelda are probably not based on *data*, but on a teacher's response to events or anecdotes from the classroom. The information collected in an anecdote, among other things, is affected by a teacher's tolerance level, the classroom setting, and the content; however, the information collected from reliable data should not be affected by these factors. When a teacher makes these kinds of statements about students, she is indicating that a student's behavior is somehow standing out in the classroom. Collecting data about how the students stand out will then help the teacher to make more objective and more effective decisions about what to do.

For example, clearer, more data-based statements would be these:

- Johnny shouts out 10 times during 15-minute intervals of teacher instruction in social studies class.

- Madeleine reads 45 words per minute with 5 errors in second-grade text. Her peers (on average) read 75 words per minute with no errors.

- Esmerelda is unable to complete any math problems correctly when directions are given orally.

When data are presented, as in the examples just given, they remove much of the potential misinterpretation or teacher bias in defining student behavior. Many a teacher has been humbled to find that the *defiant* child actually shouted out no more than the *gifted* child. We are all human in our preferences, but when making decisions about students, we, as education professionals, must attempt to create clearer understanding and eliminate bias as best we can.

Monitoring Progress. Once a classroom or school situation has been documented with data, strategies can be put into place to help the student. Are the strategies working? By collecting data similar to that collected when the problem was identified, a teacher would be able to better answer that question. So, to continue with Madeleine, the teacher decides to try repeated readings with her to improve her fluency. After trying this strategy, the teacher assesses Madeleine's reading progress by having her read connected text in a second-grade book for 1-minute intervals. Two weeks later, she is reading at 55 words per minute with 2 errors—still below her peers but making gains.

Changing Instruction. If Madeleine's teacher did not administer timed readings, she may not have a valid way of knowing whether Madeleine's reading was improving. If the teacher knows Madeleine's reading is not improving, however, he or she would know it was time to make an instructional change. In another example, if students must pass an end-of-year writing exam, a teacher can monitor the progress of the students on the appropriate skills by testing periodically and tracking performance. Fuchs and Fuchs (2002) found that teachers who used data to make instructional decisions made more changes to their instruction than those who did not. Their students also showed greater academic gains.

Reflecting on Practice. Data can also come from records that teachers keep about their teaching. These records can be in many forms, but typically teachers compile student grades, test scores, and other information in response to their practice. This allows teachers to document, for example, how instruction went, what disasters may have occurred, and what successes they might want to repeat. In addition to allowing a teacher to review areas of strength and weakness, collecting this type of data allows teachers to compare practices and outcomes across classrooms and students.

Therefore, in an effort to encourage research-based instruction and promote better informed policy and systemic decision-making, many university teacher and administrator education programs as well as school-related programs require graduate students (and sometimes undergraduate students) to conduct research in order to learn its value and to practice the necessary skills. For example, individuals who are working toward Masters of Education, Masters of Teaching, Masters of Science in Administration, Doctors of Education, and similar degrees are typically required to complete a project (sometimes called a "Problem of Practice," thesis, or dissertation) that involves identifying a relevant question, reviewing the literature base for information, developing a research or project plan, collecting and analyzing data, and drawing conclusions. This book is intended to help graduate students and school-based educators who want to engage in research so that they can be systematic and data based in their decision-making. This text provides guidance in the following:

- Developing a research question
- Searching and understanding the literature for the current state of knowledge on a topic
- Developing a research plan
- Collecting and analyzing data
- Drawing conclusions
- Sharing the conclusions with others

It is important to note that it would be impossible to include everything you need to know about research in one book. Therefore, consider this book a handbook, or field guide rather than a standard educational research or statistics textbook. The goal is not to simply teach you about research or research methods, but to help with the step-by-step implementation of a research project in a school or clinic setting.

Research Types, Designs, and Methodologies

Before learning more about how to conduct educational research, it is important to be sure you understand common research types and designs, as well as their uses. It is also important to understand some basic research terminology. Table 1.2 outlines the research types and designs included in this text.

Types of Research

For ease of discussion, research is categorized into two major types: experimental and descriptive. If a research project includes both types, it is referred to as mixed method. Within each type, there are varying designs and methodologies.

Experimental Research. Simply stated, the goal of experimental research is to identify cause-and-effect relationships; whether by doing X, the result is Y. Following is an example of an experimental study that includes many important associated terms and ideas presented in bold.

A teacher named Jennifer may want to know if using Technique A will increase the number of words read by second graders in one minute. In this example, Technique A is the **independent variable**—the variable that is manipulated and controlled by the researcher in the hope of causing an effect. The **dependent variable**—the variable that may change because of the independent variable—would be the number of words read by each student in grade-level text in one minute. The students included in the study are the **sample** chosen from a **population** or larger group with certain identifiable characteristics. In experimental research, a researcher usually chooses a **representative sample**, or one that has similar characteristics to the population, so that the results of the experiment can be considered applicable to all individuals in the population. Thus, one related goal of experimental research is to produce results that are **generalizable** to the population and not just results that are applicable to a single sample.

TABLE 1.2 ● Research Types and Designs Included in This Text	
Type of Research	**Research Design**
Experimental/ Quasi-experimental	Group (posttest only, pretest-posttest, comparison group, time-series)
	Single subject (ABA, multiple baseline)
Descriptive	Qualitative (case study, grounded theory)
	Survey
	Correlational
Mixed Methods	Includes one or more designs from Experimental/Quasi-experimental and/or Descriptive types of research

Jennifer develops Technique A for improving reading fluency. She makes sure that Technique A actually focuses on reading fluency or is like a technique that has been proven effective in other studies. In this way, Jennifer is making sure that Technique A has some aspect of **validity.** Jennifer also practices giving the oral reading fluency assessment so that she can use it in the same way with all students in the sample. In this way, Jennifer is making sure her measurement of the dependent variable has **reliability**.

Now that the preparations are completed, Jennifer is ready to conduct the study. She puts the names of all of the second graders in three local elementary schools in a hat and draws them out, one by one, assigning each student to a classroom. In this way, she is **randomly assigning** students to classes, meaning every child has an equal chance to be in any of the classrooms. After the students are assigned, Jennifer trains several teachers to use Technique A and verifies that they can use Technique A with **fidelity**. The students in the classrooms who receive instruction using Technique A are participants in the **experimental group**. The students in the classrooms who do *not* receive instruction using Technique A are participants in the **comparison group**.

Jennifer administers the oral reading fluency assessment before and after teachers use Technique A, and then compares the students' performance. Using statistics, she can determine whether or not there is a **statistically significant** difference between the students' performance before and after, as well as between the experimental and control group. For there to be a statistically significant difference in performance, the change in the number of words read in one minute by the second graders must be greater than a predicted change due to differences that may occur due to chance when the assessment was given (e.g., didn't eat breakfast that morning, fire drill just before assessment, different background knowledge of students, etc.).

In this example, the teacher was able to exert a great deal of control over the implementation of Technique A, *and* she was able to randomly assign students to classrooms. It should be noted that random assignment is often difficult in school settings. When random assignment is problematic or impossible, the research study is then called quasi-experimental (Cook & Campbell, 1979). As with experimental research, a primary goal of quasi-experimental research is to show cause and effect. However, quasi-experimental research recognizes that random assignment (and therefore, control of some related chance variables) is next to impossible in most forms of social science research, including in education, where real-life classroom settings present difficulties in randomly assigning students and techniques. When done well, however, quasi-experimental research results can be generalized broadly, especially when other research studies find similar results.

Descriptive Research. In descriptive research, unlike experimental research, the researcher attempts to report what already exists. Moreover, the researcher's purpose is to understand and report the characteristics of a current or past phenomenon. For example, the results of a study may indicate that 80% of the teachers in elementary classrooms in one state are white females and hold master's degrees. Or, in a survey of seventh graders, 3 out of 10 report having tried alcohol. Or in a review of census data, 25% of Americans over the age of 70 live alone. The purpose of each of these types of studies is *not* to determine cause and effect but to describe what already exists. Following is an example of a descriptive study using survey methods.

Superintendent Andre wants to know how teachers in his district feel about their jobs. He asks a group of teachers and administrators to tell him what types of activities make up a teacher's job (e.g., teaching classes, disciplining students, paperwork, etc.). This group of teachers may be called a **focus group**, a small group of individuals with similar characteristics to those under study who give ideas about concepts important to a study. Taking the input from the focus group, Andre creates a survey with several questions about a teacher's job. He asks teachers to rate their satisfaction with each job aspect on a scale of one (very unsatisfied) to five (very satisfied). He also asks for some demographic information such as age, number of years teaching, number of years teaching in the district, and so forth. After piloting and revising it, Andre asks all of the teachers in the district to complete the survey. In this way, he is giving the entire population the opportunity to participate. About 75% of the surveys are returned. Thus, his sample turns out to be a little bit less than the entire population (although it's still a pretty high **return rate**). The results are tabulated, graphed, and reported to school administrators and the school board.

Descriptive research can be accomplished through many research methods, including survey, qualitative, and correlational. Each method uses very different techniques. Following is an example of a descriptive study using qualitative methods.

Tiana wants to describe the instructional actions of five middle school teachers using a new curriculum. All of the teachers have attended a professional development workshop, and they are now beginning to implement the curriculum in their classrooms. Tiana observes each teacher and classroom on many occasions over a number of weeks. She also interviews the teachers several times. She then reviews the new curriculum guides. As Tiana collects the data from observations, interviews, and document reviews, she examines them for themes, commonalities, and theories about instructional actions. Tiana must identify and describe her procedures for collection and analysis of her data in detail so that the study is judged to be trustworthy or completed using appropriate techniques. After completing the study, she will be able to describe these teachers' actions in relation to their beliefs and the curriculum, but because the sample size is so small, it may not be broadly generalizable.

Mixed Methods. Some studies address questions that are best answered using **mixed methods research**. Simply put, mixed methods research either employs experimental and descriptive designs, or more than one type of descriptive research design. For example, mixed methods research could utilize a pretest-posttest comparison design to experimentally investigate group differences in math performance *and* survey teachers and students to describe their thoughts on the math curriculum. A mixed methods project could also use a correlational design to consider the relationship between gender and math performance, while also conducting interviews and focus group sessions to describe what boys and girls and their parents think about the math curriculum and their goals for the future. Designing and conducting mixed methods research will be discussed in more detail in Chapter 7, and analyzing and interpreting mixed methods research will be discussed in more detail in Chapter 11.

In sum, the broad categories of experimental and descriptive research provide an organizing framework for the purposes of research. To determine cause-and-effect relationships, research is either experimental or quasi-experimental. To provide information about what exists, research is descriptive. As presented in the research examples, research also varies by the method used.

Research Methodologies

In addition to dividing research into experimental and descriptive, many educators organize research by the methods used and kinds of data collected. Let's consider two broad categories of methods and data: quantitative and qualitative.

Quantitative Methods. **Quantitative methods** are used in both experimental and quasi-experimental research, as well as some forms of descriptive research. Quantitative methods involve assigning numbers to sequential levels of variables being studied for purposes of statistical analysis. For example, researchers may use test scores (e.g., 86 on a scale of 0 to 100) to indicate reading achievement. Participants may rate their level of exertion during activities (one is no exertion, two is mild exertion, three is moderate exertion, etc.).

Researchers analyze these numbers for a variety of purposes. In experimental or quasi-experimental research, the purpose may be to determine if an independent variable led to a significant change in a dependent variable. For example, consider these possible results from the earlier example of the second-grade reading intervention: "Following intervention, there was a statistically significant difference in the number of words read in one minute by second graders. This difference favored the group that received Technique A." In this example, Technique A was the independent variable, and the number of words read per minute was the dependent variable, measured quantitatively.

Now take a look at the possible outcomes of Superintendent Andre's survey. After analyzing the data, Andre may be able to say that the teachers in the sample have an average age of 40 and, on average, have taught for five years in the district. The average rating of satisfaction with paperwork level is 3.5, in the satisfied range. Andre may also be able to calculate correlations to let him know that the older the teacher, the more satisfied with the level of paperwork. Andre is able to describe quantitatively what exists among the teachers in his district but not to determine cause-and-effect relationships since his research purpose was descriptive and not experimental. Chapters 5 and 9 provide guidance on experimental research, and Chapters 7 and 11 detail descriptive research and methods.

Qualitative Methods. **Qualitative methods** are used in descriptive research. Qualitative researchers analyze language, written or oral, and actions to determine patterns, themes, or theories in order to provide insight into certain situations. Qualitative data might include personal interviews, observations, and document review. The qualitative researcher works at "capturing what actually takes place and what people actually say" (Patton, 2002, p. 26). There are many data analysis techniques available in qualitative inquiry, including naturalistic inquiry, grounded theory, case study analysis, and others. Consider a possible outcome of Tiana's curriculum investigation.

Tiana discovers that teachers using the new curriculum talk about its implementation using three general themes: (a) developing materials, (b) managing students, and (c) creating interest. The instructional actions she observed included many mundane tasks, such as teaching students where to find their folders, as well as intriguing discussions based upon character analyses. Chapters 6 and 10 provide more direction on qualitative research and methods.

TECHNOLOGY IN RESEARCH

Technological advances in computers, voice recognition software, phone apps, and the like have made conducting research somewhat easier than in the past. For example, researchers who use qualitative methods used to glue text from interview transcripts to index cards, which they would then sort into different categories. In today's research endeavors, software allows researchers to convert interview recordings to text files, insert the text files into data management programs, and sort and categorize data on their computers. Phone apps allow teachers and others doing research in classrooms to record observations as events occur with little intrusion. Most chapters in this book include Technology in Research, a special feature that gives a brief description of a technology relevant to the chapter's topic. The Technology in Research features are meant to introduce the topic and provide selected resources for more information.

IN THEIR OWN WORDS

It is important to understand the theory or purposes behind conducting research in schools. Understanding how to put the theory into practice, however, is critical to conducting an effective study. In each chapter, you will meet graduate students, teachers, and seasoned researchers who describe how they make research work. Each person will offer comments about successes and failures, as well as provide guidance on some aspect of the topic included in the chapter. The bits of knowledge these researchers provide can help make your research project flow smoothly.

Selected Organizations That Support Research In Education

Before the close of this chapter, I must note that there are many professional organizations and groups in education. The organizations that focus on research in education can provide valuable support and resources to beginning researchers. Some of these groups have members from all aspects of education, and others serve subsections of education professionals. Appendix A provides information about some of these organizations, including their mission statements and goals, how they support researchers, their sources of support (including funding), and how to locate or contact them for more information. It was impossible to highlight all the groups that support educational research, so groups were chosen based upon their commitment to research, their accessibility, and the reputation they have attained in education.

Putting It All Together

Given the variety of questions and designs, there is no single way to conduct research in educational settings. What you will read over and over again in this book is that the research design and methods must be appropriate to explore the initial research

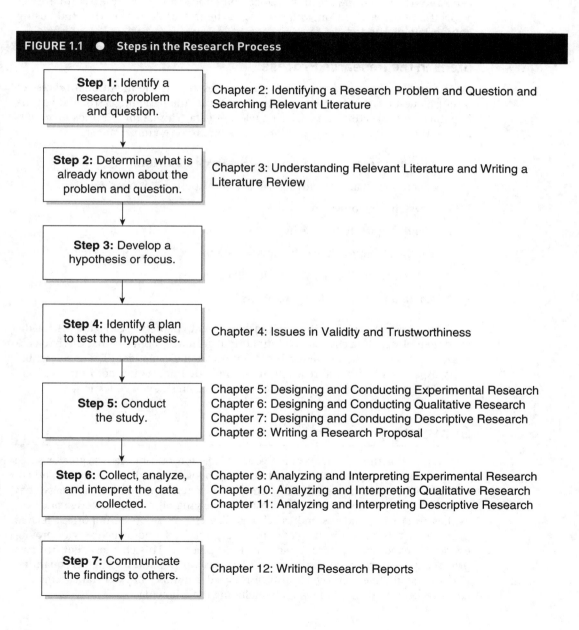

FIGURE 1.1 ● Steps in the Research Process

Step 1: Identify a research problem and question.

Chapter 2: Identifying a Research Problem and Question and Searching Relevant Literature

Step 2: Determine what is already known about the problem and question.

Chapter 3: Understanding Relevant Literature and Writing a Literature Review

Step 3: Develop a hypothesis or focus.

Step 4: Identify a plan to test the hypothesis.

Chapter 4: Issues in Validity and Trustworthiness

Step 5: Conduct the study.

Chapter 5: Designing and Conducting Experimental Research
Chapter 6: Designing and Conducting Qualitative Research
Chapter 7: Designing and Conducting Descriptive Research
Chapter 8: Writing a Research Proposal

Step 6: Collect, analyze, and interpret the data collected.

Chapter 9: Analyzing and Interpreting Experimental Research
Chapter 10: Analyzing and Interpreting Qualitative Research
Chapter 11: Analyzing and Interpreting Descriptive Research

Step 7: Communicate the findings to others.

Chapter 12: Writing Research Reports

question. In other words, you should not say, "I am a qualitative researcher," or "I am a quantitative researcher." The reality is that different types of research may work together coherently to achieve better understanding of a research question or educational situation. The balance of this book begins with guidance in developing and focusing research questions so that the most appropriate research type and design will be apparent. Once you choose a type of research to answer a specific research question, you can begin the task of designing the study using appropriate methods.

Steps in the Research Process

As noted at the beginning of this chapter, research is the intentional process of posing a question, developing a hypothesis or focus, and designing a study to test the hypothesis by collecting and analyzing relevant data. This definition leads to an outline for the research process that is broken down into seven important steps:

1. Identify a **research problem** and **research question**.

2. Determine what is already known about the problem or question.

3. Develop a hypothesis or focus.

4. Identify a plan to test the hypothesis.

5. Put the plan into place (conduct the study).

6. Collect, analyze, and interpret the data collected.

7. Communicate the findings to others.

These steps are explained in detail in subsequent chapters. (See Figure 1.1 for the alignment of steps and chapters.) It is important again to emphasize that this book is a guide for the completion of research projects, not a book that identifies and describes every aspect of educational research. It will provide information both practical and helpful to anyone completing a graduate-level research study in education.

Summary

The purpose of this text is to guide your completion of a master's degree or some doctoral-level research studies. In addition, this book can guide practitioners and clinicians in conducting research in practice. The current research-to-practice gap has contributed to too few educators accessing and relying on proven, effective practices as they work with students and in schools. Therefore, one of the important related purposes of this book is to help administrators, teachers, and related service providers develop and use scientific inquiry in their practice. This chapter identified two primary types of research, experimental and descriptive, and highlighted quantitative and qualitative methods. It also introduced a number of important terms and concepts commonly used in research, including the following:

Research

Independent variable

Dependent variable

Sample

Population

Representative sample

Generalize

Validity

Fidelity

Reliability

Random assignment

Experimental group

Control group

Statistically significant

Quasi-experimental design

Survey research methods

Focus group

Trustworthy

Qualitative research methods

Quantitative research methods

Please refer to the glossary at the end of the text for specific definitions.

Finally, the chapter described the seven steps necessary in completing a research project:

1. Identify a research problem or question.

2. Determine what is already known about the problem or question.

3. Develop a hypothesis or focus.

4. Identify a plan to test the hypothesis.

5. Put the plan into place (conduct the study).

6. Collect, analyze, and interpret the data collected.

7. Communicate the findings to others.

Activity

Fill in the blanks with the appropriate term(s).

1. _____ methods are often used in experimental, quasi-experimental, and descriptive research; methods involve assigning numbers to sequential levels of variables being studied for purposes of statistical analysis.

2. _____ is a broad term that usually means the systematic and rigorous process of posing a focused question, developing a hypothesis or focus, testing the hypothesis or focus by collecting and analyzing relevant data, and drawing conclusions.

3. The _____ _____ is the variable that the researcher manipulates and controls in the hope of causing an effect.

4. _____ is a term associated with a study that does what it claims to do.

5. The _____ _____ is the group that receives the independent variable or treatment.

6. _____ methods are often used in descriptive research; these include personal interviews, observations, and document review.

7. _____ is a term associated with study methods that can occur similarly across participants and time.

8. The _____ _____ is the variable that may change because of the independent variable.

9. _____ is a term associated with experimental procedures in a study that are done as intended.

10. The _____ _____ is the group that does not receive the independent variable or treatment.

11. _____ is a term associated with qualitative procedures in a study that were completed using appropriate techniques.

Answers can be found on page 18.

Provide an example of the following research methods:

12. Quantitative research methods

    _____

    _____

13. Qualitative research methods

    _____

    _____

14. Quasi-experimental research methods

    _____

    _____

Your Research Project in Action

At this point in your reading, you should be thinking about how research fits into your practice. As you consider this, you will be able to determine an area of focus that will be useful in developing your research study. Start by thinking about the following questions:

- Where do I go to find information about educational practices?

  _____

  _____

- Where do I look for research articles or to find out if a practice has a research base?

  _____

  _____

- Why would it be important for me to conduct research in my school/district/practice or to be guided by research findings?

  _____

  _____

- In what ways do I use anecdotal evidence instead of data-based evidence? How can I change this?

  _____

Further Reading

Cook, T. D., & Campbell, D. T. (1979). Quasi-*experimentation: Design and analysis issues for field settings*. Boston: Houghton Mifflin.

This classic research book is an excellent reference for finding examples of real-world application research studies. This book also provides examples of problems previous researchers have experienced and describes how to avoid those difficulties in one's own research. This book provides an excellent discussion of the advantages and limitations of using quasi-experiment research methodologies. Knowing the advantages and limitations helps researchers focus on what exactly they are hoping to find, achieve, or resolve and how this particular methodology will facilitate that process.

Patton, M. Q. (2002). *Qualitative research & evaluation methods* (3rd ed.). Thousand Oaks, CA: Sage.

This book is written to benefit a wide variety of audiences. Students, researchers, and even practitioners can find this book beneficial to their research. This book focuses on qualitative research methods and addresses the main concepts of problem identification, participant inclusion and observation, interviewing and note taking, decoding of messages, data analysis, and reporting of results. Included are interview guides and questions that researchers can reference when conducting their own studies. In addition, Patton provides personal narratives of his own experiences and struggles with research studies.

References

Boudah, D. J., Logan, K. R., & Greenwood, C. R. (2001). The research to practice projects: Lessons learned about changing teacher practice. *Teacher Education and Special Education, 24*, 290–303.

Carnine, D. (1997). Bridging the research-to-practice gap. *Exceptional Children, 63*, 513–521.

Cho, V. (2016). Administrators' professional learning via twitter: The dissonance between beliefs and actions. *Journal of Educational Administration, 54*(3), 340–356.

Cook, T. D., & Campbell, D. T. (1979). Quasi-*experimentation: Design and analysis issues for field settings.* Boston: Houghton Mifflin.

Crockett, J. (2004). Taking stock of science in the schoolhouse: Four ideas to foster effective instruction. *Journal of Learning Disabilities, 37*, 186–188.

Deshler, D. D., Mellard, D. F., Tollefson, J. M., & Byrd, S. E.(2005). Research topics in responsiveness to intervention: Introduction to the special series. *Journal of Learning Disabilities, 38*, 483–484.

Finn, C. E., Jr. (2000). Foreword. In D. Carnine, *Why education experts resist effective practices (and what it would take to make education more like medicine).* Retrieved May, 5, 2010, from http://www.edexcellence.net/detail/news.cfm?news_id=46

Fuchs, L. S., & Fuchs, D. (2002). Curriculum-based measurement: Describing competency, enhancing outcomes, evaluating treatment effects, and identifying treatment nonresponders. *Peabody Journal of Education, 77*, 64–84.

Glenn, J. M. L. (2015). The research-to-practice gap: Problems and possibilities. *Business Education Forum, 69*(4), 6–14.

Grifenhagen, J. F., Barnes, E. M., Collins, M. F., & Dickinson, D. K. (2017). Talking the talk: Translating research to practice. *Early Child Development and Care, 187*(3–4), 509–526.

Guckert, M., Mastropieri, M., & Scruggs, T. E. (2016). Personalizing research: Special educators' awareness of evidence-based practice. *Exceptionality, 24*(2), 63–78.

Guldberg, K. (2017). Evidence-based practice in autism educational research: Can we bridge the research and practice gap? *Oxford Review of Education, 43*(2), 149–161.

Landrum, T. J., Cook, B. G., Tankersley, M., & Fitzgerald, S. (2002). Teacher perceptions of the trustworthiness, usability, and accessibility of information from different sources. *Remedial and Special Education, 23*, 42–48.

Lee, K. A., Dewell, J. A., & Holmes, C. M. (2014). Animating research with counseling values: A training model to address the research-to-practice gap. *Professional Counselor, 4*(4), 301–315.

McIntosh, K., & Goodman, S. (2016). *Integrated Multi-tiered systems of support.* New York: Guilford Press.

National Institute of Child Health and Human Development (NICHD). (2000). *Report of the National Reading Panel: Teaching children to read.* Retrieved May 5, 2010, from http://www.nichd.nih.gov/publications/pubs/nrp/smallbook

Patton, M. Q. (2002). *Qualitative research & evaluation methods* (3rd ed.). Thousand Oaks, CA: Sage

Profession. (2018). In *Merriam-Webster's online dictionary.* Retrieved April 5, 2018, from https://www.merriam-webster.com/dictionary/profession

Thompson, R. W., Duppong Hurley, K., Trout, A. L., Huefner, J. C., & Daly, D. L. (2017). Closing the research to practice gap in therapeutic care: Service provider-university partnerships focused on evidence-based practice. *Journal of Emotional and Behavioral Disorders, 25*(1), 46–56.

Vaughn, S., & Damman, J. E. (2001). Science and sanity in special education. *Behavioral Disorders, 27*, 21–29.

What Works Clearinghouse (https://ies.ed.gov/ncee/wwc/PracticeGuides)

Activity Answers

1. <u>Quantitative</u> methods are often used in experimental, quasi-experimental, and descriptive research; methods involve assigning numbers to sequential levels of variables being studied for purposes of statistical analysis.

2. <u>Research</u> is a broad term that usually means the systematic and rigorous process of posing a focused question, developing a hypothesis or focus, testing the hypothesis or focus by collecting and analyzing relevant data, and drawing conclusions.

3. The <u>independent variable</u> is the variable that the researcher manipulates and controls in the hope of causing an effect.

4. <u>Validity</u> is a term associated with a study that does what it claims to do.

5. The <u>experimental group</u> is the group that receives the independent variable or treatment.

6. <u>Qualitative</u> methods are often used in descriptive research; these include personal interviews, observations, and document review.

7. <u>Reliable</u> is a term associated with study methods that can occur similarly across participants and time.

8. The <u>dependent variable</u> is the variable that may change because of the independent variable.

9. <u>Fidelity</u> is a term associated with experimental procedures in a study that are done as intended.

10. The <u>comparison group</u> is the group that does not receive the independent variable or treatment.

11. <u>Trustworthy</u> is a term associated with qualitative procedures in a study that was completed using appropriate techniques.

2

Identifying a Research Problem and Question, and Searching Relevant Literature

Chapter Objectives

In this chapter, the reader will

- understand the characteristics of a research problem or phenomenon.
- understand the characteristics of good research questions.
- clarify the difference between a research problem and hypothesis.
- understand the purposes of a literature review.
- understand the process for conducting a literature search.

Long before you create a research proposal, let alone conduct your research, you need to identify a problem or phenomenon to address and then a question or questions to ask about the problem or phenomenon. This chapter first discusses the nature of a research problem, where you might get ideas for a problem to investigate, narrowing down or focusing on a particular problem to address, and writing good research questions. It then discusses finding literature that is relevant to and helpful in clarifying your targeted problem and question(s).

Identifying a Research Problem

We often think we understand problems when we really don't. For example, when students encounter difficulties with word problems in math, teachers may initially think that students have not mastered the basic skills that would allow them to carry out the needed computations. However, the difficulty may actually lie in poor reading skills, which prevent the students from identifying the words in math problems. The student also might not understand or correctly interpret essential vocabulary.

As another example, when students do not hand in homework assignments or participate in class, some might be inclined to think that the students are not motivated. While there may be motivational issues, motivation may not be the only factor. A high school student may have an evening job that demands considerable time and energy. A younger student may be trying desperately to camouflage poor or nonexistent skills. In some cases, the chosen instructional strategy may not be well matched to the student's cognitive or attention level. Therefore, it is crucial that researchers accurately identify the problem they want to study.

What Is a Research Problem?

A research problem, or **phenomenon** as it might be called in many forms of qualitative methodology, is the topic you would like to address, investigate, or study, whether descriptively or experimentally. It is the focus or reason for engaging in your research. It is typically a topic, phenomenon, or challenge that you are interested in and with which you are at least somewhat familiar.

Where Do You Find a Problem or Phenomenon to Study?

Since a research problem is usually something about which you have some knowledge, that personal experience is often a good starting point. Realistically, you have to select something that you are interested in, because you are going to commit yourself to a significant investment of time and energy. Thus, if you are not personally interested, it will be difficult to sustain the effort needed to complete the research with any measure of quality or validity. You may want to talk to teachers, counselors, administrators, psychologists, or others about some of the problems they face. For example, your ideas may come out of experiences like Johnny's shout outs, Madeleine's reading rate, or Esmerelda's trouble with math that were discussed in Chapter 1. You may find an interesting idea that way and, in addition, address something that may have social significance beyond your research project, thesis, or dissertation. Moreover, by addressing the questions of practicing educators, you may develop important relationships with future research partners and participants.

Narrowing or Clarifying Your Problem

A problem statement such as "Students can't read" is not clear because many aspects of reading, including discrete reading skills and strategies, may contribute to reading difficulties. Alternatively, "Students cannot find the main ideas in reading passages," is much clearer and potentially much easier to measure and address, since one can define *main idea* and measure student performance on tasks that require students to find main ideas.

So, whether in the classroom, the physician's office, or the mechanic's shop, defining or diagnosing a problem is key to designing and implementing effective interventions or treatments to address it. Without adequately defining the problem, researchers may find themselves going off on a "goose chase" to tackle a vague phenomenon, trying to deal with symptoms rather than root causes, and wasting time, becoming frustrated, or even making the actual problem worse.

Later in this chapter, you will read about the use of standardized test scores for entrance to undergraduate or graduate school as an example research topic. While that may be a good topic, it is not well defined; it needs to be narrowed by thinking about the kind of information that the researcher wants to find out. Whether you are interested in the kinds of tests that are used, the average cutoff scores, or the degree to which scores predict college grade point average, as examples, a topic has to be specific enough to be clearly defined and yield helpful results from a literature search that will follow.

Identifying a Possible Research Question

After you have narrowed down your problem, searching and reviewing existing literature may further clarify your research approach. Moreover, by identifying where the conclusions of previous research are unclear or where gaps may exist in the literature, you will be better prepared to write good research questions.

What Is a Research Question?

A research question is a way of expressing your interest in a problem or phenomenon. Research questions are not necessarily an attempt to answer the many philosophical questions that often arise in schools, and they are certainly not intended to be an avenue for grinding personal axes regarding classroom or school issues. You may have more than one research question for a study, depending on the complexity and breadth of your proposed work. Each question should be clear and specific, refer to the problem or phenomenon, reflect an intervention in experimental work, and note the target population or participants (see Figure 2.1). Identifying a research question will provide greater focus to your research or clarify the direction of your investigation, whether the research is descriptive or experimental. Quite significantly, a well-written research question will also shed light on appropriate research methods (e.g., specify the intended actions of the variables and how an experimental intervention might be measured).

Examples of Good Research Questions

Given the characteristics of good research questions noted in Figure 2.1, let's take a look at some examples, and nonexamples, of good research questions. Table 2.1

FIGURE 2.1 ● Characteristics of Good Research Questions

> ➤ Are specific.
>
> ➤ Are clear.
>
> ➤ Refer to the problem or phenomenon.
>
> ➤ Reflect the intervention in experimental research.
>
> ➤ Note the target group of participants.

illustrates a few of each and includes explanations of why a researcher would categorize them as one or the other.

Here are some additional examples of good experimental research questions from existing literature:

- What are the effects of the flipped classroom on secondary chemistry students' performance on important constructs (Olakanmi, 2017)?

- Does participation in the professional development program increase ESL and classroom teachers' use of high-impact instructional strategies as compared to teachers in the control group (Babinski, Amendum, Knotek, Sanchez, & Malone, 2017)?

- Would a combined repeated reading and question generation intervention improve the reading achievement of fourth- through eighth-grade students with learning disabilities or who are at risk for reading failure (Therrien, Wickstrom, & Jones, 2006)?

The following are additional examples of good questions from descriptive research:

- What are the empirical factors that predict effective continuing professional development activities for school staff (Cheng, 2017)?

- How are the alternate assessments and achievement standards implemented for students with the most significant cognitive disabilities across 16 states (Kohl, McLaughlin, & Nagle, 2006)?

- How do elementary teachers anticipate and actually use iPads in the classroom over the course of the first year of 1:1 implementation (Frazier & Trekles, 2017)?

Writing a Hypothesis

A **research hypothesis** essentially is a declarative statement of how you expect the research to turn out. In a way, it is a possible answer to your research question.

TABLE 2.1 ● **Examples and Nonexamples of Good Research Questions**

Examples	Nonexamples
Do students in Algebra I classes who engage in the XYZ curriculum perform significantly differently on state tests than students who do not participate in that curriculum? This one is good. It is specific and clear. We know who the participants will be and that student performance on state tests is the problem.	*Why do students seem so apathetic?* This is not specific or clear, nor does it reflect an intervention, if one is planned, or a target group of participants. Better questions might be: Are science students more engaged in class discussions when a response strategy is used (experimental)? What are the reasons for apathy among various groups of high school students (descriptive)?
Do general education teachers evaluate student homework differently than special education teachers, based on five criteria? Assuming this is descriptive research, the problem is evident, the target participants are noted, and the question is pretty clear.	*Does computer practice improve state test scores?* Even though an intervention is mentioned and a way of measuring performance is implied (i.e., state test scores), the problem and target group are unclear.
Does the use of metacognitive strategies predict reading performance on standardized tests for immigrant Chinese children? This one is clear and quite specific, notes the target participants, and nicely alludes to the variables that will be studied.	*What strategies improve student understanding of main ideas in history texts?* The problem is pretty clear, but the target group is not. In addition, there is no specific reference to an intervention, important if this will be experimental research. If this will be descriptive research, on the other hand, that is moot.

It should be brief, note your important variables, and suggest something you can test or descriptively investigate. It is typically included in experimental research but is also found in descriptive research such as factor analyses or survey-based investigations. It is *not* typically included in qualitative methodology in which the results are intended to be emergent (refer to Chapter 6). In the case of experimental research and quantitative types of descriptive research, your research question often directly leads to your hypothesis. Therefore, it is good practice to ensure that your research topic or problem statement, research question, and hypothesis use consistent language regarding variables and any anticipated outcomes. Certainly, you would write a hypothesis for each question that you propose.

Let's go back to a couple of the good example research questions noted in Table 2.1 and see how a hypothesis might be written for each.

Question: Do students in Algebra I classes who engage in the XYZ curriculum perform significantly differently on state tests than students who do not participate in that curriculum?

Possible hypothesis: Students who participate in the XYZ curriculum in Algebra I classes will perform significantly differently on state achievement tests than students who do not participate in that curriculum.

If you wanted a directional hypothesis, one also could have written that the target students will perform significantly *better* on the tests. A **directional hypothesis** is one that implies a difference in a particular direction when one compares two groups or a group at different points in time (i.e., if one wants to project a difference in favor of one group or condition).

Question: Do general education teachers evaluate student homework differently than special education teachers, based on five criteria?

Possible hypothesis: General education and special education teachers evaluate student homework significantly different on each of five given criteria.

You may have previously heard the term null hypothesis. A **null hypothesis** is simply a statement saying that you expect no differences in outcomes between groups or that no relationships exist between the given variables in your hypothesis. Some researchers do not think that a null hypothesis adds substantial value to research, while others do. Your advisor may want you to include it in your proposal. The null hypothesis for the example above regarding the way teachers evaluate homework might be simply this: General education and special education teachers do not significantly differ on any of five given criteria for student homework evaluation.

Before leaving this discussion of research questions, let's focus for a moment on the concept of significance. You may have noticed the adjective *significantly* in front of the word *different* in each of the previous example hypotheses and null hypotheses. **Significance** refers to the notion that differences between two groups or conditions are not simply due to chance or any other known variable (Gall, Gall, & Borg, 2006). The term is also typically used in reference to statistical differences that may be noted in the analysis. Significance will be further discussed in Chapter 9.

IN THEIR OWN WORDS

Defining and Writing Research Questions

Tamara Nimkoff, doctoral student

What makes a good research question? It's a common query that graduate students face when developing their research topics. Unless a topic, and its subsequent questions, are handed to the student, there is often a period of uncertainty in which the student is developing a host of possible research questions all the while wondering if they are actually thesis or dissertation "worthy." Students often feel they need to demonstrate their sophistication by creating complex and multilayered questions. Certainly, it's important to consider the originality of a research topic, the contribution it will make to the field. But you can approach an interesting and important topic with research questions that are uncomplicated and clear. Start with the idea—what you want to know about the topic—and then break that idea down into more and more parsimonious questions. Don't be afraid of simplicity in composing research questions. A set of straightforward research questions will help you stay focused on your research topic at those inevitable times when you need to regain your footing and will demonstrate to your committee and your readers that you have a focused research agenda.

The Purposes of a Literature Review

Depending on whether you are a teacher, graduate student, administrator, or have another role, you may have one or more purposes for conducting a literature review. There are actually many potential purposes, but let's focus on a few common ones: (a) to help figure out what works; (b) to pursue a topic, problem, or question of professional and/or personal interest; (c) to pinpoint an area of further study; (d) to provide a rationale/background for study; (e) to survey or analyze research methodology. You may have one or more, or even all, of these purposes for conducting a literature review.

To Help Figure Out What Works

The introduction to this chapter alluded to the need for educators continuously to search out best practices for students, particularly struggling students. Indeed, this is an important task. Teachers, administrators, and other educators look for ideas in workshops, on the Internet, from conference exhibits, or simply in the classroom across the hall. These may provide ideas, but one may not know whether research has established their trustworthiness. By searching the literature, instead of or in addition to these efforts, educators may find valuable information about practices that have been tested with students and in situations similar to those that pose challenges for them. In that way, they may find specific information about what works and what does not.

To Pursue a Topic, Problem, or Question of Professional and/or Personal Interest

Whether you are an educator, a graduate student, or both, you may want to investigate or may be assigned to investigate a topic through a literature review. Perhaps you have a research problem in mind and have even written a tentative research question or two. Whether your problem or topic is graphic organizers, multiple intelligences, class size, or any other, a literature review may be a rewarding opportunity to ask and begin to find answers to your questions. Perhaps you tried cooperative learning as a teacher but decided it didn't work for you. You may be surprised or validated by what the literature says on the topic. Regardless of the topic, a literature review is an excellent chance to learn more about an area of interest.

To Pinpoint an Area of Further Study

Compiling and analyzing previous research will always reveal something to you. If you are interested in a particular topic, a literature review may reveal simply that little or no research exists on that topic. Let's say you wanted to study the effects of learning strategies on state competency test scores. You are likely to find very little on that subject, but if you look at research generally on the outcomes of learning strategies, you will find quite a bit. You might further discover that while there is a lot on learning strategies, there is little specifically on test taking strategies. So, you see, by searching and analyzing the literature, you may pinpoint a particular area where research is needed.

To Provide a Rationale/Background for Study

If you are a graduate student and are required to write a thesis or dissertation or engage in a research project, you will need to include a literature review as part of your final product. Thus, a literature review not only provides you with an opportunity to learn more about a given topic but also to create support or a rationale for engaging in a particular area of proposed research. For instance, if you wanted to research the use of math manipulatives, conducting a literature review would give you a chance to show others the importance of your topic and refine the problem, research questions, or hypotheses you have targeted as well.

To Survey or Analyze Research Methodology

When you select a topic to study, pinpoint a particular area of needed research related to your topic, and provide sufficient background to support further research, you may also use a literature review to look at how previous researchers studied the topic. You may clarify ideas, see flaws, or discern opportunities. For example, perhaps a topic such as token systems has been studied in certain settings through single-subject experimental designs. You may look at that literature and decide that your research questions might be best answered through a large-group experiment. Alternatively, you might decide that you would like to qualitatively describe the impact of token systems on student motivation. In short, by analyzing research methodology in a literature review, you may discover how you should design your own research study.

The Process of Conducting a Literature Search

Whether you have one or more purposes for conducting a literature review, there is a process for getting from point A to B. That is, there is a process that can take you from knowing little or nothing to understanding something meaningful and informative. This process may be referred to as conducting a **literature search**. This includes (a) determining your focus and (b) searching literature databases. Let's take a look at that here. The next chapter will help you then analyze the studies you find, as well as organize and write a literature review.

Determining Your Focus

Determining your focus for a literature search includes three important activities: picking a topic, making decisions about what to include and exclude, and translating the topic into key terms.

Step 1: Picking a Topic. Let's say you're interested in the use of standardized test scores for entrance to undergraduate or graduate school. That's a good topic, although not well defined. You may need to narrow it by thinking through what kind of information you'd like to find out. For instance, do you want to find out what kinds of tests are used? Do you want to learn about the average cutoff scores? Are you interested in how well the scores predict college grade point average or employment status after college? How about the way that admissions departments weight the scores in their decisions?

One way or the other, a topic has to be specific enough to yield useful results when you get to the actual literature search.

While you may start off with too broad a topic, you could begin too narrowly also. Perhaps you are interested in the use of metacognition among immigrant Chinese children in elementary reading. My hunch is that you might need to broaden the search to look for information about metacognition in immigrant children's reading. Looking for previous research related to Chinese children in elementary reading would likely yield little or nothing. It is, however, worth beginning your search with a narrower focus to see what you can find.

Step 2: Making Decisions About What to Include and Exclude. After thinking through your topic so that it is not too broad and not too narrow, you can make decisions about what to look for in your search. Your topic scope will also help you decide what to disregard should an initial computer search yield hundreds of possible articles. Moreover, it will help you in the next step of the process, searching more efficiently with key terms.

Inclusion and exclusion decisions may be based on many things, including the age of the students you want to study, the years of teacher experience, the location of the study (rural, urban, suburban), the date on which the study was conducted, whether the students have disabilities or not, and many, many other possibilities. For instance, in the previous example, you might want to start by including articles that address metacognition in immigrant children in any location, and you might exclude articles that address American-born children and those written before 2005 because you want to look at more recent experiences in research.

Step 3: Translating the Topic Into Key Terms. By deciding what to include and what to exclude, you prepare yourself to search more effectively and efficiently. When you begin to use online search indexes such as the Educational Resources Information Center (discussed in the next subsection), the index will prompt you to enter search terms. The index will then find articles and documents that use those terms in their descriptions.

So, to take our example further, the key search terms in the topic of "metacognition among immigrant Chinese children in elementary reading" would likely be *metacognition, immigrants, Chinese, elementary*, and *reading*. As mentioned earlier, this is a pretty narrow topic and thus has five search terms; you certainly may have fewer than five when beginning your literature review. The more terms that you decide to search, the less likely you will find a lot of literature on the topic. Still, it may be more efficient to start your search as narrowly as possible and then broaden your effort. Let's look at that next.

Searching Literature Databases

Generally speaking, you can search literature electronically or by hand. Certainly, using an online database is far more efficient than searching stacks of journals or other resources in the library. Nevertheless, even if you begin your search online, you may find yourself searching the reference lists of selected articles to find additional sources. For now, let's first walk through how you might conduct an electronic search.

Searching Online. There are many possible databases where you can conduct an online literature search, including those noted in the Technology in Research features box, as well as other generic databases such as Google (google.com). The following paragraphs

TECHNOLOGY IN RESEARCH

In addition to ERIC, there are many other electronic databases for literature searches, including PsycINFO (apa.org/pubs/databases/psycinfo/); PubMed, a service of the National Library of Medicine, which includes citations from MEDLINE (https://www.ncbi.nlm.nih.gov/pubmed); Google Scholar (https://scholar.google.com); Education Research Complete (https://www.ebsco.com/products/research-databases/education-research-complete); and JSTOR, a digital archive of academic journals and other scholarly content (jstor.org).

highlight examples using the Educational Resources Information Center (ERIC; eric.ed.gov), a database that the U.S. Department of Education has supported for many years and perhaps the most widely used database in education. ERIC is free, meaning no university login or password is required. ERIC contains over 1.6 million records, including many full text materials. Records include journal articles, reports, fact sheets, conference papers, books, and other materials dating back to 1966 and are updated monthly.

ERIC uses simple features that often eliminate the need for complex searches. A simple search will return records based on your search terms or their variants by author, title, source, abstract, and several descriptors. That is, for most searches, you can get relevant results with a simple search that includes multiple terms, rather than needing to use commands such as AND, OR, or use quotation marks.

To search the ERIC database, log in to eric.ed.gov and enter your search terms. Let's say you were interested in writing strategies for middle school students who have ADHD. Figure 2.2 shows the ERIC home page with search terms entered.

After you click on the search button, a new screen will appear with the most relevant matches to your search terms. See Figure 2.3.

Understanding Search Results. Based on this search, there were 15,045 results, as you can see from the upper right-hand corner of the screen shot. That's obviously a lot to comb through. Fortunately, you can quickly and easily narrow your search in many ways. First, you can check one or both of the boxes at the top for "Peer reviewed only" and "Full text available on ERIC," and then click on the search button again. That will narrow your search output to only records that have been reviewed by professionals and/or only to search output that has records in which the full text of the article or report is immediately available to you through ERIC.

Secondly, you can narrow or limit your search by the fields that appear on the left-hand side of the screen shot in Figure 2.3, including Publication Date, related descriptor terms, Source, Author, Educational Level, Location, What Works Clearinghouse Rating, and a few others. Numbers appear next to each limiter such as those under Publication Date, that is, there are 5,076 records (of the original 15,045) in the search available in the last 10 years. If you click on that limiter, a new search output will appear only with the 5,076 records. Thus, you have limited the search output to about a third of the original. You can add multiple limiters to your search, and they will all appear at the top of your screen. You can also click off any limiters afterwards, if you wish to expand your search again.

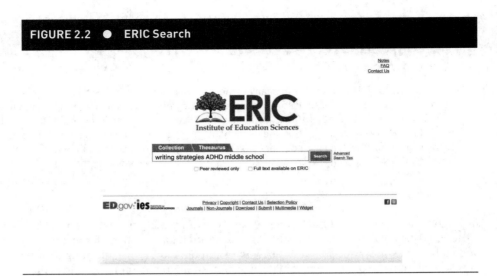

Source: US Deparment of Education, https://eric.ed.gov/

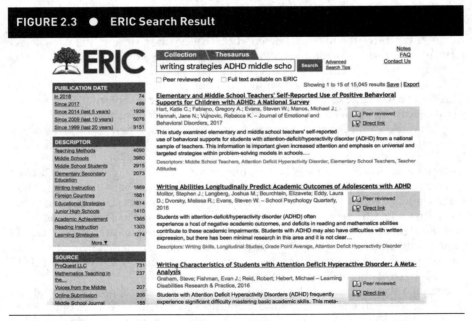

Source: US Deparment of Education, https://eric.ed.gov/

On the ERIC home page where you started (Figure 2.2), you will notice a link for "Advanced Search Tips" on the right-hand side of the screen. If you were to click on that, a new page would open that offers a YouTube video on searching ERIC, as well as information about how to conduct more specific searches if needed.

Now, let's go back to your original search output in Figure 2.3. Rather than narrowing or limiting your search right away, let's say that as you peruse the first 15 records, you see several that look promising. For instance, let's say you decide to look at the second one listed and click on the title, which is a hotlink. You will then get a screen that looks like Figure 2.4, which includes an abstract of the journal article.

You will notice that the ERIC document reference number, the title, author, and other identifying information are listed, including the publication type, which tells you this document is a journal article, and the number of pages in the document. The number of references indicates whether this document provide leads on other sources on the topic. Below the abstract, the document lists descriptors that are present in this record, including the ones from your search.

Let's look at the abstract for a moment. This article is about middle school students with ADHD and about their writing abilities. The date of the publication is very recent, fitting well within our criteria. All in all, this article would probably be worth tracking down. Sometimes ERIC provides a link to a free downloadable PDF version of the actual article. By accessing that, you will, of course, save yourself time and possibly some money. This abstract doesn't indicate that a free PDF can immediately be downloaded, but if you click on "Direct link" on the right-hand side, you can see if you can still get access to the full text. In this example, when you click on "Direct link," a new screen appears to link you to a page outside of ERIC, in this case, to the journal publisher. In this case, the publisher is not offering a free downloadable copy of the article. Therefore, you have three options: a) try to locate the actual article at your local or university library, b) back up your search to look at other records in your original search output and investigate those (Figure 2.3), or c) at your original search output, click on

FIGURE 2.4 ● ERIC Abstract of Article

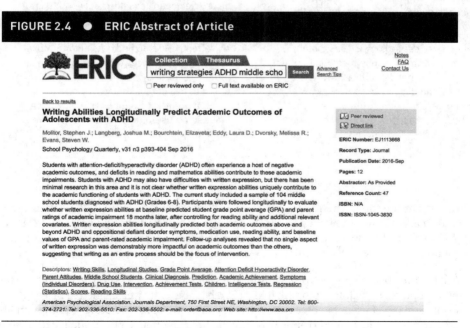

Source: US Deparment of Education, https://eric.ed.gov/

IN THEIR OWN WORDS

Tips for Conducting an Electronic Search

Courtney Valdes, master's degree student

1. *Keep it simple.* You may be researching the effects of parenting style on the language development of at-risk children, but if you enter that mouthful into a search database, you may find exactly nothing. Instead, focus on the key terms, such as *parenting style, language development*, and *at-risk children*.

2. *If at first you don't succeed, search, search again.* Didn't find much? It's more likely that you weren't searching properly than there is no literature on your subject. Most databases employ very specific descriptors (descriptive terms) for cataloging articles. Try using different, but similar terms. For example, use *literacy* instead of *language development*, or broaden the term *at-risk children* to *at-risk*.

3. *Descriptors, descriptors, descriptors.* Sometimes common sense just won't cut it, and you will need to do a little extra legwork to find descriptors that will work for your search. In these instances, you have two choices: you can search the Thesaurus of ERIC Descriptors, or you can look at the descriptors listed for the few articles your search turned up or for articles that may not exactly fit your needs but touch on some aspects of your topic.

4. *Look beyond the abstract.* Don't get seduced by a pretty abstract. Often the abstracts don't give a completely accurate picture of the article they are representing. Therefore, it is best not to stop your search after finding one or two articles that might fit your topic. If you have access to an electronic database of articles, you can actually review the articles before ending your search. Otherwise, gathering a good list of potential articles to take with you to the library could be a real time-saver.

5. *Don't forget to read literature reviews.* Even if an article doesn't exactly meet your needs, other research referenced in its literature review might. This can often be a quick and effective way to find relevant literature for your paper. Once you have a reference for an article, you can enter its author(s) or title into the database and—voila!—you've found a great article for your review, or at least some useful descriptors to help you continue your search.

the box at the top of the screen that says "Full text available on ERIC," hit the search button again, and review the records that come up there with free downloadable PDFs. You may need to do all three things in order to acquire a sufficient number of articles for an adequate review and analysis of your topic/problem.

If at First You Don't Succeed. To summarize the search process, you know that you have to pick a topic that is of interest to you. It must also be sufficiently well defined so that an electronic search is efficient but broad enough that you have enough literature to draw from in your written product. As you can see, the search process is often iterative, and requires flexibility in looking, as well as using limiters. In addition, after reading an article, it is a good idea to look at the reference list. The author(s) of the article may have cited other literature that you should look at too. Read the advice of a graduate student in In Their Own Words.

Before concluding, this is a good time to introduce you to the practice of relying on **primary sources**. Primary sources are the original literature pieces written by authors whom you wish to cite in your paper. You can also choose to cite what others have cited, but then you are relying on those authors' interpretation of those sources, now called **secondary sources**. Secondary sources might include existing literature reviews, such as those published in the *Review of Educational Research* or the *Handbook of Research on Teacher Education*. These may be great for helping you sift through a lot of literature or validating your analysis. Nevertheless, the rule of thumb is this—whenever possible, find the primary source, read it for yourself, and cite it if it fits within your review parameters.

Putting It All Together

Identify three potential research problems or phenomena of interest.

1. _____

   _____

2. _____

   _____

3. _____

   _____

Write a possible research question for each of the above research problems.

1. _____

   _____

2. _____

   _____

3. _____

   _____

Write a possible hypothesis for each of the above research questions.

1. _____

   _____

2. _____

   _____

3. _____

   _____

Summary

The first part of the chapter discussed identifying research ideas and narrowing your problem focus. It is important to point out that these efforts, while essential at the beginning of your research, sometimes reoccur later as well. That is, you may define a problem initially and then clarify, or even redefine it later after conducting a literature search and review. Keep this thought in mind as you turn to the next chapter. You see, research is a far more iterative or even recursive process than a linear one. Even though the author suggests that you take the time to focus carefully on a specific research problem and then write good questions and hypotheses (when appropriate to the method) early in the process, you will likely continue to revise your questions and hypothesis even as you later shape your research design and method. Designs and methods are discussed in Chapters 5, 6, and 7. Chapter 8 on proposal development will refer to research questions yet again in order to apply and extend your understanding as you link your questions and hypotheses to design and methods.

To conclude, consider the following anonymous "thought for the day": "A problem well stated is a problem half solved." There is a great deal of truth in that, and it is particularly true for writing good research questions and for selecting a research design and methods.

Discussion Questions

1. What is the difference between a research problem and a research question?

2. What makes a good research question?

3. What's the difference between a research question and a hypothesis?

4. Is this a good research question? Why or why not?

    Does peer tutoring affect the performance of ESL students on essays written in language arts classes?

5. Is this a good research question? Why or why not?

    How can I improve student grades in science?

6. How might making decisions about what to include and exclude from your search be valuable *before* you begin your literature search?

7. What are the advantages and disadvantages of using a database such as ERIC over using a search engine such as Google?

Your Research Project in Action

Based on your completion of activities in Chapter 2, select the research problem you are most interested in and conduct a literature search using the ERIC or another database. Use the following guide.

Research problem: _____

_____

Keywords to search by: _____

_____

Did those keywords pull up documents?   Yes   No

Were there too many documents or not enough?   Too Many   Not Enough

Redefine keywords to search by: _____

_____

Find five resources that have abstracts directly pertinent to your research problem.

1. _____

2. _____

3. _____

4. _____

5. _____

Identify which of the resources are primary or secondary sources.

Primary	Secondary
1.	1.
2.	2.
3.	3.
4.	4.
5.	5.

Further Reading

Gall, M. D., Gall, J. P., & Borg, W. R. (2006) *Educational research: An introduction* (8th ed.). London: Pearson.

This book has been highly referenced by many graduate students for many years. Qualitative and quantitative methods of study are presented, compared, and analyzed in great detail. The authors describe the interconnections among educational research, educational philosophy, and educational practice.

McMillan, J. H. (2015). *Fundamentals of educational research* (7th ed.). London: Pearson.

This book is an introduction to education research for students who want to conduct research, particularly in their own settings. Research credibility is a central theme of the book. The book includes tools to facilitate this research process, such as technology activities, personal author reflections, and self-test questions and answers.

References

Babinski, L. M., Amendum, S. J., Knotek, S. E., Sanchez, M., & Malone, P. (2017). Improving young English learners' language and literacy skills through teacher professional development: A randomized controlled trial. *American Educational Research Journal*, *55*(1), 117–143.

Cheng, E. C. K. (2017). Managing school-based professional development activities. *International Journal of Educational Management*, *31*(4), 445–454.

Frazier, D. K., & Trekles, A. M. (2017). Elementary 1:1 iPad implementation: Successes and struggles during the first year.*Journal of Educational Technology Systems*, 1–22. Downloaded April 11, 2018 from https://doi.org/10.1177/0047239517737965

Gall, M. D., Gall, J. P., & Borg, W. R. (2006). *Educational research: An introduction* (8th ed.). London: Pearson.

Kohl, F. L., McLaughlin, M. J., & Nagle, K. (2006). Alternate achievement standards and assessments: A descriptive investigation of 16 states. *Exceptional Children*, *73*, 107–122.

Olakanmi, E. E. (2017). The effects of a flipped classroom model of instruction on students' performance and attitudes toward chemistry. *Journal of Science Education and Technology*, *26*(1), 127–137.

Therrien, W. J., Wickstrom, K., & Jones, K. (2006). Effect of a combined repeated reading and question generation intervention on reading achievement. *Learning Disabilities Research and Practice*, *21*, 89–97.

3

Understanding Relevant Literature and Writing a Literature Review

Every day, educators are confronted with decisions regarding how best to teach and support students for whom many traditional methods do not seem to work. They reflect, share experiences and materials with colleagues, and check the Internet to find descriptions of practices to help. Still, they may often find it difficult to tell reliable practices from snake oil. Educators may not seriously consider picking up a research journal that reports findings about the problems they encounter. For many, an abundance of technical and statistical information in many journal articles and a perceived aloofness of researchers make such efforts anything but inviting. Such barriers are often coupled with information overload, a lack of time for reflection, and difficulty determining just what the difference *is* between "good" and "poor" research.

This situation is unfortunate. Published research articles in refereed journals and other reliable sources are a potentially valuable tool for educators. They provide an opportunity to look at research-based practices in other classrooms and settings instead of relying on word of mouth or the marketing of products and materials companies. Published research often details effective and efficient approaches that are helpful for students with a variety of characteristics. By reviewing published research, one can sharpen and focus research questions prior to conducting one's own investigations. Thus, educators need to review existing literature. In this chapter, you will learn how to analyze and understand research literature in education, as well as how to write a literature review.

Analyzing Literature Search Outcomes

In Chapter 2, you were introduced to a process for searching existing literature, using the ERIC electronic database as an example. Once you found some resource citations with abstracts, you began to analyze them in terms of the inclusion and exclusion criteria set out earlier. In an attempt to make educational research more meaningful for you, this chapter begins with a set of markers for evaluating and analyzing trustworthy and usable information. Like Carnine (1997), my hope is that if educators are better able to digest the material presented in research reports, they will find literature reviews more informative; they may be better able to find beneficial information and techniques to use in their classrooms, schools, and other settings; and the direction of their research will become clearer. Suggestions are provided for analyzing and understanding different forms of **experimental research**, as well as **descriptive research**, particularly qualitative studies.

Most research articles are set up the same way. After the **abstract**, the **introduction** provides background information and rationale for the study. Next, the researcher presents the **method** used in the study, including a description of the participants, the setting, the intervention (in experimental research) or phenomena studied (descriptive research), the measures or types of data collected, and the data analysis procedures. This is followed by a **results** section in which the researcher describes the outcomes of the measures (experimental) or findings from data collected (descriptive). The last section of a report is the **discussion** in which the author(s) provides his or her interpretation of the results and the implications of the study.

In an effort to judge the usability of a research article, the reader should look for important details in each part. However, it may not be necessary to read each part of the report in the order in which it was presented. In fact, for many educators, it might be helpful to follow an alternative sequence as presented in Figure 3.1. The following sections explain items to consider in each part of an article, following the sequence in the flow chart. This sequence is certainly not intended to be inclusive of every possible item. You might use the information in each section as a checklist (see *Check Sheet for Understanding Relevant Literature* at the end of this chapter), with the understanding that the objectives of studies may vary.

Analyzing the Abstract and Introduction

The abstract at the beginning of an article may well be the same as what you have already read from the output of a literature search. It is typically an overview of the article and, if the article presents research, should include an abbreviated description of the participants involved, as well as the outcomes.

FIGURE 3.1 ● Suggested Alternative Sequence to Reading and Analyzing Research

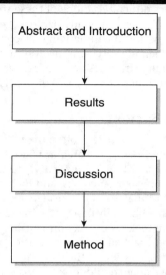

The introduction, which follows, typically includes the author's review of litera-ture, including relevant information from other articles or databases. This is not an area for the researcher's opinions, but a place where results from previous studies or other literature are reported. In a research article, the literature review typically concludes with a statement of the purpose of the research study and often specific research questions as well.

In sum, here's what to look for in the abstract and introduction:

- Relevance to the reader's topic, as well as relevance to participants of interest

- Recent and important citations of relevant articles rather than an abundance of references to outdated work

- Citations of research articles rather than an abundance of opinion or theory papers (i.e., check the reference list.)

- Clear purpose/goals of the study, including good research questions (as noted in Chapter 2)

Look back at the abstract from the example literature search in Chapter 2. You can see information about the participants, the research method, and the results. Now here's an example of part of an introduction. Look for part of the literature review and the purpose/goals of the study.

Although some studies (Jordan et al., 2013; Schneider & Siegler, 2010; Steencken & Maher, 2003) have suggested the effectiveness of using manipulatives or visual representations for enhancing fraction learning among students with mathematics difficulties, none of these studies focused on number lines specifically. The present study had two primary goals: (a) to identify error patterns and the underlying misconceptions among middle school students when identifying a fraction number on a number line and (b) to compare the faulty strategies between students with and without mathematics disabilities. (Zhang, Stecker, & Beqiri, 2017, p. 227)

Analyzing the Results Section

The results section of a research article is often the most difficult section for many educators to navigate. In experimental research articles, it may be loaded with statistics and terms that may seem daunting. In qualitative descriptive research, the results section may be called the findings or outcomes, and include a list and explanation of themes that emerged from the analysis. Some readers may skip to the discussion section in an attempt to find out what *really* happened. In either experimental or descriptive research, skipping to the discussion section can be presumptuous because the results section is meant to be a factual statement of the data, whereas the discussion section is the researcher's interpretation of the data.

In the results section, the reader should look for answers to the research questions presented in the introduction. Therefore, for any experimental intervention, the reader should look for the effects of that intervention or treatment. In qualitative descriptive research, the reader should be attentive to the specific statements and information the researchers give to support the themes noted or address questions asked. In either type of research, the results section should not include any extraneous data or opinions from the researcher.

In sum, here's what to look for in the results section:

- Explanation of outcomes or effects regarding participants

- Explanations of results with minimal jargon

- For qualitative methods, clearly defined themes with data to support/provide examples

- Displays of the results in graphs or other visuals

Here's an example of part of the results of an experimental study. Look for the characteristics just listed.

Significant differences were found between the two groups for total mathematical ability on the TEMA-3, with higher scores for the intervention group. The ANCOVA of the math ability scores was significant, $F(1, 46) = 13.59$, $p = <.001$, $n^2 = .22$ (see Table 3). The strength of the relationship between the intervention and the dependent variable was assessed as medium on the dependent measure, holding constant the pretest math achievement scores. The intervention group had the lower pretest mean ($M = 74.46$, $SD = 11.91$), but the higher posttest mean ($M = 82.29$, $SD = 13.66$) and adjusted mean ($M = 83.2$). The comparison group had the higher pretest mean ($M = 76.58$, $SD = 11.97$), and the lower posttest mean ($M = 75.81$, $SD = 11.36$) and adjusted mean ($M = 74.97$; see Table 2). Follow-up tests were conducted to evaluate pairwise differences among the adjusted means. There were significant differences among the pairwise comparison of adjusted means between the two groups ($p = < .001$). Although the intervention group experienced total math ability gains, posttest scores were still more than 1 SD below the mean for both groups (Green, Gallagher & Hart, 2018, pp. 12–13)

Now here's an example of a part of the results of a study utilizing qualitative data.

Students' perceptions of the value of their STEM education varied. Many students felt that their STEM education prepared them well for college; for instance, Ariana was "able to go straight into microbiology, organic chemistry, and physics" in college, and Benjamin's advanced STEM courses "helped develop study skills" that he needed in college. Some students, however, felt less prepared; for example, Olivia's experiences in statistics left her feeling shaky in college psychology courses: "I didn't realize there was so much math and science in [Psychology]. I wish I was more introduced to that." Iris, likewise, felt she "definitely could have learned more," but felt that overall, her STEM experience in high school prepared her well for college.

Willow described her school's AP program as "so incredible"; she took 12 AP exams and began college with 73 hours of credit. She described coming to college and "being told that I could take a graduate biochemistry class when I was a 20-year-old junior." (Mullet, Kettler, & Sabatini, 2018, p. 77).

Analyzing the Discussion Section

In the discussion section of research articles, the researcher interprets the results of the study. However, the researcher should not misinterpret the data or attempt to apply the results to people or settings that are dissimilar. This means that even though the methods of a study may be chosen to promote generalizability across situations (in an experimental study), a single study cannot have "the answer" for all educators, students, and schools. Therefore, in experimental and descriptive research, the reader should consider the credibility of the interpretation, as well as commentary about the limitations of the study, implications for practice, and future research needs.

So, here's what to look for in the discussion:

- Interpretation that does not infer beyond the results previously presented

- Discussion of limitations or shortcomings of the research

- Implications for classroom, school, clinic, or other use

Following are parts of the discussion from two different studies.

> Results of this evaluation, reflected in the data regarding absenteeism, discipline referrals, GPA, percentage staying in school, reading performance, and sense of connectedness, in particular, suggest that Prepared for Graduation has promise for at-risk high school students. In each of the two years that data were collected, results suggested that major goals were met for this group of target students. That is, absenteeism and discipline referrals decreased, students stayed in school, GPAs went up, students closed the gap in reading performance, and sense of connectedness seemed to improve. One possible simple explanation for the positive outcomes on these marker variables, and in particular, the improvements toward the end of the school year, is that job site visits occurred during the later part of the school year. Students needed to be in good standing at school in order to be eligible to leave campus for the job site visits, and that may have functioned as a significant incentive. On the other hand, or in addition, the job site visits may have added a sense of relevancy to schooling, and that relevancy led to improvements on marker variables. In other words, the job site visits may have given the target students a reason to perform better in the later part of the school year when student performance is sometimes poorer (Boudah, 2016, p. 11).

Findings of the current study should be interpreted in light of several limitations. Although these results are largely consistent with and expand upon other studies of the school experiences of treatment-seeking anxious children (Langley et al., 2004; Langley et al., 2014), future research on school-based accommodations with larger samples is needed. Second, results are based in part on measures of impairment and accommodations developed for this study. The good internal consistency of the impairment measures and their concordance with measures of anxiety symptoms provide preliminary evidence for their reliability and validity. However, the analysis of accommodations relied solely on survey responses from mothers and children. Information from IEP and 504 documents themselves would be useful in the future for validating these responses. Similarly, information on school functioning was based on parent and child report; there were no data from schools to validate these reports. Third, data were collected at one point in time when children completed an intake for outpatient clinical services. It is therefore unclear whether anxiety symptoms caused impairment or whether poor academic performance (e.g., difficulty with reading) increased anxiety. Similarly, it is unclear whether anxiety-related impairment might have improved already as a result of effective accommodations. Finally, the present findings do not speak to the school experiences of anxious youth who were not seeking outpatient treatment (Green et al., 2017, p. 230).

The excerpt from the Boudah (2016) article is a good example of a reasonable interpretation and description of implications, and the Green et al. (2017) article excerpt is a good example of a clear description of limitations.

Analyzing the Method Section

The method section gives a detailed account of how the researcher conducted the study. By analyzing the methods after the results and discussion, the reader has an opportunity to ask, "Okay, that's what the results were, but how did they go about getting those results? Do the results make sense, given the research procedures followed? Are the procedures even clear?" The most important parts of the method section for educators are the descriptions of the participants and setting, the research procedures (in experimental studies, this includes the intervention), and the data collection and analysis procedures.

Participants. For the reader to understand who was involved in the research, a description of the participants is important. In experimental studies where the researcher(s) is making a claim of generalizability of the findings, the reader needs to know to whom you might generalize the findings. For example, if a researcher is studying the way that elementary teachers instruct students in fractions, the reader needs to know a bit about the teachers in order to understand what variables (e.g., years of experience, graduate degrees) to consider in the interpretation of the results. If a qualitative study has reported that Latino children experience school success differently than non-Latinos, one should know something about the Latino children who participated in the study. For students with disabilities, the reader should know some information about the nature of the disabilities. In 1992 (Rosenberg et al.) and again in 1994 (Morris et al.), the Council for Learning Disabilities published guidelines for describing research participants who have learning disabilities. The What Works Clearinghouse has published a brief reporting guide on characteristics of general study participants (2012).

In short, whether the participants are children or adults, there are a number of details that readers should look for in order to get a sense of who the participants were; particularly in experimental studies, readers should learn whether the individuals in the study are comparable to those the reader may wish to include in his or her research. In other words, to determine whether an intervention may work in the classroom, school, or other setting, a researcher must be able to determine if the sample participants involved in the study were in some way similar to those in her or his research setting (e.g., school, classroom, clinic).

Certain minimums should be reported, and the general rule may be simply this: the more information, the better. Specific characteristics about students, educators, or other participants are preferred over mere labels such as "novice principal," "experienced teacher," "Latino children," or "students with disabilities."

Here are some things to look for in the description of student participants:

- Number
- Gender
- Age and grade level
- Ethnicity
- Social economic status (SES), if possible, or a proxy such as eligibility for free or reduced lunch

- Standardized achievement, state test scores or proficiency status

- Any behavioral characteristics that may be linked to the research questions

If the participants are teachers, administrators, parents, or other adults, the following information might be relevant:

- Number

- Gender

- Ethnicity

- Age

- Years of professional experience

- Degrees earned

- Social economic status (SES), if possible, or a proxy such as income level

The following is an excerpt from the participants section of a study that describes the students involved. Look for the participant characteristics.

To be eligible for the fluency studies, second graders read below 40 words per minute and fourth graders below 80 words per minute as the median score of three AIMSweb (Academic Improvement Measurement System; Shinn & Shinn, 2002) passages. After securing parent permission (i.e., 93% of those from whom permission was requested), participating students included 337 students with RD [Reading Disabilities]. One hundred and ninety-two of these students were in second grade and 145 in fourth grade. Sixty-one percent were eligible for special education services (40% of second-grade and 89% of fourth-grade students), with 80% of students receiving special education services under the category of LD [Learning Disabilities] that included RD. Placements for these students included general education and special education resource room for up to 2.5 hours per day. No significant differences were found in the reading rate between students with and without formal identification for disabilities; therefore, all of the poor reader sample will be referenced as students with RD. Eighty-one percent were native English speakers, and 19% were English Learners (ELs) who spoke Spanish as their first language and scored 3, 4, or 5 on a 5-point scale of English Language Development. Thus, none of the EL participants were beginning English speakers and all possessed conversational ability in English. The reading rate did not differ between students with RD with and without identified disabilities or between ELs and native English speakers (O'Connor, 2018, p. 128).

Setting. The context in which a study takes place may impact the results also. Education researchers need to understand the setting in which any study takes place in order to help them decide whether their own setting is similar or different in ways that may help interpret outcomes.

A clear description of the setting would include many of the following:

- Urban, rural, or suburban

- Overall SES of students and families in the community

- Age of the school

- Extent of school resources and support

- Size of student population and average class size

- Racial or ethnic makeup of the school or district

- Mean state test scores or proficiency status

Following is an article excerpt that includes many characteristics of a good description of the setting.

This study took place in a school district located near a large university in the Midwest. The district has two high schools, three middle schools, and 19 elementary schools. Several years prior to this study, as part of a district-level initiative, all schools had adopted a PBIS framework but were at different stages of implementation at the time of the study. Principals from three elementary schools serving grades K–6 agreed to participate in the study. These schools served between 400 and 521 students, ranged from 64.5% to 81.2% White, and had free or reduced lunch rates between 10.8% and 26.3%. About 9% of students had disabilities, and English language learners made up 0.2% to 13% of the school population (see Table 1) (Bruhn, Barron, Fernando & Balint-Langel, 2018, p. 33).

Research Procedures. Understanding the specifics of the research process is important, regardless of whether the research is experimental or descriptive. Information should be included about the relationships among the researcher, the study, and the participants in the study, as well as the critical details of the research process; these are especially common conventions in studies using qualitative methods (Spradley, 2016). In experimental studies, the intervention methods should be described in enough detail for educators to decide whether or not the intervention is applicable or practical in their settings.

A clear description of the research procedures would include many of the following:

- Step-by-step description of experimental intervention implementation

- Necessary time and materials required for an experimental intervention

- Procedures and conditions prior to implementing intervention

- Who implemented the intervention, their responsibilities, and the extent of preparation for implementing intervention

- How participants were selected and grouped

- Incentives to participants

- Monetary costs associated with implementing intervention

- Perceptions or biases of the researcher

- Role of the researcher, particularly in qualitative methodology

Here's an example research procedures section from an experimental study, followed by an example procedures section from a descriptive study using qualitative methods. Try to find at least some of the information listed above in each excerpt.

. . . instructors administered a sentence construction probe at the end of each session. Instructors handed out a sentence construction probe to students and said, "I will give you 1 min to write as many complete sentences as you can. Work quickly and accurately. Do you have any questions?" Instructors answered any questions and read any words requested by students. Students were told to pick up their pens or pencils and begin. A countdown timer was started. At the end of 1 min, sentence construction probes were collected and no feedback was given. Sentence construction probes had 10 unique picture-word prompts displayed across two pages. The pictures on sentence construction probes were not used during intervention (i.e., no overlap between probes and intervention materials). The pictures were approximately 4 cm by 4 cm with two to three words accompanying each picture. Three lines to the right of each picture-word prompt provided space for student responses. Figure 1 shows examples of picture-word prompts and formatting of probes (Datchuk, 2017, p. 65).

Five of the six authors conducted at least one focus group. All five focus group facilitators had worked in the disability field with individuals with social-communication needs; three of the focus group facilitators were also family members of individuals with disabilities. Throughout data collection and analysis, the authors engaged in reflexive practices (e.g., took field notes) to help address their biases. Each focus group had a primary facilitator who asked the protocol questions and a co-facilitator who took detailed notes. Each facilitator was trained in conducting focus groups. Specifically, three of the facilitators had prior experience conducting focus groups. The other two facilitators were trained by: observing focus groups and debriefing with the experienced facilitators, assisting with conducting the pilot focus groups, and initially only co-facilitating focus groups until they were ready to be the primary facilitator. At the beginning of each focus group, the facilitators acknowledged their relations to disability to establish rapport. All questions on the protocol were asked during each focus group. Focus groups were audio recorded and transcribed verbatim; the focus group facilitator reviewed each transcript for accuracy. On average, focus groups lasted 1.5 to 2 hr. Parent focus groups ranged from nine to 10 participants; professional focus groups ranged from six to seven participants (Burke et al., 2018, p. 194).

The excerpt from the Datchuk (2017) article provides a good example of many of the important components of experimental research procedures, and the Burke et al. (2018) article excerpt illustrates a clear description of procedures, conditions, and biases of researchers using qualitative methods.

Data Collection and Analysis. Readers should look carefully at the kind of data collected and the method of collection. For example, the author of this text conducted a study to look at the effects of an intervention on in-class student engagement (Boudah, Deshler, Schumaker, Lenz, & Cook, 1997). The researchers decided to measure only student verbal engagement. That decision meant that many other nonverbal ways in which students are sometimes engaged, including direct eye contact or head nodding, were left out of the eventual analysis. As another example, in a qualitative study, researchers might interview only certain people in a school regarding the culture of collaboration. One may never know the opinions of those who were not interviewed, yet those opinions could have changed the outcomes of the study. In short, what the reader will see in the results section is dependent on what data were collected, as well as how data were analyzed.

Moreover, the reader should see an explanation of how the data were collected, by whom, and how reliability or trustworthiness of the data was established. *Trustworthiness* is the extent to which the researcher and reader can trust the findings, a concept especially germane to qualitative methods (Lincoln & Guba, 1985).

A clear description of the data collection and analysis would then include the following:

- Description and/or examples of types of data collected

- How data collectors were trained

- How data were collected

- How the researcher made sure data collectors followed procedures (reliability)

- How data were managed (e.g., transcribed, entered in statistics program)

- If statistics were used in analyzing the data, an explanation of why each statistic was selected, and name of software used

- If qualitative data were collected, a detailed description of data analysis procedures used (with examples), and name of software used

Here are two more article excerpts, one experimental and the second descriptive (qualitative data). Take a look at them for some of the characteristics above.

Evaluators compared student performance at two points in the school year, before and after participation in XR classes. That is, students were compared to themselves to calculate growth between pre and post performance. The performance of students participating in XR classes was *not* compared to the performance of another group of students who did not participate in XR classes. Raw scores were calculated by scoring individual student pre and posttest protocols according to test guidelines and used in inferential analyses using Statistical Package for the Social Sciences (SPSS). The subtests for the GRADE include measures of Listening Comprehension, Vocabulary, and Sentence and Passage Comprehension. The GRADE also produces a total raw score that was first included in the analysis. The TOSCRF is a measure of reading comprehension and general reading fluency. The test produces a single raw score that was used in the analysis. A Paired-Samples t-test was conducted using Statistical Package for the Social Sciences (SPSS) to examine the difference in means between pretest and posttest total raw scores from the GRADE and the TOSCRF. A Paired-Samples t-test was conducted to examine the difference in means between pretest and posttest raw scores from the GRADE Listening Comprehension, Vocabulary, and Sentence and Passage Comprehension *subtests*. A split file Paired-Samples t-test was conducted to examine the difference in means between pretest and posttest total raw scores from the GRADE and TOSCRF, for students with disabilities only. Analyses were conducted only when the number of students in any subgroup was greater than one. Means and standard deviations were computed for pretest and posttest raw scores on the GRADE and TOSCRF for all students, by district, by school, and by teacher. The raw score means were then converted to Grade Level Equivalents (GEs) and pretest to posttest differences were computed. The GE differences were then displayed in Microsoft Excel bar graphs (Boudah, 2018, p. 153).

The audio files were transcribed verbatim, reviewed for accuracy and potential identifying features were anonymized. The data were then analysed using a thematic analysis (Braun and Clarke, 2006) to identify key themes at a semantic level which Boyatzis (1998) describes as not looking beyond what the participant has said. As the first author had already undertaken a systematic literature review on the positive aspects of parenting, it was important, while undertaking the data analysis, to avoid the unconscious 'seeing' of data that researchers expect to find (Crabtree and Miller, 1999) and also not to force the data into preconceived categories, affecting the confirmability of the findings. Multiple readings of the transcripts and field notes took place and annotations were added prior to coding. Coding was initially a phrase or a single word that captured the 'essence' of what a positive aspect might be and was undertaken first in individual transcripts and then across all 17 transcripts. Areas of consensus began to emerge and cluster as themes in relation to the research question, and the themes were then further clustered and assigned succinct phrases to describe the meaning that underpinned each theme. The adequacy and appropriateness of the themes were subject to interpretive rigor (Ezzy, 2002) as these were checked by two other researchers and any discrepancies or disagreements led to all the research team reading the transcript together and agreeing a coding and theme, increasing the credibility and trustworthiness of the data interpretation (Beighton & Wills, 2017, p. 329).

Many educators are unsure of what to look for when analyzing research literature and how to approach the task. The alternative sequence given here and the checklist at this end of this chapter provide direction for analyzing research. The next section of this chapter will help you organize your analyses and write a literature review.

Writing a Literature Review

First of all, writing a literature review as a part of the introduction of a research paper is a different task than writing a thorough stand-alone review. In other words, a literature review written and published in the *Review of Educational Research* is different than a review included as part of the introduction to a research report, or even a thesis or dissertation. The process may be similar, but the depth of analysis and detail presented in a stand-alone literature review will be much greater than in a report introduction.

Organizing Your Review Information

Graduate student researchers and other educators should first organize the articles that they have found through a literature search in some meaningful way. A table or matrix might be helpful. For example, Figure 3.2 is a sample matrix using the sections of a research report for organizational purposes.

Any or all of the sections could be specified in much more detail, depending on what kinds of things are important in your review. For example, in the Chapter 2 example literature search of *writing strategies of middle school students with ADHD*, you could very well decide to add several columns to the table for the specific parts of "method," such as "participants," particularly when a literature search yields studies on other populations such as elementary students, high school students, or students from other countries. You could further refine the table by creating a category called something like "type of intervention." This would very well capture a variety of experiments published in the literature. However, you might anticipate that the literature on such a topic would include descriptive studies as well. That being the case, you could either add a category called something like "focus of study," which might capture descriptive studies having to do with writing as well as reading or math.

Synthesizing the Literature Information

Fill in the table with information from each of the studies you found in your literature search. After doing so, look at the information within the categories/columns for commonalities, trends, and missing areas of study as well as discrepancies, particularly in the results. Make notes about what you find, perhaps in the cells of a summary column in the table, and include what you think the implications are for the population of interest to you, as well as for future research needs and directions.

Writing Your Review

Now you are ready to start writing. If you are writing a stand-alone literature review, you will need to begin your paper with a section discussing the purpose of

FIGURE 3.2 ● Sample Literature Organizational Table

Article	Introduction	Method	Results	Discussion
1				
2				
3				

your review and then a section that details your search process and your inclusion/exclusion decisions.

From that point on, a literature review that precedes a research paper and one that stands alone are formatted similarly. You could organize your paper in sections with headings that match the same categories/column titles you created in your organizational table. You may decide to focus on a smaller number of categories of particular interest to you and/or your research proposal (if you are writing the literature review as the beginning of a research paper, thesis, or dissertation). Each of these categories can become sections with headings for discussion of the following:

- Commonalities or trends in the results

- Inconsistencies or contradictions in the results

- Strengths and/or weaknesses in the methods

A literature review concludes with an attempt to answer the "so what?" question. That is, writers should step back to discuss the overall implications of the body of literature reviewed, including but not limited to implications for the population of interest and for future research.

In the complete text of a graduate-level literature review, Boote and Beile (2005) suggested that students be sure to do the following:

- Justify criteria for inclusion and exclusion of research in the review.

- Distinguish what has been researched on the topic from what needs to be researched.

- Place the topic or problem in the broader scholarly literature and historical context.

- Articulate important variables and phenomena relevant to the topic.

- Identify the main methodologies used in the research and their advantages and disadvantages.

- Rationalize the practical and scholarly significance of the research problem.

- Write with a coherent and clear structure.

If you are writing a stand-alone literature review, look at examples in the journal *Review of Educational Research* (http://journals.sagepub.com/home/rer), which includes only literature reviews and syntheses. Many other high-quality journals in the field of education also publish literature reviews and syntheses; find and review some of those too. Research syntheses can be either narrative (e.g., a researcher makes subjective comparisons related to the research question) or quantitative (e.g., a researcher makes numerical comparisons related to the research question). A popular form of quantitative research synthesis is the meta-analysis. A **meta-analysis** is "the statistical analysis of a large collection of analysis results from individual studies for the purpose of integrating the findings" (Glass, 1976, p. 3).

Revisiting and Revising Research Questions

In Chapter 2, you read that it is important to narrow and specify your research problem of interest and to craft research questions to guide your research efforts. You also should recall that these efforts, while essential early on in your research, sometimes reoccur later as well. That is, you may initially define a problem and then, after conducting a literature search and review, revisit your questions to clarify, refine, or revise. Therefore, after you draft your literature review, I suggest that you take the time to look again at your research problem, questions, and hypotheses (when appropriate to the method) and revise your questions and hypothesis as necessary, given what you have learned through your review and analysis of existing literature. Your analysis of the research methods used in previous studies may well have given you some excellent ideas on how to design your study, and your questions should reflect the key aspects of your method (e.g., participants and variables).

Putting It All Together

If you haven't already done so, take a look at the *Check Sheet for Understanding Relevant Literature* on the next page. Make copies of and use the check sheet as you read each article in order to direct your analysis. Make additional notes as necessary. This documentation will help you later when you organize your analyses prior to writing your review.

Summary

Ultimately, educators decide whether research studies have utility for them and their classrooms or schools. Many proven practices require administrative and teacher support, training, and additional materials to realize similar results. There are no quick fixes when working with students or understanding the nature of many aspects of education. Nevertheless, to find effective practices, educators should be aware of what researchers have already done in many classrooms, schools, or other related settings. Thus, research reports are a vital source of information about innovative practices and other important phenomena.

Education professionals will not find the answers to all of their questions by reading one research article, but through a thoughtful search and evaluation of what researchers have done, educators can ask better questions, find direction, and discover many reliable sources of help. In other words, as suggested in Chapter 2 and in this chapter, conducting a literature review can give you a chance to show others the importance of your topic and refine the problem, research questions, or hypotheses you have targeted.

Check Sheet for Understanding Relevant Literature

What to Look for in the Abstract and Introduction

Relevance to my topic, as well as relevance to participants of interest

❑ Recent and important citations of relevant articles rather than an abundance of references to dated work

❏ Citations of research articles rather than an abundance of opinion or theory papers (i.e., check the reference list)

❏ Clear purpose of the study, including good research questions

What to Look for in the Results

Explanation of outcomes or effects regarding participants

❏ Explanations of results with minimal jargon

❏ For qualitative methods, clearly defined themes with data to support/provide examples

❏ Displays of the results in graphs or other visuals

What to Look for in the Discussion

Interpretation that does not infer beyond the results previously presented

❏ Discussion of limitations or shortcomings

❏ Implications for classroom or other use

What to Look for in Research Procedures

❏ Step-by-step description of experimental intervention implementation

❏ Necessary time and materials required for an experimental intervention

❏ Procedures and conditions prior to implementing intervention

❏ Who implemented the intervention, their responsibilities, and the extent of preparation for implementing intervention

❏ How participants were selected and grouped

❏ Incentives to participants

❏ Monetary costs associated with implementing intervention

❏ Perceptions or biases of the researcher

❏ Role of the researcher, particularly in qualitative methodology

What to Look for in Participants

❏ Number

❏ Gender

❏ Age and grade level

❏ Ethnicity

❑ Socioeconomic status (SES), or proxy such as free or reduced lunch, or income level

❑ Time in special education placement

❑ Standardized achievement, state test scores or proficiency status

❑ Any behavioral characteristics that may be linked to the research questions

❑ Degrees earned

❑ Years of professional experience

What to Look for in the Setting

❑ Urban, rural, or suburban

❑ Overall SES of students and families in the community

❑ Age of the school

❑ Extent of school resources and support

❑ Size of student population and average class size

❑ Racial or ethnic makeup of the school or district

❑ Mean state test scores or proficiency status

What to Look for in Data Collection and Analysis

❑ Description and/or examples of types of data collected (may be found in appendixes or tables)

❑ How data collectors were trained

❑ How data were collected

❑ How researcher made sure data collectors followed procedures (reliability)

❑ How data were managed (e.g., transcribed, entered in statistics program)

❑ If statistics were used in analyzing the data, an explanation of why each statistic was selected, and name of software used

❑ If qualitative data were collected, a description of data analysis procedures used (with examples), and name of software used

Discussion Questions

1. Is the presented alternative sequence for analyzing research articles helpful (Figure 3.1)? Why or why not?

2. What minimum descriptors regarding student participants should be included in a method section?

3. What key parts of the description of data analysis should you look for in any qualitative research report?

4. Why is it important to understand the limitations of a study?

5. How might your literature review inform revisions to your research questions?

Your Research Project in Action

First, select a research article from your search of the literature and use the check sheet to guide your analysis. Organize the critical information from your analysis into a larger version of the table below. Complete this table as you read and analyze each article from your literature search.

Article	Introduction	Method	Results	Discussion
1				
2				
3				
4				
5				
6				

Further Reading

Boote, D. N., & Beille, P. (2005). Scholars before researchers: On the centrality of the dissertation literature review in research preparation. *Educational Research, 34*(6), 3–15.

In this article, the authors' goal is to improve the quality of literature reviews by providing criteria all individuals should both reference and abide by when producing their own works. The authors of this article suggest that to become an educational scholar and productive researcher, an individual must be able to collect and analyze previous studies, collect and analyze personal study information, and then advance the collective understanding and knowledge through presentation of personal study. The authors examine three dissertation literature reviews at three universities, checking for content and quality.

References

Boote, D. N., & Beille, P. (2005). Scholars before researchers: On the centrality of the dissertation literature review in research preparation. *Educational Researcher, 34*(6), 3–15.

Boudah, D. J., Deshler, D. D., Schumaker, J. B., Lenz, B. K., & Cook, B. (1997). Student-centered or content-centered: A case study of a middle school teacher's lesson planning and instruction in inclusive classes. *Teacher Education and Special Education, 20*(3), 189–203.

Carnine, D. (1997). Bridging the research-to-practicegap. *Exceptional Children, 63*(4), 513–521.

Glass, G. (1976). Primary, secondary, and meta-analysis of research. *Educational Researcher, 5*(10), 3–8.

Lincoln, Y. S., & Guba, E. G. (1985). *Naturalistic inquiry.* Newbury Park, CA: Sage.

Morris, R., Lyon, G. R., Alexander, D., Gray, D. B., Kavanagh, J., Rourke, B. P., et al. (1994). Editorial: Proposed guidelines and criteria for describing samples of persons with learning disabilities. *Learning Disability Quarterly, 17,* 106–109.

Rosenberg, M. S., Bott, D., Majsterek, D., Chiang, B., Gartland, D., Wesson, C., et al. (1992). Minimum standards for the description of participants in learning disabilities research. *Learning Disability Quarterly, 15,* 65–70.

Spradley, J. P. (2016). *Participant observation.* Long Grove IL: Holt, Waveland Press.

What Works Clearinghouse. (2012). *What works clearinghouse reporting guide for study authors.* Downloaded April 18, 2018 from https://files.eric.ed.gov/fulltext/ED534326.pdf

Literature Examples

Beighton, C., & Wills, J. (2017). Are parents identifying positive aspects to parenting their child with an intellectual disability or are they just coping? A qualitative exploration. *Journal of Intellectual Disabilities, 21*(4), 325–345.

Boudah, D. J. (2016). Prepared for graduation: A multi-faceted and multi-tiered intervention to support at-risk high school students. *Journal of Education & Social Policy, 3*(2), 1–15.

Boudah, D. J. (2018). Evaluation of intensive reading strategies intervention for low-performing adolescents with and without learning disabilities. *Insights into Learning Disabilities,* 15(2), 149–159.

Bruhn, A., Barron, S., Fernando, J., & Balint-Langel, K. (2018). Extending the direct behavior rating: An examination of schoolwide behavior ratings and academic engagement. *Journal of Positive Behavior Interventions, 20*(1), 31–42.

Burke, M. M., Meadan-Kaplansky, H., Patton, K. A.,Pearson, J. N., Cummings, K. P., & Lee, C. (2018). Advocacy for children with social-communication needs: Perspectives from parents and school professionals. *The Journal of Special Education, 51*(4), 191–200.

Datchuk, S. M. (2017). A direct instruction and precision teaching intervention to improve the sentence construction of middle school students with writing difficulties. *The Journal of Special Education, 51*(2), 62–71.

Green, J. G., Comer, J. S., Donaldson, A. R., Elkins, R. M., Nadeau, M. S., Reid, G., & Pincus, D. B. (2017). School functioning and use of school-based accommodations by treatment-seeking anxious children. *Journal of Emotional and Behavioral Disorders, 25*(4), 220–232.

Green, K. B., Gallagher, P. A., & Hart, L. (2018). Integrating mathematics and children's literature for young children with disabilities. *Journal of Early Intervention, 40*(1), 3–19.

Mullet, D. R., Kettler, T., & Sabatini, A. (2018). Gifted students' conceptions of their high school STEM. *Journal for the Education of the Gifted, 41*(1), 60–92.

O'Connor, R. E. (2018). Reading fluency and students with reading disabilities: How fast is fast enough to promote reading comprehension? *Journal of Learning Disabilities, 51*(2), 124–136.

Zhang, D., Stecker, P., & Beqiri, K. (2017). Mathematics disabilities use when estimating fractions on number lines. *Learning Disability Quarterly, 40*(4), 225–236.

Issues in Validity
and Reliability

Chapter Objectives

In this chapter, the reader will

- explore the differences among validity, reliability, and trustworthiness.

- learn about the various types of validity and selected threats to validity.

- learn about the various types of reliability.

- learn about trustworthiness and credibility.

- learn about ways to address credibility.

As you have already learned, one initial step in a quality research project is the development of a focused research question(s). Once a research question is generated, the researcher considers how best to complete the study to address the question(s). Validity, reliability, and trustworthiness are central to the design of a study. Only studies that have adequate validity or trustworthiness, as well as reliability, enhance the knowledge base in education and can inform future decisions of educators.

What Are Validity, Trustworthiness, and Reliability?

In Chapter 1, you read that validity is a term associated with a study that does what the study claims to do. More explicitly, validity is the degree to which the conclusions drawn by the researcher come from the actual study results rather than from chance or erroneous sources. Though the term is sometimes used with regard to qualitative methods, validity is generally associated with designs that include quantitative data, whether experimental or descriptive research. **Trustworthiness**, on the other hand, is a term associated with qualitative methods, but is closely related to the construct of validity. Trustworthiness is the degree to which a researcher convinces the audience that the research was completed using appropriate techniques, the findings described are credible, and interpretations that are appropriate and fully developed (Patton, 2015).

Reliability is integral to both validity and trustworthiness. In Chapter 1, you read that the term *reliable* is used to describe study methods that can occur similarly across participants and time. In other words, reliability is the degree to which a study can be repeated with similar results. For example, in a quasi-experimental study, a researcher must be confident that the measure (e.g., a reading test) used to evaluate the dependent variable (e.g., reading fluency) would produce similar results if given on separate occasions to the same student. In a descriptive qualitative study, a peer should be able to duplicate the researcher's analytical methods. If a researcher cannot assure the reader that the same outcomes are likely to be reached if the study were run again, then the reader cannot be confident that the results are meaningful.

Validity, trustworthiness, and reliability are important criteria by which the quality of a study is judged, and therefore, they exist along a continuum. In every study, a researcher makes choices about how to handle issues of validity, trustworthiness, and reliability. The choices should be described and documented so that they are clear to the reader. The issues to consider and the choices available are the subject of this chapter.

Types of Validity and Their Threats

Validity is used to judge the quality of quantitative, experimental and quasi-experimental studies. For our purposes, three major types of validity are important: **internal validity, external validity**, and **construct validity**. In every study, decisions made to increase one type of validity may affect another type of validity. For example, conducting a study in a classroom instead of a clinical situation may affect both external and internal validity. The researcher must consider the interplay of effects in terms of the purpose of the research.

Variables or actions that could reduce a type of validity are called **threats to validity**. There are potentially an infinite number of threats to the overall validity of a study; virtually every variable encountered may be a threat. The way to increase each type of validity is to address the most obvious and serious threats. This section briefly describes each type of validity and gives examples of some of the associated threats. (For a more in-depth discussion, see Cook and Campbell, 1979, as well as Rumrill, Cook, and Wiley 2011.)

Internal Validity

Internal validity is "the approximate validity with which we infer that a relationship between two variables is causal or absence of relationship implies absence of cause" (Cook & Campbell, 1979, p. 37). So internal validity begs the question, "Did this study truly indicate that A, not some other variable, caused B?" Or "Did this study truly indicate that A, not some other variable, did *not* cause B?" For example, students in an experimental group are given a pretest about frogs. They do not score well on the pretest. The researcher teaches the students a test-taking strategy and, at the same time, they complete a unit on frogs in another classroom. At the end of the instruction on test taking, a posttest is given on frogs. The students do much better on the posttest. The researcher concludes their improvement is due to the test-taking strategy. Is this a valid conclusion? It could be, but the instruction on frogs threatens the validity of that conclusion.

Threats. Threats to internal validity affect the confidence with which a researcher can state that the independent variable caused an effect on the dependent variable. The five major threats to internal validity are (a) **history**, (b) **maturation**, (c) **measurement issues**, (d) **group differences**, and (e) **alternative causes**. Table 4.1 gives a brief description and example of each type of threat.

The way to address many of these threats may be quite obvious: find equivalent groups, use appropriate measurement devices, and understand the context of the study so that history or maturation does not affect the outcomes. In some studies, however, addressing each of these threats to internal validity may be difficult. Despite the difficulty, a researcher must determine the most important threats to a specific research question and address them unequivocally. Following is an example of how one group of researchers addressed internal validity issues related to group differences, a particularly important form of internal validity for graduate researchers to consider.

Boardman et al. (2016) conducted a comparison group study to examine the effectiveness of systematic reading intervention for elementary students with disabilities in inclusive classrooms. Here is how they addressed the threat of group differences:

> Because teachers were randomly assigned to conditions such that in each school some teachers taught CSR [Collaborative Strategic Reading] and others did not, we are not aware of any systematic differences in the way students with disabilities were distributed across classrooms or in the types or amount of special education services they received. Considering the distribution of students with LD across classrooms, classes were similar (e.g., similar ratio of students with LD to students without LD) with the exception that in the CSR condition, only 42% of classrooms had students with LD, whereas 76% of classrooms in the control condition included students with LD. Twenty-two additional students in the CSR group and 18 additional students in the comparison group had a disability other than LD. Categories included deaf, emotional disability, physical disability, speech and language, autism spectrum disorder, significant limited intellectual capacity, and multiple disabilities. Our sample was representative of national percentages of students with LD and other disabilities (Cortiella & Horowitz, 2014). (pp. 413–414)

In this example, the researchers carefully examined the ratio of students with disabilities randomly assigned to groups, provided those data to the reader, and deemed the groups equivalent. By making the effort to do this relatively simple analysis, the researchers enhanced the internal validity of the study by avoiding initial group differences.

Threat	Definition	Examples
TABLE 4.1 ● Examples of Threats to Internal Validity		
History	Something occurs during the study that impacts the dependent variable but is unrelated to the independent variable.	A researcher may be interested in getting the opinions of special educators on the amount of paperwork required in the job. He sends the survey to 1,000 teachers across the United States, first on the east coast and, a few months later, on the west coast. After the researcher receives responses from the east coast surveys but before the researcher gets them from the west coast, Congress changes federal law and eliminates Individualized Education Plans. Thus, the paperwork burden is dramatically reduced in the middle of this researcher's study.
Maturation	The study occurs over a period of time in which participants get older; their incidental learning or experience affects the dependent variable.	A researcher wanted to know if a writing strategy improved seventh-graders' performance on the state writing test. She collected student scores from sixth grade and compared them to scores the next year, after the students received instruction in the writing strategy. In addition to receiving the writing strategy instruction, the students experienced an entire year of writing practice and other instruction.
Measurement issues	The frequency and practice of assessment and/or the assessment devices used affect the dependent variable.	1. A researcher administers the same standardized test with the same items to participants within a short period of time. 2. A researcher asks participants to complete an online survey about participant comfort and skill in using online material.
Group differences	The experimental and control groups are not equivalent in terms of important variables or characteristics.	A researcher wants to compare the effects of a peer-assisted math program to traditional instruction. She chooses an experimental and control group. The experimental group consists of students who are above grade level in math. The control group consists of students who are below grade level in math.
Alternative causes	Changes in the dependent variable are the result of effects of the dependent variable on the independent variable, rivalry between groups, resentful control by comparison group participants, or interaction between groups.	1. Does variable A cause variable B to change or vice versa? 2. "I'm in the group that doesn't get the new resources or treatment, so I'm going to work harder so my group will show them!" 3. "I'm in the group that isn't getting fancy treatment. I'm not going to do anything." 4. "Hey! This is cool stuff. I'm going to tell my colleagues about it."

External Validity

External validity is the extent to which the results of a study can be generalized to other similar groups, individuals, or situations (Rumrill, Cook, & Wiley 2011). In other words, "How do the conclusions of this study apply elsewhere? Can they be applied elsewhere?" For example, external validity may impact a study's design in the choice of participants or the inclusion of a sample. A study with a large, representative sample of participants has greater external validity than one with a small, distinctive group of participants. Again, the purpose of the research guides decisions about sample and about setting. If a researcher is at all interested in generalizing study results beyond the sample included, the study must include participants who are similar to the population, not just those on hand or easily available.

Threats. Threats to external validity challenge the extent to which a study can be generalized to other settings, conditions, or the population. Three major factors in the study are important: the sample characteristics, the treatment characteristics, and the setting characteristics. The first, **sample characteristics**, affects the ability to generalize to other groups not included in the study. For example, if Juan wants to generalize results of his study to students in seventh-grade mathematics classes, then he must choose a sample that has characteristics of that population, including (but not limited to) ethnicity, gender, age, academic achievement levels, socioeconomic levels, etc. Although the focus of the research determines the important characteristics of the sample, choosing participants because they are convenient, or because they happen to be at the right place at the right time, threatens the external validity of a study because the sample might not be representative of the population. In any case, detailed participant descriptions, as noted in Chapter 3, are essential.

The second consideration, **treatment characteristics**, is how the experimenters and the intervention affect external validity. If Gabriel experiments with an instructional strategy that requires 50 hours of professional development for teachers, the success of the instructional strategy may not generalize to those who have not gone through the same process. If John studies the effects of a writing strategy on high school students and the students believe that the writing samples are going to be used for entrance into a local college, they may perform better than if they believed the writing samples were being used simply as part of an experiment.

Finally, **setting characteristics** include all of the resources and situations used by the researcher to implement the intervention and collect data. For example, does Linda conduct a study in a lab setting where most variables can be controlled and influenced? If so, how would the results generalize to a general education classroom? Does Joe provide a tremendous amount of resources for the teacher's classroom, such as computers, printers, and the like? If so, how do the results generalize to classrooms that do not have those resources? Does Tameka include the target students in classrooms with students not involved in the study? When considering the external validity of methods, a researcher must address issues related to the sample, treatment, and setting characteristics proposed.

Continuing the Boardman et al. (2016) example, here is the description of how the school sites were chosen in an effort to address possible threats to external validity based on sample characteristics:

The study took place in 14 elementary schools located in three urban/ near urban school districts, two in one state (Site 1) and one in another state (Site 2). Each district served a diverse population of students. Sixty teachers, 31 randomly assigned to treatment and 29 to control, participated in the study. Selection and consent of both teachers and students followed Institutional Review Board procedures at the participating universities.

Due to uneven numbers of teachers by site (31 in Site 1 and 29 in Site 2), randomization resulted in an additional teacher in the treatment condition at each site (16 treatment and 15 control in Site 1 and 15 treatment and 14 control in Site 2). Ninety-five percent of the teachers were female. The majority (65%) were Caucasian, followed by Hispanic (27%), African American (6%), and Asian (2%). Teaching experience ranged from 1 to 30 years, with a mean of 9.23 and a median of 7 years. Roughly 40% of teachers had a master's degree. Nearly half of the teachers (48%) held at least one certification in addition to being elementary certified (e.g., English language arts, bilingual, reading, special education, English as a second language). There were 1,372 students in the initial sample (686 in treatment and 686 in the comparison condition; see Table 1). The average age was 10.6 for students in CSR treatment and 10.52 for students in comparison. The majority of the student sample was Hispanic, and about half were ELLs. (p. 413)

In this study, the researchers believed it was important for the intervention to be tested in a sample that included a large number of EL learners in schools with a large population of EL learners. They chose the school sites with this purpose in mind. Thus, the results could generalize to a larger group of schools with this specific population, enhancing the external validity of the results of this intervention. Also note that this excerpt also includes the IRB statement as well as demographic information regarding the participating teachers.

Construct Validity

Construct validity is the degree to which a researcher truly measures the construct of focus in the study. Reading, intelligence, and academic achievement are frequently studied constructs in education. Defining *reading* is actually a difficult task for some researchers. What aspect of reading is the focus of the study? Reading comprehension? Reading fluency? Phonemic awareness? How a researcher defines and measures a construct affects the study's construct validity.

Let's say Maria wants to determine if Reading Program Q improves the reading skill of third graders more than the current program. She divides students into experimental and control groups and assesses each student's *reading* by having the student read isolated words on a page for 1 minute. Many would argue that this is not an assessment of a student's *reading* but a measure of a student's performance in reading isolated words (e.g., sight words) or decoding words. These are component skills of reading, but did the researcher measure the learner construct of *reading*? Arguably not.

Threats. The researcher is responsible for making explicit the construct of interest in the study and the components of the construct that will be measured. If these descriptions are not given, then construct validity is threatened. There are three major threats to construct validity to consider:

1. Inadequate description of construct
2. Inadequate measurement of construct
3. Inadequate attention to levels of independent variable

An inadequate description of the construct of interest could mean the researcher focused on a limited number of components of a construct but concluded that the research evaluated the entire construct. To continue our previous reading example, if Maria is interested in measuring students' *reading fluency*, she may want to measure words read per minute (WPM). WPM may not be an adequate measure of a student's total reading performance, but at least Maria would have more validly identified *fluency* as the construct, not *reading*.

The inadequate measurement of a construct also makes a study suspect. Using only one measure or only one method to gather data about a construct can be a problem. For example, if Omar wants to describe a school's climate, it would be inappropriate merely to interview the teachers and ask them how they felt about the principal. That would be a description of the teachers' views of the principal, not of the school climate. To measure school climate, Stephen would need to conduct interviews with many people involved in the school and ask questions about a range of topics. In addition, he might want to consider additional ways to collect data, such as questionnaires, to get multiple sources of data.

Another threat to construct validity is inadequate attention to different levels of the independent variable. This threat occurs when only one or two levels of a multilevel variable are implemented. The results may indicate that at level 1, this intervention had no impact, but, in fact, it might have had impact if level 2 or higher had been implemented. For example, Rodney wants to determine if using a graphic organizer will improve the descriptive writing of his students. He may tell the students to use the graphic organizer but not provide them with guided and independent practice in using the organizer when they write. He sees no differences in their writing after an essay assignment and concludes that graphic organizers do not help. Had Rodney required the students to use the organizer in their prewriting and turn in the organizer with their papers, there may have been an effect on their essays. Again, the focus of the research will help to determine the major threats to construct validity and how best to address them.

In the Boardman et al. (2016) example again, the purpose of the research was to investigate the effects of a reading intervention in diverse elementary classrooms. To address the purpose, the researchers aptly described how the dependent variable was measured:

> The student outcome was reading comprehension performance, as measured
> by the reading comprehension subtest of the Gates-MacGinitie Reading
> Test (fourth edition; MacGinitie, MacGinitie et al., 2000). The GMRT is a
> timed paper-and-pencil, group-administered survey that assesses student

achievement in reading and was administered by researchers prior to beginning the intervention (August) and prior to winter break (December). The comprehension subtest is designed to measure students' abilities to read and understand different types of prose from passages in published books and periodicals. Some questions relate to a literal understanding of the passage whereas others require students to make inferences or draw conclusions. In addition, the comprehension subtest is designed to measure students' ability to determine the meaning of words in an authentic text context. Two parallel forms permit pre- and posttesting. Alternate-forms reliability for the GMRT is estimated to range from .90 to .95, and test-retest reliability has been estimated as above .88 (MacGinitie et al., 2000). (p. 415)

In this case, the authors detailed the test used to measure the dependent variable, including each of the different subtests. The author's description also provided information about when the test was administered, the parallel test forms, as well as the test-retest reliability. This level of detail certainly enhanced the construct validity of their study by allowing the audience to determine exactly what was being assessed (reading) and whether a similar construct of reading comprehension might be used in other schools.

These examples from Boardman et al. (2016) illustrate the factors you must consider in addressing issues of validity. They are meant to help you understand the different types of validity. It is important to remember that you may not eliminate all of the threats to validity, but by focusing on the research purpose, you will prioritize the threats that your study most needs to address.

Reliability

Reliability has an important relationship to validity in any study. Reliability is the degree to which a study can be repeated with similar results. If it can be determined that some aspect of a study is not reliable, then the validity of that study's conclusions is suspect as well. For ease of discussion, this section considers two essential types of reliability: internal reliability and external reliability. **Internal reliability** is the degree that data collection, analysis, and explanations or conclusions are similar under comparable research conditions, and **external reliability** is the extent to which an independent researcher could replicate the study in other settings.

Internal Reliability

There are two major areas to address related to internal reliability: reliability of an instrument and reliability of observation. The reliability of the measure chosen for evaluating the dependent variable in a study is crucial to the reliability and validity of the study as a whole. Researchers have a choice in establishing the reliability of the measures used to assess the dependent variable: (a) use a measure that has been published and standardized or (b) create their own measure. If a researcher uses a published assessment device (e.g., a standardized math test), the researcher must determine from the technical data whether or not the device has adequate reliability. If a researcher decides to develop a measure or instrument, the researcher must determine its reliability.

Reliability of an Instrument. Reliability of an instrument (e.g., test or paper/pencil measure) is described by parallel forms reliability, test-retest reliability, split-half reliability, or Cronbach's alpha. **Parallel forms reliability** indicates the degree to which a person's score is similar when the person is given two forms of the same test. A person's results on Test Form A are compared to results on Test Form B. **Test-retest reliability** is the degree to which a person achieves a similar score on an assessment measure when the entire measure is administered once and then is administered again. Katie may take a math test on day 1 and again on day 14, and then the results are compared. **Split-half reliability** is the degree to which a person receives a similar score on one half of the test items as compared to the other half. Drew may compare a student's responses on the even-numbered questions to those on the odd-numbered ones. **Cronbach's alpha** is a statistical formula used to determine reliability based on at least two parts of a test. Both split-half reliability and Cronbach's alpha require only one administration of the measure.

The reliability of an instrument is measured by a **reliability coefficient**. Reliability coefficients indicate the relationship between multiple administrations, multiple items, or other analyses of evaluation measures. The degree of similarity of results from parallel forms, test-retest, split-half, and Cronbach's alpha test results in a reliability coefficient of between 0 and 1. If the reliability coefficient is 0, there is no relationship between results and, therefore, no reliability. If the coefficient is 1, the results are exactly the same and are perfectly reliable. In most cases, researchers attempt to use measures that have a reliability coefficient of .8 or better. (see Figure 4.1.)

Reliability of Observations. Researchers measure the reliability of observations by calculating interobserver agreement and interscorer agreement or intraobserver agreement and intrascorer agreement. **Interobserver agreement** is the degree to which two independent observers record observational data of the same situation similarly. Chris may determine interobserver agreement by having two observers sit in the same classroom at the same time recording data. The degree to which the two

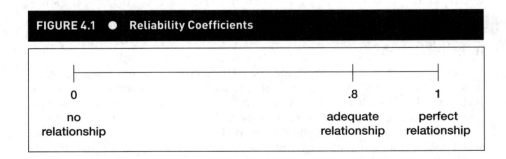

FIGURE 4.1 ● Reliability Coefficients

observers' data is the same is the degree of reliability of observation. The agreement is simply calculated in this way:

$$\frac{\#agreements}{\#agreements + \#disagreements} = \%$$

Typically, researchers aim for a minimum of 80% reliability on at least 15–20% of the observations. *Interscorer agreement* is similar in that two data collectors score an item (e.g., a test, writing sample) and their scores are compared and calculated in a similar manner as interobserver agreement and with similar minimum standards.

Intraobserver agreement and intrascorer agreement, on the other hand, are the degree to which an observer or scorer records similar data about the same observation or test on *two different occasions*. For example, Jon's study includes the evaluation of writing samples based upon a scoring rubric. *Intrascorer agreement* in this study would be the degree to which the scorer gives the same score to a single writing sample scored on Monday and again on Friday.

In an example from a quasi-experimental study, Floress, Jenkins, Reinke, and McKown (2017) observed the rate of verbal praise among a sample of elementary classroom teachers. Here is a portion of how the researchers achieved reliability of their observations:

> At the beginning of each semester, the first author trained all the assistants even if they had been involved in the project (or a similar project) the previous semester . . . During the last 2 weeks of training, students were required to accompany an assistant, who collected data the previous semester, to the schools to collect direct observation data in the classroom. The assistant needed to obtain at least 80% interobserver agreement (IOA) on three observations prior to collecting data independently. After training was complete (and to combat observer drift over time), assistants attended weekly research meetings led by the first author. These meetings gave assistants the opportunity to discuss various coding issues, discrepancies, and questions that came up during the classroom observations. It also ensured that all assistants were continuing to code similarly. In addition, immediately after reliability data were collected, the assistants examined the data for discrepancies, discussed the discrepancies, together decided on the correct codes, and finally calculated IOA. Observers reported IOA at the weekly meetings and if IOA fell below 80%, it was discussed with the first author and additional training (e.g., reviewing examples and nonexamples) occurred to ensure that the coding definitions were understood. (p. 5)

In this example, the researchers addressed interobserver agreement (IOA) through very thorough training of observers. When scorers disagreed, further discussion regarding coding followed, all in an effort to achieve high rates of IOA and minimize threats to internal reliability.

The second major consideration with regard to internal reliability is the fidelity to which a treatment or intervention is implemented. This is simply referred to as **treatment fidelity** (although otherwise known as fidelity to implementation). If Janice conducts a study in a school and trains teachers to instruct students in a strategy for taking tests, she must ensure that the teachers teach the strategy in the same way it was intended. That is, if one teacher teaches the strategy for 25 minutes a day for ten days, all teachers should teach for 25 minutes per day for ten days. If Janice prompts the teachers to use certain techniques during instruction, she needs to make sure they do so. Researchers should make sure to check the fidelity to implementation throughout experimental and quasi-experimental studies.

Once more in the Boardman et. al. (2016) intervention study, teachers were taught how to instruct students to use reading comprehension strategies. Here is how the researchers ensured treatment fidelity:

> Fidelity of implementation denotes the degree to which a program is implemented as originally planned (O'Donnell, 2008). Fidelity is operationalized in this study in terms of dosage (frequency of implementation), quality (how well CSR instruction was delivered), and program differentiation (the degree to which instructional strategies within each condition can be differentiated). To measure dosage, we used teacher logs, in which teachers in the treatment condition self-reported the number of CSR sessions and minutes they taught throughout the intervention. The Implementation Validity Checklist (IVC; Vaughn et al., 2011, 2013) classroom observation tool was used to assess quality of CSR instruction and program differentiation. (p. 415)

In this example, the researchers clearly specified how treatment fidelity was defined in terms of dosage, quality, and program differentiation, as well as how each one of those constructs were measured using teacher logs and an observation checklist.

External Reliability

External reliability, again, is the degree to which a study can be replicated by other researchers. The extent to which a study has external reliability is based upon factors such as the thorough description of methods; the complexity of intervention, training, and measurement; and the setting. For example, if Matilda does not adequately describe the methods used in her study, it is difficult for others to replicate the study. This threatens the study's external reliability. Likewise, if the intervention Matilda uses is extremely complex and requires training that only a few people are qualified to give, it may be very difficult or impossible to replicate the study. Again, external reliability is threatened. Finally, if Matilda uses a contrived or restrictive setting, it might be difficult for other researchers to create a similar environment. All of these issues threaten the external reliability of a study, and it should be easy to see how these issues parallel those of external validity.

Here is a good example of setting description from McDermott & Gormley (2016):

> We selected this particular school because it offered teachers a variety of technologies to use in their classrooms, all of its classrooms had operating Smart Boards (Smart Technologies, 2014) as well as five desktop computers, and moreover, the school recently invested in a web-based literacy program that offered personalized reading practice with diagnostic printouts of children's reading performance. The intermediate grades (4–6) also provided personal laptops for every student. In addition, we have conducted other inquiries in this school (e.g., Gormley & McDermott, 2013 & 2014) and had ready access to its classrooms. The school is located in a small northeastern city. It serves a large percentage of children in poverty, with 85% of its students eligible for free and reduced lunch. Data from the school's "Report Card" revealed that this school served children from high poverty neighborhoods, and more than three fourths of the student population was from minority backgrounds. Two-hundred two children attended the school in the 2011–12 academic year, of which 52% of the families identified their children as African American, 28% Latino, 11% Caucasian, and 8% multiracial. During the same academic year, 46% of its third-grade children, 35% of the fourth-grade children, 24% of the fifth-grade children, and 59% of the sixth-grade children passed the statewide examination in English language arts. Results of the 2012–2013 statewide testing in English language arts, which were based on the Common Core State Standards, revealed a severe downturn in children's test performance, with only 6.5% of the children in Grades 3 and 6 passing the new statewide examination, although these scores were similar to comparable urban schools in the state and sometimes better than those in the local district. (pp. 125–126)

In this example, the researchers described the setting and later detailed the research methods. There is excellent detail regarding where the study took place, and that enhances the external reliability of the study.

This discussion of validity and reliability has used examples of experimental or quantitative descriptive studies. When discussing qualitative research methods, validity and reliability are interrelated in the concept of trustworthiness.

Trustworthiness

When conducting descriptive research that uses qualitative methods, validity and reliability are viewed a little differently, and there is debate as to whether the experimental concepts of validity and reliability are even appropriate to qualitative methods. Certainly, they take different forms in qualitative inquiry. In response, many researchers who use qualitative methods use the idea of trustworthiness. Trustworthiness is based on the concept of *credibility*; that is, establishing the truth value of the study. There are many important components to credibility. These include the credibility of the researcher, methods, and conclusions. As Patton (2015) stated:

> The credibility of qualitative inquiry depends on four distinct but related inquiry elements:
>
> - *Systematic, in-depth fieldwork that yields high-quality data*
> - *Systematic and conscientious analysis of data with attention to issues of credibility*
> - *Credibility of the inquirer, which depends on training, experience, track record, status, and presentation of self*
> - *Readers' and users' philosophical belief in the value of qualitative inquiry* (p. 653)

Let's first discuss Patton's third and fourth elements and the heavy reliance on the researcher as instrument in descriptive studies using qualitative methods. Then we'll elaborate on the first two elements related to rigorous methods.

Credibility of the Researcher

In qualitative inquiry, considerable emphasis is placed on the capabilities of the researcher. The researcher is the one who enters the situation and makes participants feel comfortable (or not), collects and analyzes data, and reports interpretations and conclusions. Though qualitative methodology includes procedures for decisions within a study, the researcher processes the data in a unique way, based upon training, experience, bias, and other factors. This is different from the processing of statistical data. Therefore, it is imperative that researchers consider and make explicit their characteristics, such as training, experience, ideas, and **conceptual framework**, when making design decisions.

When beginning a study, a researcher must consider any and all personal and professional information that may affect data collection, analysis, and interpretation—either negatively or positively. Therefore, the researcher should make the following explicit:

- Professional training
- Biases and experience in the situation
- Understanding of the method of data analysis
- How issues of entry and continued evaluation or observation were handled
- The conceptual framework upon which the study was built

Since the point of qualitative research is to present a description of the situation studied, it is impossible to be completely objective. As a researcher, you have only one perspective on the situation. If your study is designed and conducted well, however, the results you present will include a multitude of perspectives from the participants. The readers must be satisfied that you were capable of conducting the study in an appropriate manner—that you understood how to use the methods you chose; that you dealt with issues of your entry into and exit from the research setting; and that you adequately described your conceptual framework, thereby establishing the credibility of both researcher and research.

Unfortunately, this breadth of information is often missing from journal articles and reports of qualitative research. In the Sylvan study (2018), however, the background and potential biases of the researcher were adequately addressed, increasing the credibility of the researcher and enhancing trustworthiness:

> The author is an experienced pediatric SLP [Speech Language Pathologist] with close to a decade of experience in public school settings. This allowed the researcher to establish credibility (Lincoln & Guba, 1985) with interview participants and gather data over the course of the school year that was detailed and varied enough to provide a full and revealing picture (Holloway, 1997). The author, mindful of personal bias, ensured analyst triangulation by involving multiple researchers in continually reviewing the research process including reading and analyzing interview transcripts and documents throughout this study (Lincoln & Guba, 1985; Patton, 2002). (p. 607)

Credibility of Methods and Findings

Once the credibility of the researcher is established, the credibility of the methods chosen must be addressed. The methods should fit the research question(s). Four issues about trustworthiness must be addressed. Table 4.2 lists these issues and the methodological questions they invoke.

Truth Value. The first issue of concern regarding credibility of methods and findings is that of truth value. How does a researcher establish that the findings presented are true? To address this concern, researchers must ensure that they are getting a view of the context from multiple perspectives and over a reasonable period of time. Lincoln and Guba (1985) and others (e.g., Marshall & Rossman, 2015) recommend three initial actions in the design of a study: **prolonged engagement**, **persistent observation**, and **triangulation**. In addition, consider **peer debriefing**, **negative case analysis**, and **member checking** in order to increase truth value and enhance credibility of qualitative researcher findings (see Table 4.3).

Prolonged engagement means that the researcher becomes familiar with a setting and the people in the setting and then engages in data collection for a period of time that would provide for observation of both everyday and out-of-the-ordinary occurrences. Prolonged engagement allows those in the setting to become comfortable so that observation is not obtrusive and does not cause the participants to change behavior.

Persistent observation "is to identify those characteristics and elements in the situation that are most relevant to the problem or issue being pursued and focusing on

TABLE 4.2 ● Methodology Questions to Address Issues in Trustworthiness	
Issue	**Methodology Questions**
What is the "truth value?"	How can one establish confidence in the "truth" of the findings of a study?
How is the information applicable?	How can one determine the extent to which the findings of a study have applicability in other contexts or with other subjects (respondents)?
Is the information consistent or dependable?	How can one determine whether the findings of a study would be repeated if it were replicated with the same (or similar) subjects (respondents) in the same (or similar) context?
Is the research neutral or not?	How can one establish the degree to which the findings of a study are determined by the subjects (respondents) and conditions of the inquiry and not by the biases, motivations, interests, or perspectives of the researcher?

Source: Adapted from Lincoln & Guba (1985).

TABLE 4.3 ● Techniques to Increase Truth Value	
Technique	**Description**
Prolonged engagement	Being in the situation or context of study for an extended period of time
Persistent observation	Conducting observations consistently and of sufficient duration
Triangulation	Using more than one source of information to confirm a concept or idea
Peer debriefing	Having a peer review data and analysis to play "devil's advocate" as the researcher makes decisions
Negative case analysis	Reviewing cases that do not fit into the current analysis scheme to determine how the scheme might change
Member checking	Asking participants in the study to review conclusions and observations or interviews

them in detail" (Lincoln & Guba, 1985, p. 304). If Fontaine wants to describe the interactions between veteran teachers and students who speak English as a second language, she would want to observe many of these interactions in order to begin noticing typical qualities and patterns. Once these patterns or qualities are identified, she could begin to observe for these patterns or qualities specifically. Only then would Fontaine be able to explicate the examples and nonexamples of these patterns.

Triangulation is another way to increase truth value. Triangulation may be across data sources or within data sources. For example, if Miller wanted to describe the interaction of co-teachers in general education classrooms, he would want to interview both the general educator and the special educator involved, not just the special educator. Or if William wanted to describe the feelings of teachers about accountability policies at a school, he would want to interview teachers, observe classrooms and teacher workshops, and examine policy documents. In a sense, he would attempt to get more than one perspective on a situation.

Peer debriefing involves talking through research design and analytic ideas with a peer researcher who is uninvolved in the study, to face questions about decisions, and to make explicit what may be going on while conducting a study. The peer often plays a devil's advocate role and questions every aspect of data, data collection, and data analysis. This process can eliminate or at least identify a researcher's unknown biases.

Negative case analysis is the refining of a hypothesis about a phenomenon until it accounts for all known cases or pieces of information. Essentially, it means reviewing pieces of data that do not "fit" into the current data analytic scheme and revising that scheme until the cases do fit. This may be quite difficult to do, but it focuses data collection and analysis to provide the best description of data possible. Using negative case analysis, a research must explicate all of the pertinent characteristics of a pattern of data that leads to devising a hypothesis.

Finally, member checking is a potent way to establish trustworthiness by way of increasing truth value. In member checking, the participants in the study actually review the hypotheses, patterns, characteristics, analysis, interpretations, and conclusions. They offer suggestions, or they confirm or deny ideas. Of course, there are difficulties inherent in member checking. Participants may be wary of how the interpretations are to be used or about what they may say. These situations may be overcome by prolonged engagement, but each case is unique and must be considered.

In a study of secondary teachers' adaptations of a reading intervention program, Leko, Roberts, and Pek (2015) presented the following information about peer debriefing, triangulation, and member checking:

> To promote trustworthiness and credibility, we used a series of procedures including the use of multiple data sources that allowed for triangulation (Brantlinger, Jimenez, Klingner, Pugach, & Richardson, 2005). We also engaged in investigator triangulation by peer debriefing throughout the entire study (Brantlinger et al., 2005). During interviews, we used member checking to verify our information and interpretations. We also engaged in intercoder agreement whereby the first two authors independently coded

the interview and observation data during the open and selective stages, compared codes and emerging themes, discussed discrepancies, and came to consensus regarding the core and component concepts and how they were related. (p. 172)

Applicability. The second way that the credibility or trustworthiness of qualitative research methods and findings can be enhanced is by applicability. Researchers who complete descriptive studies using qualitative methods do not, generally, conduct the studies for purposes of broad generalization. In fact, the purpose in most cases is to describe a context in tremendous detail so as to understand that situation, not necessarily others. Therefore, researchers who conduct descriptive studies using qualitative methods are required to include rich description of every aspect of the study (e.g., researcher, participants, methods, and analysis techniques). It is then incumbent upon the person who wants to generalize the research to another situation to "match" the situation (Lincoln & Guba, 1985). Thus, to address the issue of applicability, a researcher must provide as much detail about the components of a study as possible.

Consistency. Consistency also enhances the credibility of qualitative methods and findings. In all measurement, consistency or reliability is of paramount importance. In qualitative methodology, consistency means that researchers could come to conclusions similar to those of the original researcher but the means by which they do so may not be identical. Again, rich description of data collection and analysis is required to evaluate the consistency of a study.

Confirmability. Is the study a true indication of the situation and not a description of the biases of the researcher? It is incumbent upon the researcher to keep detailed notes of each of these categories throughout the study. These notes, most often kept in various journals or electronic devices, can also become parts of the data analysis. In a formal audit, another individual reviews these materials to establish the ***confirmability*** of the study. Even if a formal audit is not completed, having the materials for review at any time, if questioned, is a great asset.

Ways to Address Challenges to Trustworthiness

As previously stated, it is virtually impossible to address every issue related to trustworthiness or validity. One way, however, is to include multiple researchers who conduct data collection and analysis simultaneously. The researchers later discuss their interpretations and conclusions to guide further collection and analysis techniques. The purpose is similar to peer debriefing in that each decision is made explicit and brought out in discussion. The difference is that the researchers are all involved in the study, participating in the data all the time. In doing this, though, researchers can guide each other back to the research question and refocus on important items.

An alternative to creating multiple researcher teams is to conduct an inquiry audit. According to Halpern (as cited in Lincoln & Guba, 1985), an inquiry audit includes six categories of materials for examination:

1. Raw data

2. Data reduction and analysis products

3. Data reconstruction and synthesis products

4. Process notes

5. Materials relating to intentions and dispositions

6. Instrument development information

However researchers choose to address potential issues in trustworthiness, it is imperative that they describe how the study does address the issues, especially during data analysis. For example, Leko, Roberts, and Pek (2015) provided a well-defined description of the steps of their analysis, some examples of the outcomes of the steps, and how they completed the analysis process by representing the outcomes in a visual.

> We began the grounded theory process by open coding interview transcripts and observation field notes line by line using the constant comparative method. The codes were not identified a priori; rather, they emerged from the data and were continually redefined throughout the analysis process. *Steep learning curve, incorporates additional assessments*, and *combination classes* are some open code examples from this study. We completed memoing for the implementation fidelity rating tool and artifacts and used these memos as support for the derived codes and categories. For example, in analyzing the implementation fidelity rating tool, we used memos to make note of instructional practices that teachers either omitted or inserted within the *System 44* program. Next, we completed axial coding by reassembling the data by making connections between categories and subcategories. For example, we grouped the open codes of *combination class, large class size*, and *lacks adult support* among others that were conceptually linked and labeled them with the axial code of *adult to student ratio*. Finally, we completed selective coding to formulate our theory. In this stage, we grouped axial codes into more abstract units and identified the core and component concepts (see Table 2 for sample codes). The last step was to visually represent the relationships among the core and component concepts through the use of a figure. (pp. 171–172)

As with validity and reliability in experimental, quasi-experimental, and quantitative descriptive research, in order to address vital issues that may threaten the trustworthiness of a descriptive study using qualitative methods, the researcher must continually focus on the research question(s) and purpose of the study.

IN THEIR OWN WORDS

Lora Lee Canter, upon completing her dissertation

My tip for any student wishing to engage in research is to pay very specific and careful attention to validity and reliability because if you do not, your research is much less meaningful. Let me give you some examples. You decide to conduct research on how to improve reading comprehension in young children. You introduce an intervention you design (your measures), and the students in your study make miraculous gains in the area of reading recognition and comprehension. In fact, they increase their overall reading level to the college level. Wonderful, right? Time to market your intervention and make the big bucks? Not so fast—your study lacks reliability. No one can replicate your results after they implement your intervention. It worked for that group of students in your study, but it cannot be replicated. So what does that say about your intervention? Now just imagine you decide to increase children's reading skills by instituting a gum-chewing regime. So you measure gum chewing rates in the class and then institute a gum-chewing intervention program. Sure enough, your measures work, and gum chewing increases. You replicate this in hundreds of classes and, yes, gum chewing increases in all of them. Your measures were reliable; however, there were no increases in children's reading skills. Why? Because your measures to increase reading skills through gum chewing had no validity.

Putting It All Together

Keeping in mind what you have learned in this chapter, read the following excerpt from Torres and Stefkovich (2009). List at least one potential threat to internal validity and one potential threat to external validity, and describe how you might address the threats. Then note one potential issue with internal reliability, as well as how you might address that.

> While the NCES had on prior occasions collected "anecdotal" data regarding school crime and safety indicators, the 2000 data file served as the first "systematic" attempt to gather nationally representative data on relevant indicators, including the rate of violence in school, measures employed to prevent violence, and the relationship of violence to the school environment. Safety data were collected from a sample of 2,270 schools and classified into six clusters (nominal variables). Variables for this study were selected exclusively from the discipline and school characteristics clusters. The sample also included weighted percentage indicators by geographical location of the school and involved a variety of respondents. . . .
>
> Slightly more than 90% of the 2,270 respondents served as either a principal or vice principal. Approximately 24% were employed in schools serving minority

student populations of 50% or greater. Nearly 62% were employed in urban or urban fringe school districts. Twenty-five percent of the respondents were employed in elementary schools, 33% in middle schools, 33% in high schools, and the remaining 9% in combined grade level schools. . . .

The proportion of student incidents reported to the police for the 1999–2000 academic year served as a dependent variable. This variable was calculated by dividing the "total number of student incidents reported to police" by the "total number of student incidents." The variable "total number of incidents reported for 1999–2000" summarizes the totality of serious crime within the respondent's school and reflects the aggregate sum of incidents per type of serious offense per respondent's campus. . . .

Among the independent variables, the variable "school did not regularly use law enforcement" was described as a "summary" indicator based on coders' assessment of responses to items gauging police involvement in various ways (yes/no). . . .

The *Common Core of Data* files for 1998–1999 (National Center for Education Statistics, 2001) provided demographic indicators including the minority composition of the school (0%–5%, 6%–20%, 21%–50%, and greater than 50%), percentage of students receiving free and reduced-price lunch (less than 20%, 21%–50%, 51% and greater), and geographical location of the school, or urbanicity (city, urban fringe, town, and rural). . . .

Researchers employed a factorial analysis of variance (ANOVA) to examine weighted mean differences in proportions of student offenses reported to police and used descriptive statistics to secure overall observations from the data. Factorial ANOVA was selected to test mean differences in student offenses reported by examining the effect of two explanatory variables (Ott, 1993). Independent demographic characteristics of the school (i.e., urban city, minority composition, and percentage free and reduced-price lunch) and whether the school paid for off-duty law enforcement security (yes, no) were assigned as the fixed factors in measuring mean differences in student offenses reported (a = .05). Variable interactions between use of law enforcement and the selected demographic factors were also examined. (Torres & Stefkovich, 2009, pp. 461–463)

Potential Threats to Internal and External Validity:

1. _____

_____

2. _____

_____

Ways to Address and Overcome Validity Threats:

_____

_____

_____

Potential Issues With Internal Reliability:

_____

_____

Ways to Address and Overcome Reliability Threat:

_____

_____

_____

Now, keeping in mind what you have learned in this chapter, read the following excerpt from Bustamante, Nelson, and Onwuegbuzie (2009) and list two potential issues with credibility and how you might address them.

> We developed a mixed research Internet questionnaire, consisting of open- and closed-ended questions, to collect both quantitative and qualitative data. Specifically, school leader participants were first asked to rank the importance of each SCCOC item to schoolwide cultural competence on a 4-point, Likert-type scale and then asked to describe how relevant each item was to cultural competence in actual school settings and how they might characterize each item in terms of a school-related domain (e.g., curriculum). Domains were not prescribed or restricted by the questionnaire format. Participants were free to comment openly and describe their own domains or categories by writing their responses in text boxes. . .

> To ensure the credibility of the data analysis process, several steps were followed in analyzing the narrative responses from the SCCOC instrument fidelity questionnaire. First, responses to each question were downloaded, creating a packet of narrative responses for each researcher to review. Next, to enhance intercoder agreement, individual members of the research team read and reread responses to each item and then unitized them (Glaser & Strauss, 1967). Specifically, key words and phrases for each response were highlighted, which then served as the basis for extracting a list of nonrepetitive, nonoverlapping significant statements (i.e., _horizontalization_ of data; Moustakas, 1994), with each statement being given equal weight. Units were eliminated that contained the same or similar statements or key words such that each unit corresponded to a unique response. Meanings then were formulated by explicating the meaning of each significant statement. Next,

each ensuing significant statement was compared with previous codes such that similar clusters were labeled with the same code. After all the responses had been coded, the codes were grouped by similarity, and a theme was identified and outlined on the basis of each grouping. . . . Once each research team member generated themes and subthemes for each SCCOC fidelity questionnaire item, team members met to compare individual researcher results and reached intercoder agreement at 95%. (Bustamante, Nelson, & Onwuegbuzie, 2009, pp. 803–805)

Two Potential Issues With Credibility and Trustworthiness:

1. _____

_____

2. _____

_____

Ways to Address and Overcome Potential Trustworthiness Issues:

_____

_____

_____

Possible Responses

Torres and Stefkovich (2009). Possible threats to internal validity include group differences and alternative causes. Given that this is an existing database, it is hard to control for a validity threat based on history, but one has to consider whether the data would have been different across studies during the time that they were collected, particularly given changes in laws that may have occurred in any of the locations from which the data were drawn. Given that the data are several years old, external validity may be an issue as well. To address this, the authors could provide some documentation or notes about the stability of these data over the time in which they were collected.

Although the researchers did an excellent job of attempting to draw data from representative locations and school systems, group differences may still exist based on how individual schools and systems chose to define and report students based on certain variables, such as those related to SES or suspensions. The authors could have addressed whether common definitions were used for student characteristics/variables when reported by school administrators.

Although most of the variables are generally well described, a number of other variables that may have affected the dependent variable may not have been measured. The authors clearly had to make some decisions about what to measure, based on the purposes of the research and their questions, but possible alternative causes should be noted in the limitations discussion later in the article.

Threats to reliability may be minimal, but the researchers did report that "proportion of student incidents reported to the police for the 1999–2000 academic year served as a dependent variable" and how it was calculated. They did not report any sort of reliability on the calculation, although it might be assumed that the calculation was computer generated. This could be clarified.

Bustamante, Nelson, & Onwuegbuzie (2009). The authors did a far better job than many qualitative researchers in all aspects of reporting characteristics of the study that can call trustworthiness into question. They did gather data from several sources (triangulation), but member checking would certainly enhance the overall trustworthiness of the data collection and analysis. The authors also reported intercoder reliability, but they did not describe how the percentage was calculated or on what percentage of data the reliability was calculated.

Summary

Issues of validity, reliability, and trustworthiness can affect every aspect of a study's design and outcomes. Validity is the degree to which the researcher and the audience are satisfied that the conclusions drawn are true and are not from erroneous sources. Though the term is sometimes used in qualitative inquiry, *validity* is generally associated with designs that include quantitative data, whether experimental or descriptive. *Trustworthiness*, on the other hand, is a term used more frequently in qualitative inquiry. It pertains to how a researcher can convince others that the study is credible and, in fact, provides insight that is appropriate and fully developed.

In this chapter, three types of validity were identified:

1. Internal validity

2. External validity

3. Construct validity

You also read about major threats to each type of validity and examples of how these threats may be addressed.

Reliability was described as the degree to which a study can be repeated with similar results. Reliability can also be subdivided into internal and external. Internal reliability is the degree to which a study's measures would produce similar results upon repeated applications of the treatment or repeated observations. Internal reliability can be threatened by faulty measures, inaccurate observations, and poor implementation of an intervention. External reliability is the degree to which a study's results can be generalized to other groups or situations. It can be threatened by such factors as an inappropriate choice of sample and overly complex interventions.

In addition to validity and reliability, trustworthiness was described as it relates to descriptive research using qualitative methods. Trustworthiness includes the credibility of the researcher and of the methods used. Credibility of the researcher can be established by description of the researcher's professional credentials and biases. Credibility of the methods can be established by considering their truth value, applicability, consistency, and neutrality.

Although it may be impossible to address every threat to validity or trustworthiness in a study, researchers must remain focused on the purpose of the study and their research questions. Once you have determined the appropriate method to use to answer your research question(s), you can design the study. As the design process begins, you should set priorities for the types of validity and areas of trustworthiness that will be addressed. Then, a systematic analysis of the study design and how the design addresses threats to validity and trustworthiness should be conducted. Without adequate detail about every aspect of a study, readers will question, rightly, the validity and trustworthiness of its conclusions.

In short, it is essential that you consider issues related to validity, reliability, and trustworthiness when designing and conducting, as well as analyzing and interpreting, your research. Therefore, you should refer back to the concepts presented in this chapter as you develop and carry out your research. Material in later chapters will, indeed, prompt you to recall and address validity, reliability, and trustworthiness in your study.

Discussion Questions

1. What is the difference between internal and external validity?

2. What are some of the possible threats to internal validity?

3. Why is the concept of construct validity important for teachers and administrators in understanding student test results and making instructional or policy decisions?

4. Two education researchers observed video recordings of student behavior on buses. They observed 28 behavioral events. The two researchers agreed that 20 of the events were considered inappropriate behavior. What was the interobserver reliability?

5. Explain two ways to increase truth value or credibility in qualitative research.

Your Research Project in Action

Given the research problem and question(s) you identified in Chapter 3, if your research appears to be experimental, quasi-experimental, or quantitative descriptive, complete this matrix for possible threats to validity.

Validity Type	Threat	How to Address?
Internal	History	
	Maturation	
	Instrumentation	
	Selection	

Validity Type	Threat	How to Address?
	Mortality	
	Ambiguity about direction of effect	
Construct	Inadequate description of construct	
	Inadequate measurement of construct	
	Confounding constructs and levels of constructs	
External	Sample characteristics	
	Treatment characteristics	
	Setting characteristics	

Given the research problem and question(s) you identified in Chapter 3, if your research appears to be qualitative, complete this matrix to address potential issues in trustworthiness.

Trustworthiness Issue	Threat	How to Address?
Credibility	Researcher	
	Method	
	Analysis techniques	
Transferability	Inadequate description	
Dependability	Researcher	
	Method	
	Analysis techniques	
Confirmability	Method	
	Analysis techniques	

References

Cook, T. D., & Campbell, D. T. (1979). *Quasi-experimentation: Design and analysis issues for field settings*. Boston: Houghton Mifflin.

Gall, M. D., Gall, J. P., & Borg, W. R. (2006). *Educational research: An introduction* (8th ed.). Boston: Allyn & Bacon.

Lincoln, Y. S., & Guba, E. G. (1985). *Naturalistic inquiry.* Newbury Park, CA: Sage.

Marshall, C., & Rossman, G. B. (2015). *Designing qualitative research* (6th ed.). Thousand Oaks, CA: Sage.

Patton, M. Q. (2015). *Qualitative research & evaluation methods* (4th ed.). Thousand Oaks, CA: Sage.

Rumrill, P. D., Cook, B. G., & Wiley, A. L. (2011). *Research in special education: Designs, methods, and applications* (2nd ed.). Springfield, IL: Charles C. Thomas.

Strauss, A. L., & Corbin, J. M. (2014). *Basics of qualitative research: Techniques and procedures for developing grounded theory* (4th ed.). Thousand Oaks, CA: Sage.

Literature Examples

Boardman, A. G., Vaughn, S., Buckley, P., Reutebuch, C., Roberts, G., & Klingner, J. (2016). Collaborative strategic reading for students with learning disabilities in upper elementary classrooms. *Exceptional Children, 82*(4), 409–427.

Bustamante, R. M., Nelson, J. A., & Onwuegbuzie, J. A. (2009). Assessing school-wide cultural competence: Implications for school leadership preparation. *Educational Administration Quarterly, 45*(5), 793–827.

Floress, M. T., Jenkins, L. N., Reinke, W. M., & McKown L. (2017). General education teachers' natural rates of praise: A preliminary investigation. *Behavioral Disorders*, 1–12. https://doi .org/10.1177/0198742917709472

Leko, M. M., Roberts, C. A., & Pek, Y. (2015). A theory of secondary teachers' adaptations when implementing a reading intervention program. *The Journal of Special Education, 49*(3), 168–178.

McDermott, P., & Gormley, K. A. (2016). Teachers' use of technology in elementary reading lessons, *Reading Psychology, 37*(1), 121–146. DOI: 10.1080/02702711.2015.1009592

Sylvan, L. (2018). Similar populations, differing service levels: Exploring factors that drive variability in the provision of speech-language services. *Educational Policy, 32*(4), 598–630.

Torres, M. S., & Stefkovich, J. A. (2009). Demographics and police involvement: Implications for student civil liberties and just leadership. *Educational Administration Quarterly, 45*(3), 450–473.

5

Designing and Conducting Experimental Research

Chapter Objectives

In this chapter, the reader will

- understand the characteristics of experimental and quasi-experimental research designs.
- understand the link between research questions and research designs.
- understand commonly used experimental and quasi-experimental designs.
- understand the characteristics of single-subject designs.
- understand common ways to measure dependent variables and types of data.
- understand how to align research questions with design, measurement, and data.
- be prepared to implement experimental research.

As discussed in Chapter 2, good research questions and hypotheses will lead you to your research design and method, and in the case of experimental research, there are numerous designs from which you can choose. Therefore, it is important to understand the purposes and characteristics of each type of design in order to determine the best match between a research question and methods to conduct the study. You have already been introduced to many of the different designs in previous graduate coursework or through other resources. This chapter will highlight several commonly used group designs, as well as single-subject designs, and help you to connect these designs with ways of measuring outcomes using potential data sources.

Experimental and Quasi-Experimental Research

The objective of experimental research is to make inferential links between variables as opposed to describing them. In other words, in experimental research, the researcher attempts to establish cause and effect relationships (to determine whether by doing X, the result is Y). Researchers often intentionally intervene in the natural order of events and observe to see if a change will produce or contribute to a different outcome. For example, a researcher might want to know if using a new writing technique in elementary classrooms (independent variable) will result in better scores on a state writing test (dependent variable). To study this, researchers may find participants in several schools in which to implement the new writing technique (experimental group) as well as other participants willing to be involved for comparison purposes (**control group**). The researchers would then introduce teachers at the experimental schools to the new technique, and teachers would teach it to their students. Researchers would control for variables related to age, gender, disability status, and so forth. Students would complete the state test at the beginning of the school year, prior to intervention, as well as at the end of the year. Finally, the researchers would analyze the data to find out if, on average, students in the experimental group performed better than those in the control group.

Experimental designs, as in the previous example, typically include these key characteristics: (a) randomized selection of experimental participants, (b) direct manipulation of an independent variable, (c) control of extraneous variables, and (d) measurement of outcomes (e.g., Gall, Gall, & Borg, 2006; Mills & Gay, 2015; Sytsma, 2009; see Figure 5.1). High levels of control of the independent variable and random assignment of participants to conditions (e.g., classrooms) may be impractical and difficult to implement in educational and social sciences research. Thus, research that has an independent variable, dependent variable, and outcome measures, but does not include random assignment of participants for comparisons is referred to as *quasi-experimental*.

Quasi-experimental research, like experimental research, attempts to determine if an independent variable (e.g., a new writing technique) has a direct impact

FIGURE 5.1 ● Characteristics of Experimental Designs

- Randomized selection of experimental participants
- Direct manipulation of an independent variable
- Control of extraneous variables
- Measurement of outcomes

on a dependent variable (e.g., student performance on a state test). If done well, quasi-experimental research still can be generalized beyond the context in which it was conducted to similar situations. For the purposes of this discussion, the author typically refers to both experimental and quasi-experimental research simply as *experimental research*.

There is one other characteristic common to experimental research: quantitative methods and data are utilized. As discussed in Chapter 1, using quantitative methods, a researcher assigns numbers to variables or levels of variables being studied for purposes of statistical analysis. In the writing research example, researchers would collect and analyze actual performance numbers on the state test (e.g., 78, 95, 62) or rating numbers if that form of measurement was used (e.g., 1 equals low nonproficient, 2 equals nonproficient, 3 equals adequately proficient, 4 equally highly proficient) to draw conclusions about the intervention.

Questions Point to Designs

In Chapter 2, it was noted that a research question is initially a way of expressing your interest in a problem or phenomenon and that you may have more than one research question in a study, depending on the complexity and breadth of your proposed work. A good research question is clear and specific, refers to the problem or phenomena, reflects an intervention in experimental work, and notes the target population or participants. A research hypothesis follows a research question, and sometimes a question can be directional and include a null hypothesis as well. Perhaps most importantly, research questions point to important parts of your research design and method; that is, your key variables. Take another look at the following research question and hypothesis first presented in Chapter 2.

Question: Do students in Algebra I classes who engage in the XYZ curriculum perform significantly different on state tests than students who do not participate in that curriculum?

Possible hypothesis: Students who participate in the XYZ curriculum in Algebra I classes will perform significantly differently on state achievement tests than students who do not participate in that curriculum.

Not only is the problem noted in the question and addressed in the hypothesis, but the method is clearly foreshadowed. The participants are Algebra I students. The intervention (independent variable) is the XYZ curriculum, and the response to the intervention will be measured by the state test (dependent variable). Therefore, you have a pretty good head start in making decisions about the design of a study when questions are well defined.

In making specific decisions about the design of your study, consider following a series of systematic steps (see Figure 5.2). As you might expect, the first step in the process is to define what variables you are interested in and how you might address issues of validity. Before proceeding to discuss the second, third, and fourth steps in this chapter, let's review a few concepts related to variables and validity. The last step regarding analysis will be explored in Chapter 9.

FIGURE 5.2 ● Steps in Experimental Research Design

1. Define what variables you are interested in and how you might address issues of validity.

2. Select a design that will enable you to investigate the variables.

3. Decide how you want to measure the impact of independent variable on the dependent variable.

4. Decide what kind of data you want to collect through your measurement.

5. Think about how you want to analyze the effects of the intervention on the dependent variable.

What Variables Do You Want to Investigate?

Variables, sometimes called factors, are the parts of studies that researchers may want to manipulate. An **independent variable** is the intervention or **treatment** (that is, the conditions created by the researcher to produce a result). A dependent variable is the outcome, effect, or result of the intervention, which is measured in some way. Table 5.1 lists some examples of both kinds of variables.

In the algebra intervention example, engagement in or learning the XYZ curriculum is the independent variable, and student math performance is the dependent variable, as measured by the state test scores. You may be interested in other variables or factors too, so as to compare outcomes for different populations.

Brainstorm a list of possible interventions and think about the pros and cons of each intervention option. Strive to focus interventions on a fairly specific outcome rather than one that is broad. It is easier to measure the results of specific dependent variables. You might also choose a multistage intervention, but simpler may be better, particularly if your research is in classrooms, given the multiplicity of demands. Detail your independent variable, especially one that is classroom-based, by thinking about the characteristics of effective interventions, planning procedures, conditions, and activities (see Figure 5.3).

Next, define with whom, when, where interventions will occur, as well as any materials or other resources needed. You'll also want to draft a timeline for implementation. Take the time necessary to think through the details thoroughly, not only of what the intervention will entail but when, how often, how long, with which participants, and under what conditions (e.g., during class discussions, during one-to-one work, on Monday afternoons). Here is an example of what one pair of teacher researchers decided:

Data were collected at a residential outdoor science school and in an adjacent state park. Circle formation data were collected in both outside and inside classroom settings, with 12 to 15 students per group. The four predetermined circle arrangements were tested over a four-week period. Each instructor performed and collected data on all four of the

FIGURE 5.3 ● Characteristics of Good Interventions

- Possess a strong rationale.
- Are clearly organized.
- Lead to measurable outcomes.
- Benefit many participants.
- Are doable or realistic for implementers.

In classrooms,

- Focus on how to learn, as well as on what to learn.
- Connect new learning with previous knowledge.
- Involve teacher demonstration/modeling of expected student performance.
- Include both guided and independent practice.
- Incorporate active student participation.
- Include immediate and specific feedback for students.
- Feature frequent review.

TABLE 5.1 ● Examples of Independent and Dependent Variables

Independent Variables	Dependent Variables
Reading instruction	State test scores
Parent education	Rate of spoken reinforcement
Stipends	Participation in professional development
Positive notes to home	Student behavior ratings
One-on-one tutoring	Number of math problems completed correctly
Vocabulary strategy instruction	Science lab report grades
After-school detention	Out-of-seat behavior
Use of graphic organizers	History test scores
Immediate verbal feedback	Correctly spelled words
Staying in at recess	Rate of homework completion
Mentoring	Suspension and expulsion rates
Teacher communications with home	Parent satisfaction

predetermined circle arrangements in order to control for the external factors associated with instructor quality, knowledge, and enthusiasm. The four instructors collected data on circle arrangements with a different group of students each week, completing a total of 86 observations. Lesson content and teaching methods when collecting data were relatively the same for each instructor, covering science topics through discussions, activities, and lectures. (St. Onge & Eitel, 2017, pp. 2–3)

In addition, determine if additional time is needed for intervention development and schedule time to complete that work. Decide if additional resources are needed and establish a time and method to acquire those resources.

Moreover, before you finalize your plans, it is helpful to receive outside feedback about your ideas. You may want to arrange feedback sessions with senior teachers, department heads, principals, curriculum directors, or others prior to refining the details of interventions. By doing so, you will be able to receive valuable insights about interventions and possible evaluation plans. Respondents' feedback should include both strengths and recommendations for improvement of interventions and/or evaluation designs. After receiving the feedback, modify and refine your intervention and implementation details as necessary.

Revisiting Validity

Broadly speaking, validity is the extent of truthfulness in a score or interpretation of results. With regard to measurement, construct validity is the extent to which a test or measurement tool measures the concept that it claims to (e.g., memory, intelligence, reading fluency). Internal and external validity are particularly important to consider as you make decisions about experimental designs, because if you do not address issues of validity in experimental research, others may challenge, or even disregard, your conclusions.

Internal validity is the extent to which one can accurately conclude that the results of an experiment or differences in a dependent variable are due to the independent variable and not to other factors. A key question related to internal validity is then "Did this study truly indicate that A, not some other variable, caused B?" Whether the threat is history, maturation, or measurement, perhaps internal validity is most often questioned when the differences in experimental and control group results can be explained by differences in the demographic characteristics of the groups. That is, you want to have equivalent groups in each condition. For example, in the writing or the algebra intervention research mentioned earlier, you do not want all of the students who are struggling in one group and all of those students who are high performers in another group.

External validity has been defined as the extent to which the results of a study can be generalized to other similar groups, individuals, or situations. In other words, the evaluative question is "How do the conclusions of this study apply elsewhere?" If the larger purpose of our research is to better understand and improve education, the results of studies should be applicable to other situations either through close attention to external validity or through **replication** of study results. The ability to generalize to the target population and other populations requires an adequate sample of the population included in the study. The characteristics of the intervention can also affect external validity. For example, if an intervention is complicated and the teachers who implemented the instructional strategy all had 50 hours of training, can the success of the program be generalized to classrooms whose teachers have not gone through the same process?

In short, it is important to remember that while you cannot possibly eliminate all of the variables that could reduce internal or external validity in a study, you must make careful decisions about the elements of your design to reduce threats to validity. As noted in Chapter 4, it is important to consider your research question before addressing threats. For example, conducting a study in a classroom instead of a clinical situation may increase the external validity of the study, but this setting may also decrease the internal validity. These important decisions, which reflect your dependent and independent variables, will be central to your design and will be recorded in the methods section of your research proposal (see Chapter 8 for further detail on your research proposal).

Group Designs

Once you have a good idea of which variables you want to include in your study, you are ready to consider your research design (step 2 in Figure 5.2). As noted earlier, an experimental design is the way you go about answering your research question. Your selection of a design, then, depends on what kinds of information you want to obtain. It typically includes (a) selection of experimental participants, (b) direct manipulation of an independent variable, (c) control of extraneous variables, and (d) measurement of outcomes (e.g., Gall et al., 2006; Mills & Gay, 2015; Sytsma, 2009). For the purposes of this discussion, let's assume that you have selected your participants. So now let's explore five commonly used experimental and quasi-experimental group designs that you might consider in order to manipulate an independent variable while controlling extraneous variables and to measure the outcomes of the manipulation in terms of a dependent variable. Afterwards, this chapter will also discuss single-subject designs. The five group designs are posttest-only, pretest-posttest, comparison group, factorial, and time-series.

Posttest Only

The **posttest-only group design** is sometimes referred to as the "one-shot" design (e.g., Gall et al., 2006). In this very simple research design, participants are selected, are introduced to an intervention (independent variable), and then are observed for some behavior or have their performance measured in some way of interest (dependent variable). The posttest-only design may be represented in this way:

Group →Intervention →Posttest

For example, let's say you taught a group of students a new strategy for finding main ideas in their reading. You might then give them a page from a textbook and ask them to identify the main idea. In such a design, no comparisons are made to the participants' performance prior to the intervention or to any other group's performance; therefore, the potential for internal and external validity problems exists. Among the possible validity concerns, it's hard to tell if the intervention caused the result, and you don't know for certain that the results are generalizable to any population. Therefore, this design is considered relatively weak. That said, if you can control for extraneous variables prior to and during the intervention that could affect the outcomes, the posttest-only design is certainly simple and inexpensive to implement (McMillan, 2015).

Pretest-Posttest

With the **pretest-posttest group design**, the researcher has an opportunity to address the obvious threats to internal validity that exist when there is no pretest by which to compare performance on the dependent variable. Thus, in the pretest-posttest design, participants are identified, pretested, given an intervention, and posttested through observation or some other measurement. The posttest performance can be compared to the pretest to see if there is a difference. This appears to be a very common design in educational research (Sytsma, 2009). This design may be simply represented this way:

Group →Pretest →Intervention →Posttest

For example, let's go back to the reading for the main idea study for a moment. If one simply pretested the students prior to instruction in the strategy, then posttested with the same measure, one would have a pretest-posttest design. Some concerns with validity remain, however; because there is no group of students to which to compare the treatment group's performance, readers may not be convinced that the treatment group is representative of the larger population.

In this design, as well as in any others discussed in this section, one way that you can address threats to external validity is by **random sampling**. You can employ random sampling when you have substantial resources and authority to make group selection decisions. Such resources and authority, however, are often unachievable or impractical, even in larger-scale experimental research in education.

In short, when you can use the same measure for the pretest and posttest, without retesting effects due to insufficient time in between, and you can be certain that history, maturation, or another intervention isn't responsible for outcomes, the pretest-posttest design could work for your study (e.g., McMillan, 2015).

Comparison Group

Comparison group designs move perhaps one step further than pretest-posttest designs in terms of strengthening the validity of the research. Because of that, as well as their utility, comparison group designs are often used in educational research. In a comparison design, also called *control group* or *static group* design, you have two groups matched by similar characteristics. Both are pretested and posttested. Only the experimental group, however, receives the intervention. This design can be represented this way:

Experimental Group →Pretest →Intervention →Posttest

Comparison Group →Pretest →Nonintervention→Posttest

Let's go back to the example of the algebra students study. If you were to provide the XYZ curriculum to one group of students after a pretest and prior to a posttest and administer the pretest, conduct classroom business-as-usual (or provide an alternate intervention), and then posttest the comparison group, you would have employed this design. With this design, you can look at pre- to posttest differences in the experimental group, while controlling for threats to internal validity if the pretest performances of the two groups are similar but the posttest scores are significantly different. Validity does hinge on the comparability of the two groups, as well as whether the participant experiences between and pre- and posttesting differed only by the intervention (Mills & Gay, 2015). As mentioned previously, you can enhance internal validity by random assignment of participants, if that is feasible.

One other note in relation to the comparison design: An enhancement of the basic comparison group design, considered by some to be a variation of a factorial design, is called the **Soloman four-group design**. In this design, you can control for possible pretest sensitization, as well as look at possible interactions of pretest and experimental conditions, by adding two additional groups that do not receive the pretest (Gall et al., 2006). The potential effort and cost of this design, however, sometimes make it impractical for educational researchers.

Factorial

You may be interested in looking at more than one independent variable in your experimental research. For instance, you might be interested in how students within your groups respond to an intervention based on characteristics such as age, grade level, disability category, or ethnicity. Let's say that in the earlier example regarding the new writing technique, you are interested in understanding how groups of children from four different racial backgrounds respond to the technique. In that case, the writing technique and the type of student each become independent variables, or factors. If you had a comparison group, considered a form of (non)intervention in this design, one would call this a 4 × 2 **factorial group design**. That is, there are four **levels**, or subgroups, for the ethnicity variable/factor and two levels or conditions for the intervention variable/factor. One way to represent this design is as follows:

Experimental Group →Pretest →Intervention →Posttest

(1, 2, 3, 4)

Comparison Group →Pretest →Nonintervention →Posttest

(1, 2, 3, 4)

From a two-factor design, you can get information about the **main effects**—that is, the effects of each independent variable on or its relationship to the dependent variable—as well as the **interaction effects**, the interrelated effects of the two independent variables on the dependent variable. If you were to look at the effects of the writing technique on the entire experimental group as compared to the control group, you would be looking at the main effects. If you looked at how different subgroups within the experimental group differentially responded to the writing technique, you would be looking at the interaction effects.

With a factorial design, you may decide to look at more than two factors as well, including two types of intervention rather than simply an intervention and non-intervention. In sum, the factorial design is very helpful in educational research, particularly in enabling the researcher to capture some of the complexity typically found in schools, because it is often difficult to reason that a single independent variable might be responsible for the effects observed. See Gall et al. (2006), Mills & Gay, (2015), and Campbell and Stanley (1963) for a much more elaborated discussion of factorial designs.

Time-Series

In a **time-series group design**, a group of participants is observed or administered some form of measurement (e.g., test or quiz) at multiple given intervals to establish a valid baseline, and then an intervention is introduced. After the introduction of the intervention, participants are observed or administered the same form of measurement at multiple given intervals to see if there is a change in behavior or performance. A time-series design might be represented this way, where M represents measurement and I represents the intervention:

$$\text{Group} \rightarrow M \rightarrow M \rightarrow M \rightarrow I \rightarrow M \rightarrow M \rightarrow M$$

As an example, let's say you wanted to research the effects of gifts and other recognition on the frequency with which middle school teachers referred students to the principal for behavioral issues. You could collect data on daily office referrals for a month, then introduce the intervention and measure office referrals again for a month.

The time-series design has some of the characteristics of the posttest-only and pretest-posttest designs in that one group is included in the design, and it has some of the characteristics of the next type of design we will discuss in this chapter, single-subject design, in that there is repeated measurement of the dependent variable. Certainly, the frequency of measurement enhances the internal validity of this design, which is often used to study behavior in fields including counseling and special education (e.g., Cook & Campbell, 1979; Mills & Gay, 2015).

Single-Subject Designs

Single-subject designs, also called *single-case designs*, are frequently used in special education and counseling research. Single-subject designs are not group designs, but instead attempt to capture the effects of an intervention for individuals rather than pooling individual differences as in group designs. That is, the unit of analysis is the individual, even if several individuals are studied, rather than a group. A couple of the key elements of the design are repeated measurement of the dependent variable before and after the intervention, and interventions that consist of more than a single event (e.g., more than one day of new instruction). Also, data are typically charted or graphed, rather than statistically analyzed, so that change in the dependent variable can be visually observed over time, thereby enhancing the internal validity of the results. For example, let's say you wanted to research the effects of positive notes and phone calls to home on the behavior of students with a history of behavior problems in a history class. You might collect data on behaviors such as raising hand, positive verbal responses, staying on-task, or homework completion from each of five students for several days before and after sending positive notes and making positive phone calls to home on a regular basis. You would then plot the results on a graph for a student (see Figure 5.4).

With repeated measurement of the dependent variable and well-defined and graphically illustrated baseline and intervention conditions, the effects of an independent variable can be seen with reasonable internal validity in a single-subject design. Variations on single-subject designs include the **A-B-A-B design** (also called reversal design) in which there are four conditions: baseline, intervention, return to baseline, and return to intervention. With this classic variation, you enhance the internal validity (i.e., causal determination) of your findings by demonstrating that after the withdrawal of an intervention, a behavior or performance returns to baseline levels of measurement, and then again to intervention levels of measurement with the reintroduction of the independent variable (see Figure 5.5).

Whereas group designs may include design features and procedures, including randomization and treatment integrity, to enhance internal validity, demonstrating experimental control is necessary in single-subject designs for enhancing causal determination. Tincani and Travers (2018) suggested that since experimental control

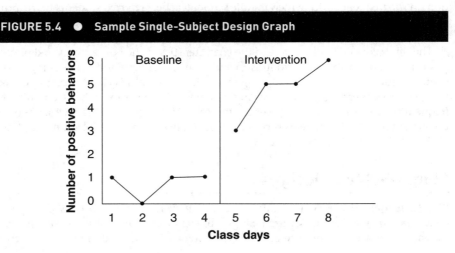

FIGURE 5.4 ● Sample Single-Subject Design Graph

FIGURE 5.5 ● A-B-A-B Design Graph

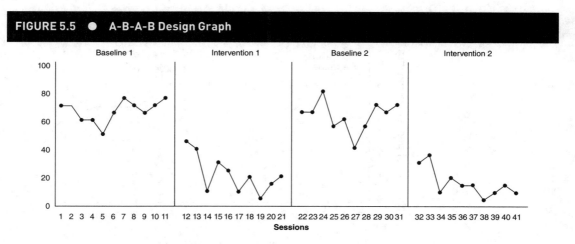

is demonstrated when an intervention (independent variable) reliably produces change in a behavior or performance (dependent variable), then an A-B-A-B design is considered a best practice in single-subject research designs. That is, if a researcher can illustrate reliable change in behavior or performance from baseline to intervention and back again, she can more confidently conclude that the intervention was effective. In fact, the What Works Clearinghouse standards stipulated that without three demonstrations of an effect (i.e., use of an A-B-A-B design), there is no evidence of a causal relationship between the independent and dependent variables (WWC, 2014). Moreover, Kratochwill et al. (2013) agreed that single-subject design standards should include A-B-A-B reversal designs as well as alternating treatments and multiple-baseline designs.

In a **multiple-baseline design**, the intervention begins at different points in time for two or more participants. The graphs of the results are lined up in such a way as to enhance the internal validity of the design (i.e., the reader can readily see the intervention effects not only in baseline and intervention conditions but across more than one participant). Figure 5.6 shows a sample multiple-baseline graph. See Tawney and Gast (1984) and Kratochwill et al. (2013) for a more thorough discussion of single-subject designs in experimental research.

Measurement of Dependent Variables

Before launching an experimental intervention, you need to consider the question "How will I measure the outcomes (dependent variable) of the intervention (independent variable)?" or perhaps "How will I know if my intervention had the intended effect?" You can measure change in hundreds of ways. Is the best way to measure body temperature with a ruler? A speedometer? Of course not. But take this example: Is the best way to measure change in physical height over a period of one year in yards or feet? Neither: You probably want to capture change that is more

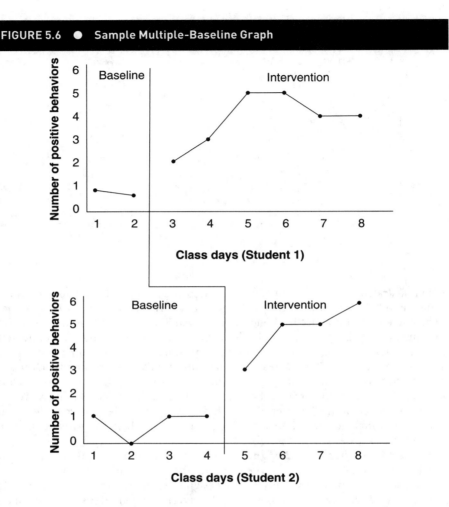

FIGURE 5.6 ● Sample Multiple-Baseline Graph

incremental than that. That's why one measures change in height for growing children in inches or centimeters.

What does this have to do with your designing your research? A lot, as I am sure you realize. You have to have *valid* ways of measuring change in performance. You also have to have *meaningful* ways. And *reliable* ways too. Measuring body temperature with a ruler is not any more a valid evaluation than teaching kids concepts and testing them on details. Unfortunately, we have all had teachers who have done that.

Now, about meaningfulness: Try to answer the "So what?" question. Or to put it another way, how will you know whether your intervention made a difference? It is not any more meaningful to measure change in physical height in terms of feet or yards than it is to measure change in reading or writing skills by simply having kids answer questions at the end of the chapter. There could be dozens of reasons why students answer end-of-chapter questions the way they do.

You must determine the instruments or tools you will use, as well as how and when you will use them and to whom you will administer them. You may have to create a measurement instrument to capture a behavior or performance that you wish to observe, or you may never have to administer an instrument but can instead rely on the permanent records of an administration, such as a state test score.

Salkind (2016) suggested that when you select a dependent variable, you should try to find measures that have been used before and in which validity and reliability have already been established. If you are using a test, be sure to get the latest version and assure yourself that the test is normed to participants with the same characteristics as those in your research. You can find information about many widely used tests online from the Buros Institute (buros.unl.edu/buros/jsp/search.jsp).

Not surprisingly, perhaps, Swanson and Hoskyn (1998) suggested that intervention effects were greater when researcher-developed measures were used than with broader, standardized measures. Still, Gersten et al. (2000) contended that if a study shows significant effects for the intervention on broader measures as well as more explicit, researcher-developed ones, then those findings are substantially more important. In short, it probably makes sense to use more than one measure of your dependent variable and perhaps to pilot them to see which give you the clearest and most meaningful data for analysis. The remainder of this section of the chapter highlights several types of dependent measures, including observations, tests and permanent records, and interviews, and the kinds of data that they yield.

Observations

Broadly speaking, there are two types of observation: *formal* and *informal*. In **formal observations**, researchers identify and record (quantitatively) a discrete target behavior. **Informal observations**, on the other hand, typically utilize anecdotal records and field notes that provide loosely structured records of observations. For experimental researchers, formal observations enable them more easily to quantify and later analyze data, whereas informal observations are more likely used as qualitative methods in nonexperimental/descriptive research. See Chapters 6 and 7 for further discussion of observations used in qualitative and nonexperimental/descriptive research.

In measuring a dependent variable through formal observations, the researcher must first decide whether it's more important to determine how often the behavior occurs (**event-based observations**) or how long the behavior lasts (**time-based observations**). More specifically, event-based observations involve identifying a behavior, counting the number of times it occurs, and keeping a tally. Time-based observations involve keeping track of the duration (amount of time) a particular behavior occurs. In time-based observations, the researcher targets a behavior that has a beginning and an end.

Event-sampling observation is helpful for determining the exact number of times a behavior occurs during a predetermined period of time. It involves identifying a behavior and simply tallying the number of times it occurs during the predetermined period. **Time-sampling observation** is helpful for determining the extent or duration of a behavior during a predetermined amount of time. It involves keeping track of whether a particular behavior occurs or not during preset time intervals. For time-sampling observation, you target a behavior that has a beginning and an end.

Event sampling would be appropriate for assessing a behavior like students talking out in class without raising their hands but would not be appropriate for measuring wandering around the room. The difference is that talking out is a discrete event with a relatively instantaneous beginning and ending. Wandering around the room may also be a single behavior, but a student may wander for several minutes at a time. Wandering around the room might be better measured by time sampling. That way, you would get an idea of how much time the student is wasting, a variable with an obvious impact on academic work. Observations of students having their heads down and sleeping would, again, be better assessed through time sampling for the same reasons as wandering around the room.

Event sampling might be helpful for assessing the number of times a student mispronounces or cannot identify words in a text passage. Like talking out, this is a pretty discrete behavior. Another possible use of event recording would be to record the number of times that students raise their hands or are called on in class. With event sampling, you want to measure behaviors that have short durations and, again, for which you want an exact count of the number of times the behavior or error occurs during a period of class time. This is not the same as counting the number of homework errors a student makes, although that data may be helpful to know also.

For time sampling, you count the number of time intervals in which something occurs, not the number of instances. You may miss a lot of instances of behavior, but again, the objective is to note the extent of behavior and how it may impact other tasks that are expected of the student. Time intervals may be in seconds or minutes, but the longer the interval, the potentially less accurate the data may be. For instance, if a student seems to wander around the room for several minutes at a time, you might want to set 2- or 5-minute intervals. You would then observe the student every 2 or 5 minutes and tally whether he was or was not wandering around the room during three consecutive class days. After collecting the data, you could look for patterns and see, for example, that the student wanders at certain times but not at others. That data should prompt you to think about what is going on during class during the times he wanders and consider why the wandering behavior might happen, given what you already know about the student.

Figures 5.6 and 5.7 give examples of event-based and time-based observation tools, respectively. The example in Figure 5.6 might be used one-on-one with a student to record the number of types of reading errors made from three selected textbook passages, as well as across passages. In cases like this one, you may get data similar to that which might come from a test. The example time-based observation tool may be helpful to measure the extent or duration of out-of-seat behavior during class on three dates. You could use this or a variation of this for measuring other behaviors that are not discrete but where the extent of student behavior affects other expected behaviors or classroom tasks. You may need to vary the interval lengths to capture enough instances of the behavior.

Tests and Permanent Records

Tests and permanent or existing records generally include a variety of material related to student performance. Whether looking at algebra, discipline referrals, or absences, many researchers create measures that attempt to match closely or are sensitive to the intervention/independent variable. Data from student performance on state tests in reading, math, and content areas, or results from individualized tests used in special education, provide broader information that may also be helpful as dependent measures. Some of these measures are **norm referenced** (i.e., student performance scores are calculated and compared to "norms" or the statistical average performance of others of the same age or grade level, for instance). In addition, you could use records of attendance, office referrals for behavior incidents, and student grade point averages, depending on your research questions.

You may also consider other student performance products, such as homework assignments, workbook pages, or written compositions, and analyze them in terms of accuracy, speed, number of items completed, percentage correct, time to complete, and type(s) of errors made.

Criterion-Referenced Assessment

One way to measure student performance is by periodically assessing performance with criterion-referenced items, such as 90% mastery or items correct, rather than compared to an age- or grade-level norm calculated external to a school or classroom, as is the case with norm-referenced tests or items. A **criterion-referenced** item might be a vocabulary term, math problem, musical scale, Spanish verb conjugation, or a social behavior that you select in advance and expect a student or group of students to master at a certain criterion level. What criterion level? The one set by you, a school district, or state education agency. You can easily create a list of related criterion-referenced items for any subject area. Your state standard curriculum may be a good reference with regard to selecting specific topics and even items.

FIGURE 5.7 ● Measure for Conducting Event-Based Observations

Student: _____ Date: _____
Target Behavior: _____

Type of error	Passage title: page #:	Passage title: page #:	Passage title: page #:	Total errors by type
Mispronunciation				
Substituted letter or word				
Could not identify				
Other				
Total errors in passage				

FIGURE 5.8 ● Measure for Conducting Time-Based Observations

Student: _____

Target Behavior: _____

X = occurrence of behavior

O = nonoccurrence of behavior

Interval	Date:	Date:	Date:	Total for the Interval
1.00				
1.05				
1.10				
1.15				
1.20				
1.25				
1.30				
1.35				
1.40				
1.45				
1.50				
Total for observation				

Here's what you do:

1. Select your topic objective (e.g., writing complete sentences, vocabulary).

2. Set your criterion level of performance (e.g., 85% of attempts).

3. Select or develop a series of specific items (e.g., spelling words, vocabulary terms, math word problems, sentences that are not complete).

4. Pretest the student on all items.

5. Assess the student at frequent intervals as you teach the words, terms, types of problems, and so forth. This may be daily, every other or third day, weekly, and so forth.

6. Record the results.

7. Graph the results in a way that best illustrates progress (e.g., line graph, bar graph).

Whether you decide to develop criterion-referenced assessments, select a test, or use permanent records to measure your dependent measure, be sure to communicate that clearly in your research proposal (see Chapter 8) as well as in your research report (see Chapter 12). Here is an example of a reasonably well-communicated dependent measure reported by teacher researchers:

> The quizzes consisted of ten multiple-choice questions randomly drawn from a bank of 25 questions. I chose these specific instruments because the students were accustomed to using them with their regular classroom teacher and because they provided a consistent number of questions that assessed student knowledge of text at the comprehension level of Bloom's taxonomy. The students took each of the quizzes online during class. . . I began the data collection process with a benchmark quiz that was used as a baseline measurement of student comprehension for comparison to later quizzes following use of the ReQuest technique. The students read a text selection using the accustomed IRE technique and took the corresponding benchmark quiz. The data collection process continued with the ReQuest instructional technique discussed above. The students completed a series of three chapter sections using the ReQuest technique and took the corresponding quiz for each section. (Peleaux & Endacott, 2014, p. 6)*

While the description of the measurement of the dependent variable (quiz scores) may be pretty reasonable, the use of classroom-based tools also may be subject to threats to internal and external validity (refer back to Chapter 4) that need to be addressed and discussed by the researchers.

Continuous Assessment

A well-developed line of research has measured and improved student achievement using **curriculum-based measurement** (CBM) with observation or criterion-referenced instruments. Shinn and Bamonto (1998) described CBM as

> a set of standard simple, short-duration fluency measures of reading, spelling, written expression, and mathematics computation . . . developed to serve as general outcome indicators measuring "vital signs" of student achievement in important areas of basic skills or literacy. (p. 1)

CBM probes are constructed using state or district curricula, and teachers administer them in time periods of minutes on a frequent basis so that they can evaluate how students are performing in the curriculum and whether instructional change is necessary to improve achievement. For example, a standard reading fluency CBM probe

* First published by New Prairie Press

TECHNOLOGY IN RESEARCH

Using Apps to Collect Data

Mobile phones and electronic tablets have become common in schools and clinics. Among their many purposes, teachers, administrators, and clinicians regularly use these devices to monitor students and collect data. A wide range of apps can quickly and easily be downloaded for use on phones and portable devices. They could prove invaluable for conducting classroom research projects and for making data-based decisions. Here are some basic types:

- *Gradebook assistants*—These programs (e.g., Powerschool) allow you to enter grades in your device as you walk by student desks and then sync your device to your desktop gradebook.

- *Network apps*—These applications (e.g., google docs) allow educators to connect to networked files, which could include student data files, other word processing documents, spreadsheets, student assessment results, etc.

- *Data collection apps*—These programs, such as the ones described below, allow you to keep track of points while you are teaching. Enter the names of the students in your classroom on your handheld device and use it to add or subtract points from each student merely by tapping on their names.

One example data collection app is called *Behavior Observation Plus*. This free app allows you to record frequency of behaviors during set intervals. After selecting a student and using the dropdowns to select behaviors and observation interval times, you push a button each time a behavior occurs. The app also times the length of the observation so you can easily calculate rate of behavior and run reports. Another app is *Observation Timer*. This app is also free to download to your device and allows the user to customize labels, times, and intervals. It records and time stamps data accurately, and allows you to easily export data into Excel spreadsheets for further analysis or graphing.

includes a passage of 250 words taken from a grade-level text. Students are asked to read as many words as possible in 1 minute while the teacher notes both words read correctly and errors. In another example, to measure reading comprehension, a teacher chooses a passage of 250 words taken from a grade-level text and deletes every seventh word. Given three alternatives to choose from, students are given 5 minutes to read and select words to fill in the blanks. Probes are administered weekly, along with instruction, to measure progress in performance over time.

Research has shown CBM to be a valid and reliable indicator of performance and progress in major skill areas, including math, reading, and writing (e.g., Keller-Margulis, Mercer, & Thomas, 2016; Methe, Briesch, & Hulac, 2015; Jitendra, Dupuis, & Zaslofsky, 2014). With the use of CBM data, educators can track student data in a formative way that is relevant to the curriculum and facilitates data-based decision-making regarding student performance.

Interviews

As a broader and more dynamic assessment included in experimental research, individual or group interviews may be helpful in understanding the effects of the

IN THEIR OWN WORDS

Joy LaFrance-Phipps, MAEd Student

Deciding how you want to measure the effects of the intervention is a key component of research design. Unless the effects of the intervention are measured and then analyzed correctly, the whole experiment has been a waste of time and resources. The question I asked myself before beginning data collection was: "What do I want to get out of my intervention?" In other words, what behaviors do I want changed and why? When a researcher knows exactly what kind of outcome she desires from the intervention, measuring the dependent variable is actually quite simple. That goes back to using the hypothesis in order to help with this part. For example, if a researcher wanted to increase the time on-task for a particular participant, then the hypothesis should state that the intervention will do that. When analyzing the effects of the intervention, all the researcher has to do is look at the data collected and see if the time on-task increased. If so, the intervention would have had a positive effect on time on-task.

independent variable, either by gaining insight into other reasons why participants may have responded as they did or by measuring the learning process as it relates to performance of a skill. For instance, educator researchers may want to ask study participants about their perceptions of structured note taking, small-group work, or some other aspect of the class to gain insight into aspects of the class that may affect student performance with regard to the dependent variable.

Another purpose of interviews in experimental research is to gain information about student cognition or strategy use—that is, how students approach specific reading, writing, or math activities or some other task you attempt to measure. This kind of interview can provide valuable information about why student outcomes on tasks or in a subject area are different than what might have been expected. One way to capture such information is to ask a sample or particular group of students to "think aloud" as they complete a task that measures the dependent variable. The task might be reading a passage from a history text in order to infer the main idea, completing a set of algebra problems, or writing a paragraph about a favorite food. Using interviews, as a form of what is referred to as **Mixed Methods**, in conjunction with a researcher-developed test, for example, is also a way to enhance the internal and external validity of your study. Descriptive interview procedures and Mixed Methods research are further detailed in Chapters 6 and 7.

Types of Data

You have just learned that the way you measure the effects of an intervention on your dependent variable is important. That is, by using an appropriate and effective measurement, you will be able to answer the question: How will I know if my intervention worked? Measurement, as discussed, is an essential link between your research questions and your outcome data. That said, what kind of data might you get, given your selected way of measuring outcomes? This is important to consider also, because the type of data you collect has implications for how you ultimately analyze your results. Now this chapter takes a brief look at four types of data (also called scales of measurement) found in experimental as well as descriptive research: nominal, ordinal, interval, and ratio.

Nominal Data

Nominal data are arranged by unordered, categorical groups. For example, the question "Are you male or female?" puts respondents in groups without order. Likewise, recording a student behavior as on-task or off-task categorizes the data in a dichotomous fashion.

Ordinal Data

Ordinal data place responses in a certain order or rank, but this order does not have equal intervals between items (Alreck & Settle, 2004). This continuum includes descriptors that are ordered in some fashion. With ordinal data, you can compare responses or behaviors across groups or individuals, or you can compare responses or behaviors from comparable samples over time (Fowler, 2014). For example, a question such as "How would you rate your fitness level—excellent, good, fair, or poor?" asks respondents to describe their fitness levels along a continuum, but the difference between *excellent* and *good* is not necessarily interpreted as the same as that between *good* and *fair*. Rating student written performance along a similar continuum would also yield ordinal data.

Interval Data

Interval data are numeric and have equal intervals between values, but they do not necessarily have a zero value. These data are similar to ordinal data, except defined numerical values are used for the ratings. The Fahrenheit temperature scale is a well-known example of interval data. In surveys, interval data is obtained with linear, numeric scales. For example, a question may read, "Rate the following items on a scale of 1 (*unimportant*) to 5 (*extremely important*)." Likewise, if one assigned numbers to the student performance ratings that were noted in the previous paragraph as ordinal data, one would then have interval data. You may use most descriptive statistics with interval data (i.e., mean, median, mode).

Ratio Data

Finally, **ratio data** have the characteristics of interval data, but the equal intervals are also related by ratios. For example, someone who weighs 40 pounds is twice as heavy as someone who weighs 20 pounds. Ratio data also have an absolute zero where nothing of the characteristic exists. There are no limitations on statistical operations with ratio data; however, few items (other than age) lend themselves to ratio data.

This discussion of types of data will be linked to the discussion of data analysis in Chapters 9, 10, and 11.

Putting It All Together

In this section of Chapter 5, the objective is to help you pull together research questions and designs with means of measurement and possible data sources. In this way, you will see how the different parts of your research are interrelated, as suggested by the steps outlined in Figure 5.2 for designing your study. Here you will use some of the research examples mentioned in the discussions of the highlighted group designs and of single-subject designs.

To begin, take a look at Table 5.2. The "Design" column lists the five group designs and single-subject design. In the far left column are research questions that might lead to each of the listed designs. The right-hand columns list types of measurement and possible data sources that might come from each of the designs.

Now let's highlight the information in each row of Table 5.2, consistent with the process discussed in this chapter and previous chapters. Essentially, the process is this: create your research question(s), determine your variables and address validity, select

TABLE 5.2 ● Matching Research Questions With Design, Measurement, and Data			
Research Question	**Design**	**Measurement**	**Possible Data**
Can students find main ideas after learning a new reading strategy?	Posttest only	Verbal prompt to identify main ideas from text passages	Correct or incorrect responses
Can students more accurately find main ideas after learning a new reading strategy?	Pretest-posttest	Prompts from a standardized test	Correct or incorrect responses
Do students in algebra I classes who engage in the XYZ curriculum perform significantly differently on state tests than students who do not?	Comparison group	Prompts from state tests	Correct or incorrect responses, scaled, or other scores provided
Does the performance of children from different racial backgrounds differ in response to a new writing technique?	Factorial	Writing prompt	Rating scores (e.g., based on organization of ideas, details, mechanics)
Do gifts and other recognition affect the frequency with which middle school teachers refer students to the principal for behavioral issues?	Time-series	Discipline referrals over designated period of time	Frequency counts
Do students with disabilities engage in a greater number of positive classroom behaviors after positive notes and phone calls are regularly made to home?	Single-subject	Event recording protocol	Frequency counts

your design, decide on your measurement and what data to collect, and finally determine how you will analyze the data. Data analysis will be discussed in Chapter 9.

In the first row, if your research question is something like *Can students find main ideas after learning a new reading strategy?* you may be limited to a posttest-only design. In this example question, there appears to be no reference to comparing pretest and posttest performance, nor is there reference to more than one group. The independent variable would be the new reading strategy, and the dependent variable would be some measure to find main ideas. Perhaps you could administer a researcher-created measurement that simply has students read from a text passage and respond to a prompt to identify the main idea(s). This test could be individually administered, and student responses could be verbal, rather than paper and pencil, so as not to confound reading with possible writing problems (i.e., addressing construct validity—see Chapter 4). The data might consist of simply correct or incorrect responses (nominal data).

In the second row, if your research question is *Can students more accurately find main ideas after learning a new reading strategy?* then you probably could employ a pretest-posttest design. The words *more accurately* and *after* imply more than one condition to the experiment; hence, pretest and posttest measurement conditions would fit here. The variables are the same as in the posttest-only design above. You could use a similar form of measurement, or as suggested, add a broader measure, such as prompts from a standardized test. If the test was also individually administered and student responses were verbal, for the sake of construct validity, the data would likely consist of correct or incorrect responses.

In the third row, if your research question was *Do students in Algebra I classes who engage in the XYZ curriculum perform significantly differently on state tests than students who do not?* you would use a comparison group design. Clearly, two groups are involved in this study. Engagement in the XYZ curriculum is the independent variable, and performance on state tests is the dependent variable. Therefore, your measurement is pretty clear—likely the prompts from a state test that would probably yield correct or incorrect responses, or at least scaled or other scores provided by the state.

In the fourth row, if your research question was *Does the performance of children from different racial backgrounds differ in response to a new writing technique?* you could employ a factorial design. In this question, multiple conditions or groups are not obvious, but the researcher is clearly interested in multiple factors. That is, one independent variable appears to be a new writing technique, and the other is the multilevel factor called racial background. If you did have a comparison group, you would call the exposure or nonexposure to the new writing technique the two levels of the first factor. You could measure performance in regard to the dependent variable through a researcher-developed tool and/or use a broader measure such as a state test. A paper-and-pencil or computer-based writing prompt may very well produce rating scores (e.g., based on organization of ideas, details, mechanics).

The fifth row starts with the question *Do gifts and other recognition affect the frequency with which middle school teachers refer students to the principal for behavioral issues?* For this question, you might select a time-series design. Surely, you could look at preintervention and postintervention differences, in what would be equivalent to a pretest-posttest design, to illuminate the changes in a single group of participants, as well as to see if the effects linger for any period of time. The independent variable is clearly the gifts and other recognition, and the dependent variable is the frequency of referrals.

Thus, your measurement and data source are straightforward. You can just collect frequency counts of discipline referrals over some designated period of time.

The question in the last row is *Do students with disabilities engage in a greater number of positive classroom behaviors after positive notes and phone calls are regularly made to home?* While you could certainly use a pretest-posttest or even a comparison group design, if you had a comparison group, you might be interested in looking at responses to the intervention by individual students who have unique needs. In that case, you would use a single-subject design. The independent variable is positive notes and phone calls, and the dependent variable is positive classroom behaviors. In terms of measurement, an event-recording protocol might be helpful, where you might use categories of defined positive student responses and tally them in class before and after the intervention begins. From that measurement, you would have a frequency count of the number of positive student responses in each of the experimental conditions.

From these examples, you should be able to see how your research question, variables, design, measurement, and data need to fit together. Having a clear plan in place will make carrying out the experiment far easier.

Implementing Interventions

If you are conducting experimental research, some of your most important decisions will have to do with the details of what the intervention will entail; who will provide or administer the intervention; as well as when, how often, how long, under what conditions the intervention will occur (e.g., after school, during lecture or small-group work, as a review before a test). Clearly, if part of your purpose for the research is to address a need or problem, you want to flesh out how you plan to conduct your intervention. In addition, if your experiment entails training others (e.g., teacher participants or other researchers), to carry out an intervention, you'll want to take steps to ensure treatment fidelity (sometimes called *implementation fidelity, intervention fidelity,* or *fidelity to implementation*). That means, at a minimum, setting standards for consistent training of implementers and observing to check that implementation is consistent with expectations across settings. Without fidelity to implementation, you raise threats to internal validity, as mentioned in Chapter 4.

Moreover, if you want the research to be generalizable and, ultimately, if you want to share it with others with similar problems, you'll want to document your procedures well. Chapter 8 will address documentation in your research proposal, and Chapter 12 will discuss writing research reports.

Consent for Participation

Prior to implementing an intervention, research participant information and consent forms will need to be obtained, including forms from the parents of students who participate in your study. This is typically true for research conducted as a part of a university degree requirement or if the researcher plans to talk publicly or write about the study.

Consent forms are likely to have most of the language required by a school or district, but it is best to check with an administrator. You may need to plan well ahead in order to get forms approved. Refer to Figures 8.2 and 8.3 in Chapter 8 for sample parent and student information and consent forms.

Set dates for distributing and collecting the signature forms. It is necessary to distribute the forms early in order to give parents and/or other participants ample time to respond ahead of your timeline for the study. In addition, you may want to buy a bag of candy bars, nice pens, or something to distribute to students or other prospective participants as an incentive for returning the signed consent forms.

Once you have acquired consent from participants and have ironed out all the details in terms of what, who, when, where, and how, you are ready to implement your experimental intervention according to your research design and collect data for analysis. As with most of the research designs discussed earlier in the chapter, don't forget to collect **baseline** or preliminary data regarding your dependent variables in order to establish current performance prior to introducing your independent variable (i.e., intervention).

Summary

Experimental designs, in a sense, provide the "blueprint" for your study. Thus, it is important to understand the purposes and characteristics of various designs in order to determine the best fit for your research question, address validity issues, and the select ways to measure your dependent variable. This chapter highlighted several commonly used group designs, as well as single-subject designs. A goal was to help you think about the importance of sound measurement of your selected variables and consider possible sources and types of data.

This material is not intended to provide you with the depth of information that you should receive in an entire graduate course on experimental design, but instead highlight the critical steps to guide you through the process. From the discussion in this chapter, however, you should see the importance of connectedness in your study, from your research question to the design, measurement, and data. If you are engaging in experimental research, Chapter 9 will guide you through the next step, learning how to analyze and interpret experimental data.

Discussion Questions

1. What is the difference between a group design and a single-subject design?

2. Why would a comparison design have greater validity than a pretest-posttest design?

3. Would it be better to use event-sampling observation or time-sampling observation to measure the number of correct math problems on a fifth-grade test? What form of observation would be better suited to measuring the extent to which a teacher is engaged in lecture as opposed to classroom discussion?

4. What type of data would be generated from measuring the number of correct math problems? What type of data would be generated from teacher observation of students?

Your Research Project in Action

Refer to the research problem you identified and elaborated on in earlier chapters. Use this guide in the design of your research.

Research problem/question:

_____

_____

Type of research design you are going to use:

_____

Why use this design for your study?

_____

_____

_____

Variables investigating:

1. Independent (intervention) _____

_____

2. Dependent _____

_____

Who will receive intervention?

_____

_____

When will intervention take place?

_____

_____

How often/how long will intervention take place?

_____

_____

How will intervention be introduced to participants?

_____

_____

Where will intervention take place?

_____

_____

How will you measure the dependent variables?

_____

_____

_____

What data will you collect?

_____

_____

How will you organize your collected data?

_____

_____

Further Reading

Gall, M. D., Gall, J. P., & Borg, W. R. (2006). *Educational research: An introduction* (8th ed.). Boston: Allyn & Bacon.

Some students may use this text as their primary research methods text. The authors provide a sound, in-depth explanation of the major types of educational research designs. Each chapter provides guided questions and answers and has been used by thousands of graduate students for many, many years.

References

Alreck, P. L., & Settle, R. B. (2004). *Survey research handbook* (3rd ed.). New York: McGraw-Hill/Irwin.

Campbell, D. T., & Stanley, J. C. (1963). *Experimental and quasi-experimental designs for research*. Boston: Houghton Mifflin.

Cook, T. D., & Campbell, D. T. (1979). *Quasi-experimentation: Design and analysis issues for field settings*. Boston: Houghton Mifflin.

Fowler, F. J. (2014). *Survey research methods* (5th ed.). Los Angeles: Sage.

Gall, M. D., Gall, J. P., & Borg, W. R. (2006). *Educational research: An introduction* (8th ed.). Boston: Allyn & Bacon.

Gersten, R., Baker, S., & Lloyd, J. W. (2000). Designing high-quality research in special education: Group experimental design. *Journal of Special Education, 34*(1), 2–18.

Jitendra, A. K., Dupuis, D., & Zaslofsky, A. F. (2014). Curriculum-based measurement and standards-based mathematics: Monitoring the arithmetic word problem-solving of third-grade students at risk for mathematics difficulties. *Learning Disability Quarterly, 37*(4), 241–251.

Keller-Margulis, M. A., Mercer, S. H., & Thomas, E. L. (2016). Generalizability theory reliability of written expression curriculum-based measurement in universal screening. *School Psychology Quarterly, 31*(3), 383–392.

Kratochwill, T. R., Hitchcock, J. H., Horner, R. H., Levin, J. R., Odom, S. L., Rindskopf, D. M., & Shadish, W. R. (2013). Single-case intervention research design standards. *Remedial and Special Education, 34,* 26–38.

McMillan, J. H. (2015). *Educational research: Fundamentals for the consumer* (7th ed.). London: Pearson.

Methe, S. A., Briesch, A. M., & Hulac, D. (2015). Evaluating procedures for reducing measurement error in math curriculum-based measurement probes. *Assessment for Effective Intervention, 40*(2), 99–113.

Mills, G. E., & Gay, L. R. (2015). *Educational research: Competencies for analysis and applications* (11th ed.). London: Pearson.

Rumrill, P. D., Cook, B. G., & Wiley, A. L. (2011). *Research in special education: Designs, methods, and applications* (2nd ed.). Springfield, IL: Charles C. Thomas.

Salkind, N. J. (2016). *Exploring research* (7th ed.). London: Pearson.

Shinn, M. R., & Bamonto, S. (1998). Advanced applications of curriculum-based measurement: "Big ideas" and avoiding confusion. In M. R. Shinn (Ed.), *Advanced applications of curriculum-based measurement* (pp. 1–31). New York: Guilford Press.

Swanson, H. L., & Hoskyn, M. (1998). Experimental intervention research on students with learning disabilities: A meta-analysis of treatment outcomes. *Review of Educational Research, 68,* 277–321.

Sytsma, S. (2009). *The basics of experimental design (A quick and non-technical guide).* Retrieved May 15, 2018, from http://liutaiomottola.com/myth/expdesig.html

Tawney, J. W., & Gast, D. L. (1984). *Single subject research in special education.* Columbus, OH: Merrill.

Tincani, M., & Travers, J. (2018). Publishing single-case research design studies that do not demonstrate experimental control. *Remedial and Special Education, 39*(2), 118–128.

What Works Clearinghouse (2014). *Procedures and standards handbook. Version 3.0.* Princeton, NJ: What Works Clearinghouse. (ERIC Document Reproduction Service No. ED544775)

Literature Examples

Peleaux, J., & Endacott, J. (2014) ReQuest in the secondary history classroom: How does the introduction of a purposeful reading technique effect comprehension of text? *Networks: An Online Journal for Teacher Research, 15*(1), 1–10. Retrieved May 20, 2018 from http://dx.doi.org/10.4148/2470-6353.1063

St. Onge, J., & Eitel, K. (2017) Increasing active participation and engagement of students in circle formations. *Networks: An Online Journal for Teacher Research, 19*(1), 1–10. Retrieved May 20, 2018 from http://dx.doi.org/10.4148/2470-6353.1014

6

Designing and Conducting Qualitative Research

Chapter Objectives

In this chapter, the reader will

- understand the steps for designing and conducting research using qualitative methods.

- understand the importance of determining a focus of inquiry and fit of paradigm.

- identify various qualitative methods of data collection.

- identify the major types of sampling and researcher notes.

- determine the successive phases of research using qualitative methods.

As described in Chapter 1, descriptive research is used to understand a situation that exists. Researchers who conduct descriptive research do not manipulate the subject of study in order to determine cause and effect; instead they seek to describe accurately "what is." Descriptive research is important when research questions take the form of "What is going on here?" The "here" in this statement may be a classroom, a social program, a teacher or student's mind, a cultural group, or some problem of practice in a school district. The possibilities are endless, but the researcher must be clear about the study's purpose in order to use descriptive methods correctly.

Broadly, descriptive research includes research that utilizes qualitative methods and nonexperimental/quantitative methods. Qualitative methods include data collection and analysis primarily grounded in observation, interview, and document review. Nonexperimental descriptive methods of data collection and analysis may rely on responses of participants to specific questions of interest or data collected from existing databases. Mixed methods, as we will note in the next chapter, may employ both methods. This chapter explains the specific steps and considerations for designing and conducting research using qualitative methods (i.e., qualitative research).

What Is Qualitative Research?

Qualitative research involves the systematic analysis of language, actions, and documents to determine patterns, themes, or theories that describe and provide insight into situations. Figure 6.1 provides an overview or context for the traditions within

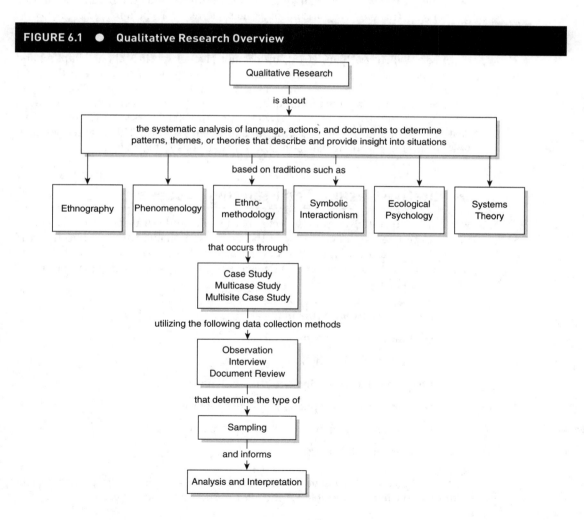

FIGURE 6.1 ● Qualitative Research Overview

the essential elements of the qualitative research process. As a systematic process of description and to provide insight, qualitative inquiry is based on one or more **traditions** and takes the form of a **case study**, **multicase study**, or **multisite study**. The data for qualitative research primarily come from some form of observation, interview, and document review. There are varying ways to conduct observations and interviews, as well as review documents, but qualitative studies typically have one or more of these sources. The traditions of qualitative research and data collection drive the process of **sampling** events or phenomena, and analyzing and interpreting results. Again, the specifics about how to go about these data analysis activities change based upon the conceptual focus of the research, but there are guidelines for the procedures.

One of the other commonalities across traditions in qualitative inquiry is that the researcher begins with a working plan that is meant to guide the inquiry but not be prescriptive. This **working plan** (sometimes referred to as the *working design* or *emergent design*) outlines participants for study, length of time for data collection, possible variables for consideration, conceptual framework, and basic data analysis procedures (Fraenkel, Wallen, & Hyun, 2015). It does not give all specifics about sampling and coding decisions because these decisions are made as the researcher collects data. The iterative process of data collection and analysis will be explained more thoroughly in Chapter 10 on data analysis techniques. This is not to say that qualitative inquiry is haphazard or unplanned in any way. Planning qualitative research requires a great deal of thought and insight into the situation being studied. This chapter describes how to develop a working plan and how to begin a qualitative study.

Qualitative Design: The Planning Process

Planning for qualitative research occurs both before and during the study. As noted, unlike experimental design, many of the specifics of qualitative data collection and analysis evolve as the study progresses. Even though a researcher will not be able to make all of the decisions about a study before beginning, the research plan must consider the following:

1. Determine a focus for the inquiry.

2. Determine fit of paradigm to focus.

3. Determine instrumentation.

4. Determine data collection and recording procedures.

5. Determine successive phases and logistics of the inquiry.

6. Plan data management and analysis procedures.

7. Plan for trustworthiness.

The balance of this chapter will address steps 1–5. The last two steps will be addressed in Chapter 10. Table 6.1 includes a brief description of each step.

TABLE 6.1 ● Steps in Planning Process	
Step	**Description**
1. Determine a focus for the inquiry.	The focus or research question(s) for the study may be broad or include several subtopics that may become the major focus of the study once data collection begins. The focus of the study allows the researcher to determine where to start with sampling and data collection. Once data collection begins, the focus may shift a bit or narrow in scope. For example, you may begin a qualitative inquiry by wondering about the culture of middle school English teachers, but the more interesting aspect of this culture may be the interaction of these teachers with their curriculum specialists. In this case, you would change from sampling dialogue during meetings of the teachers to sampling dialogue from meetings with teachers and their curriculum specialists.
2. Determine fit of paradigm to focus.	Once a focus is determined, a researcher must examine whether or not a qualitative approach is the best way to examine the issue. Do the tenets of the paradigm fit the focus? Is there a better way to do the inquiry?
3. Determine instrumentation.	In most cases, researchers include observations, interviews, and review of documents. The purpose is to understand the situation and not to impose outside ideas on it.
4. Plan data collection and recording modes.	This includes planning sampling events, finding participants, determining how data will be collected (e.g., written notes, electronic notes), and deciding how long (approximately) the study will take. Will interviews be audio-recorded and transcribed?
5. Determine successive phases and logistics of the inquiry.	There are generally three phases of a qualitative study: entry, data collection and analysis, and exit. You must make decisions about when each phase begins and ends. For example, do I have enough data on this event to say that I have enough? Have I seen a broad enough spectrum of behavior to be able to say "I've got it?" Are the participants relaxed enough with me that I can begin to collect data on natural occurrences?
6. Plan data management and analysis procedures.	In this step, you must consider your research purpose (descriptive or interpretive) and determine the best data management and analytic techniques. You must also consider how you will complete data analysis (electronic or paper?) and who else will be involved in it. Will you use a computer program to help in the analysis?
7. Plan for trustworthiness.	What techniques for trustworthiness will you use? Who will help? If peer debriefing will take place, who will be the peer? How often will trustworthiness activities take place? What will be audited?

Determine a Focus for the Inquiry and Fit of Paradigm

As previously noted, all research is based on its driving purpose and questions. Once a researcher has formulated an appropriate research question, the next task is to determine how best to answer the question. Descriptive research questions do not seek to change or manipulate variables in a setting; rather, they seek to explain something that occurs in a setting, and they often include the word *what*. For example, *what* are the interactions of female teachers and male students? *What* are the beliefs about education in Spanish culture? *What* instructional actions do co-teachers take in general education classrooms? *What* are the educational backgrounds of elementary teachers? *How* and *why* may also be addressed. Table 6.2 gives examples of research question types and strategies to consider.

Qualitative or Survey Research? Though both are included in the term *descriptive research*, survey and qualitative methods are quite different. **Survey research** is appropriate when individual responses to a protocol of questions are the best form of data to answer the research question(s). For example, "What is the educational background of elementary teachers?" is a descriptive question that can best be addressed with survey methods because it can be answered by responses to specific questions, such as "What degree have you obtained?" Descriptive research

TABLE 6.2 ● Research Question Types and Strategies		
Purpose of the Study	**Research Question**	**Research Strategy**
Exploratory 1. To investigate little-understood phenomena 2. To identify/discover important variables 3. To generate hypotheses for further research	What is happening in this social program? What are the salient themes, patterns, and categories in participants' meaning structures? How are these patterns linked with one another?	Case study Field study
Explanatory 1. To explain the forces causing the phenomenon in question 2. To identify plausible causal networks shaping the phenomenon	What events, beliefs, attitudes, policies are shaping this phenomenon? How do these forces interact to result in the phenomenon?	Multisite case study History Field study Ethnography
Descriptive 1. To document the phenomenon of interest	What are the salient behaviors, events, beliefs, attitudes, structures, and processes occurring in this phenomenon?	Field study Case study Ethnography
Predictive 1. To predict the outcomes of the phenomenon 2. To forecast the events and behaviors resulting from the phenomenon	What will occur as a result of this phenomenon? Who will be affected? In what ways?	Experiment Quasi-experiment

Source: Adapted from Marshall, C., & Rossman, G. B. (2016), p. 78.

using survey methods is similar to experimental research in that most of the meth-odological components of the study are determined by the researcher before the study begins. For example, in survey research, a sample is chosen, a survey form is determined, and question/response formats are written. By contrast, in qualitative research, Patton (2015) stated that

> Sociologist John Lofland posited four people-oriented mandates in collecting qualitative data. First, the qualitative methodologist must get close enough to the people and situation being studied to personally understand in depth the details of what goes on. Second, the qualitative methodologist must aim at capturing what actually takes place and what people actually say: the perceived facts. Third, qualitative data must include a great deal of pure description of people, activities, interactions, and settings. Fourth, qualitative data must include direct quotations from people, both what they speak and what they write down. (p. 33)

That said, after deciding that the research question is best answered through quali-tative methods, the researcher must decide which paradigm or tradition best matches the focus of the study. There are many traditions to guide how a researcher will con-duct a qualitative study.

Traditions/Domains. Traditions in qualitative research (also called domains) guide the researcher's actions and analysis. They are the philosophical backbone upon which a researcher builds a study. That is, qualitative methods are grounded in the tradition, domain, or the "lens," if you will, through which the researcher views her study's purpose and later outcomes. The qualitative researcher needs to be cog-nizant of the tradition or "lens" through which she views her study's purpose and questions. For example, is your focus on understanding the culture of a classroom or school? Then your qualitative research may be based in holistic ethnography. If your research focus is to understand the meaning involved in the interactions between female teachers and male principals, your work may be driven by ideas of symbolic interactionism. While these may seem very abstract descriptions or pro-cesses, the choice of tradition does, in fact, shape a study's purpose, data collection, and data analysis tremendously. Another example might be a study of the inter-actions between co-teachers in a classroom. Using ethnography, a researcher may answer the research question by providing a rich description of developed **themes** of interactions between teachers. A symbolic interactionist would develop a theory of the meaning made through the interactions. Subtle differences in wording, yes, but less subtle differences in approaches and potential outcomes. Thus, the qualita-tive researcher should acknowledge the tradition from which his research questions and methods emerge. Table 6.3 gives examples of the traditions/domains qualitative researchers use to conduct research.

For example, in a study of special educators by Weiss and Lloyd (2002), the authors determined it was necessary to describe the symbols of power, the interactions between the teacher and the students, and the actions taken by the special educator in response to classroom situations. These purposes drew directly from the tradition of **symbolic**

TABLE 6.3 ● Examples of Qualitative Research Traditions, Roots, and Central Questions		
Tradition	**Disciplinary Roots**	**Central Question**
Ethnography	Anthropology	What is the culture of this group of people?
Phenomenology	Philosophy	What is the structure and essence of experience of this phenomenon for these people?
Ethnomethodology	Sociology	How do people make sense of their everyday activities so as to behave in socially acceptable ways?
Symbolic interactionism	Social psychology	What common set of symbols and understandings have emerged to give meaning to people's interactions?
Ecological psychology	Ecology, psychology	How do individuals attempt to accomplish their goals through specific behaviors in specific environments?
Systems theory	Interdisciplinary	How and why does this system function as a whole?

Source: Adapted from Patton (2015).

interactionism and led to the use of techniques of **grounded theory**. This was very well detailed in the following excerpt:

> Because we were interested in exploring and interpreting the actions and roles of special educators, the principles of **symbolic interactionism** guided our study and formed our methods of inquiry. The first main premise of symbolic interactionism is that "human beings act toward things on the basis of the meanings that the things have for them and such things include everything that the human being may note in his world" (Blumer, 1969, p. 2). For the teachers we studied, this included, among other things, the students, co-teachers, schedules, classrooms, and content area involved in their teaching and required us to interview teachers to determine their meanings. The second premise is that "the meaning of such things is derived from, or arises out of, the social interaction that one has with one's fellows" (p. 2). This premise fits particularly well with the study of two teachers in one classroom and required us to directly observe classrooms and ask questions of teachers about those classroom interactions. The third premise is that "these meanings are handled in, and modified through, an interpretative process used by the person in dealing with the things he encounters" (p. 2). Again, we observed teachers in their classrooms and asked them to describe the meanings behind certain roles and actions. (Weiss & Lloyd, 2002, p. 60)

In another example, a researcher wanted to understand the culture and dilemmas of African American and Latino boys with regard to going to college. This led directly to **ethnography**.

Data are derived from an ethnographic case study that sought to understand the ways a high school's rigorous college-going culture served to influence the educational and occupational aspirations of Black and Latino teenaged boys. Presented here is a qualitative case study of one school, Metropolitan Collegiate Public Charter School (Metro Collegiate; pseudonym), and the experiences of two of its students. Merriam (2009) defined a qualitative case study as "an in-depth description and analysis of a bounded system" (p. 43); thus, and given this definition, this study was bounded by both space and time. (Carey, 2018, pp. 254–255)

Clarifying the qualitative tradition behind a study will help you determine research instrumentation and data sources.

Determine Instrumentation and the Sources of Data

As we have noted, there are three main sources of data used in qualitative inquiry: observation, interview, and document review. An introduction to each is provided here.

Observation. Observation of people, settings, and situations is paramount in qualitative research. The purpose of observational data is

to take the reader into the setting that was observed. This means that observational data must have depth and detail. The data must be descriptive—sufficiently descriptive that the reader can understand what occurred and how it occurred. The observer's notes become the eyes, ears, and perceptual senses for the reader. The descriptions must be thorough without being cluttered by irrelevant minutiae and trivia. (Patton, 2015, p. 28)

In qualitative research, you first determine what is important to observe in a general sense. For example, will you observe classrooms, individual students, individual teachers, groups of teachers or students, or something else? Unlike in experimental research, the objects of observation may change during a study as the researcher seeks more valid answers to the research question. For example, you may begin a study by observing entire classrooms for interactions between a teacher and certain students. As the study continues, you may identify the interactions between female teachers and Asian students as noticeably different from other teacher-student interactions. You may then decide to focus observations on these interactions only. Every aspect of a situation is a candidate for observation, including the physical environment, the social environment, verbal and nonverbal interactions, activities, and so forth. Since it is very easy to get distracted by events going on in the classroom or in any given situation, you must remember your purpose and focus your observations to answer your research question.

After determining the foci of observation, the researcher must determine the type(s) of observations to conduct. There are several items to consider (see Figure 6.2). The first consideration is how the observer will function in the setting. This may vary from participant observer to onlooker. In participant observation, the observer actually takes part in what is going on in the setting. For example, a participant observer in a classroom may help the teacher with instruction or even do some teaching. Observations are then made from that perspective. At the other end of the continuum, an observer may be an onlooker. In this case, the observer does not participate in any way in the setting. For example, the observer may sit at the back of the classroom and not interact with anyone in the classroom, even when asked by a student, "What are you doing here?" There are many observer roles between these two extremes. You must decide which role will provide the best data for the research question.

The second decision regards whether or not the participant(s) will know they are being observed. The continuum here runs from overt to covert observation and the decision is not necessarily either-or. For example, an observer may view a clinician testing a student by sitting behind a one-way mirror, or an observer may be introduced to a group of administrators and conduct a few practice observations to make sure everyone is comfortable with the situation. Again, the researcher must decide

FIGURE 6.2 ● Observational Considerations

Role of the Observer

Full Participant Observation	Partial Observation	Onlooker Observation

Portrayal of the Evaluator Role to Others

Overt Observations	Observer	Covert Observations
Participants know that observations are being made and who the observer is.	Role known by some, not by others.	Participants do not know observations are being made or that there is an observer.

Portrayal of the Purpose of the Evaluation to Others

Full Explanation	Partial Explanations	Covert Evaluations	False Explanations
		No explanation given to staff or participants.	Deceives staff and participants about evaluation purpose.

Duration of the Evaluation Observations

Single Observation	Long-Term, Multiple Observations
Limited duration	

Focus of the Observations

Narrow Focus	Broad Focus
Single element or component in the program is observed.	Holistic view of the entire program and all of its elements is sought.

Source: Adapted from Patton (2015).

what technique will best answer the question(s) with the least disruption to the natural environment.

Two other decisions must be made: What will the duration of the observations be, and what will the focus of the observations be? The decision regarding duration is important, particularly if the focus of study is to develop a rich description or an integrated theory. In very few instances can a researcher gather all the necessary observational data in a single observation or in a short-term observation. The researcher may begin by planning a certain number of observations over a certain period of time, but that may change over the course of the study. Disruptions will always occur. A researcher may not plan for a pep rally, but the class had to leave to attend. The fire chief may decide it is a good day for a fire drill but not tell anyone it was going to happen. The administrator being observed could be out of school with strep throat for a week. All of these things will affect the duration of the observation phase.

The final, and perhaps most important, consideration is that of focus. In the beginning of a study, the researcher's observations may have a broad focus. This may change as the study continues. Chances are, nearing the end of the study, observations will be very focused and will flesh out specific characteristics of categories or themes or fill in gaps in the data.

Returning to the example of a study of co-teachers, here is the description of the observations:

> We observed teachers on 54 occasions in co-taught and special education settings, averaging nine observations per teacher. Each observation lasted 30 minutes. We observed each special educator in either English or math special education classrooms and the corresponding content in co-taught classrooms. Two teachers did not teach corresponding content in the co-taught classroom so we observed them in all of their co-taught classrooms. During each observation, we recorded all of the actions of the special educator in a narrative form for later analysis. (Weiss & Lloyd, 2002, p. 61)

The working design for this study initially did not include an observational focus on different types of activities in these teachers' classrooms. When the authors began observations of the teachers, they noted that instructional actions (one of the inquiry's foci) were much different during teacher-directed activities than during student-directed activities. This realization forced the researchers to focus the research question even more (more interest in the teacher-directed activity actions) and to complete observations during these times in the classrooms. The researchers completed the observations in an overt fashion as onlookers, not as participants.

Interview. Interviewing is very important in qualitative research. An interview is an opportunity for the researcher to get information about beliefs, perspectives, and views from a participant. However, the researcher must understand the filter through which this information comes. In other words, an interview is an excellent opportunity to get valuable information, but it can also result in getting only what the participant thinks the researcher expects or wants to hear.

There are several types of interviews a qualitative researcher could conduct. These include the following:

- Informal conversational interview
- Interview guide approach
- Standardized, open-ended interview
- Closed, fixed-response interview (Patton, 2015)

Each type of interview has a unique purpose, as well as strengths and weaknesses. They may be used individually or in combination. The **informal conversational interview** often occurs within the setting where the study is taking place. The researcher engages the participant in conversation about the situation and asks questions about specific events, interactions, or perceptions relevant to this situation. This is helpful in making sure that questions regarding what was observed are answered or that rationales for actions are explained. The disadvantage of this type of interview is its randomness—questions come up in the situation and are not always consistent across participants or interviews.

The second type of interview is the **interview guide approach**. In this type of interview, the researcher has developed a general outline of the types of questions to ask, but specifics about wording and elaboration are not included. The advantages of this type of interview are that the researcher has a general idea about topics to be covered in the interview and can focus on elaboration of those topics and filling in gaps in data. A disadvantage may be that some areas of interest may be missed or not connected, depending on how the guide was developed or what has transpired since the guide was created.

A **standardized, open-ended interview** is one in which the researcher has already determined the questions to be asked but the responses can vary by individual. In other words, the questions are set up to require more than one-word answers and may allow the participant to take the response into an area that the researcher did not consider. This type of interview allows for more standardization across researchers or situations and reduces some potential issues related to trustworthiness. However, it does not allow the researcher the spontaneity or flexibility to pursue an area of emergent interest.

Finally, an interview could be a **closed, fixed-response interview**. In this type of interview, the researcher has developed both the questions and the alternative responses for the participant. The participant then just chooses the most suitable response. This type of interview has the advantage of being efficient and standard across researcher and participant. Data analysis is also relatively easy. However, it does not allow for unique participant responses or for flexibility in questioning.

Interviewing is a critical component of qualitative research and one that requires much skill. Researchers should practice conducting interviews before beginning a study in order to avoid practices that increase unwanted bias, decrease participant willingness to respond, or predetermine outcomes. In addition to being vigilant about interview techniques, it is important, again, to consider the purpose of the research

TABLE 6.4 ● Types of Interview Questions	
Question Type	**Description**
Experience/Behavior	To find out what a person does or has done
Opinion/Values	To understand the cognitive and interpretive processes of people
Feeling	To understand the emotional responses of people to their experiences and thoughts
Knowledge	To find out what factual information the respondent has
Sensory	To find out what is seen, heard, touched, tasted, and smelled
Background/ Demographic	To find out the identifying characteristics of the person being interviewed

Source: Adapted from Patton (2015).

and the types of questions required to address this purpose. Table 6.4 gives examples of interview question types. A balance of several types of questions makes interviews more effective.

Here is the researcher information about interviews conducted in a study on the impact of teacher evaluations:

> The semi-structured telephone interviews took 20–30 minutes to complete. Interviews were audio-recorded and transcribed verbatim. Initial interviews focused on teachers' knowledge and feelings about VAM scores, the extent to which teachers changed their instructional practices after receiving their evaluation scores, and their expectations or current school-year VAM scores. Questions included, for example, "How do you feel having Value-Added Model scores used as part of your teacher evaluation?" Follow-up interviews focused on changes in teachers' knowledge of VAM scores, teachers' feelings about VAM scores being public, the accuracy of VAM scores, and the impact of VAM scores on teachers' collaboration and instruction as the state test approached. Example questions included, "How worried are you about having your VAM scores being public information?" and "To what extent has the use of VAM scores in your teacher evaluation changed your instruction as you prepare students for the upcoming state tests?" We also asked about the observation component: "How often does your administrator come into your classroom and is it announced?" (Pressley, Roehrig & Turner, 2018; pp. 26–27)

Document Review. School and clinical settings generate many documents such as lesson plans, intervention notes, district policies, and school board meeting minutes. In studying the culture of a school, minutes from faculty meetings as well as school mission statements and attendance policies may be of value. Generally, documents related to what takes place in a setting are important and can round out the view given in observations and interviews. Documents may also give the researcher information about why participants' interview responses may not match their actions during observations. Perhaps during classroom instruction, a teacher isolates and ignores a student with a severe disability, but in an interview, the teacher states that all children, no matter the disability, should be included in classrooms in neighborhood schools. The researcher may then read the school mission statement and district policy manual to find that they state that students with disabilities shall be fully included in the general education classroom. Conclusions then may be drawn.

Document review can be done to guide observations and interviews or to enhance their content. The researcher must decide what documents are important to the research question and how to obtain these documents. Some will be archival records; others will be documents created as research continues. Again, the focus of document review may change as important items are discovered during research. In the following excerpt, the researchers noted documents they collected for review in a study of teacher implementation of a computer science curriculum in an elementary school.

> Artifacts and images of the teachers' meetings were captured as data files (e.g., scanned lesson plans, digital pictures of meetings) and stored in a secure, cloud-based file storage system. Additionally, we used Dedoose, a visual data organizer, to aid in managing and organizing the data. These data helped the research team capture the context of the meetings and the developmental progress of the teachers' planning and implementation of integrated CS. (Ozturk, Dooley & Welch, 2018; p. 154)

Though there are three main sources of data in qualitative research, the researcher has tremendous flexibility in determining what and how to collect the data. Sampling and notes, the subject of our next section, are thus important components of a research study.

Data Collection and Recording Procedures

Data collection and recording procedures include determining the sample and participants as well as maintaining notes about the processes involved in the study. The procedures also involve decisions about whether or not to transcribe interviews, whether or not to use computers to gather observational data, and how to involve other researchers.

Sampling. Again, the purpose of the study determines the unit of analysis in a qualitative study. In most cases, a sample will include specific participants, but it may be focused on the actions, words, or interactions of those participants. For example, you may want to describe the interactions between boys and girls in science lab experiments. In this case, the **unit of analysis** may be individual lab sessions, and you would want to sample as many lab sessions as possible to collect data. In another example, you may want to examine the feelings of girls about their fathers after their parents' divorce. In this case, the unit of analysis may be each girl. There are two levels of sampling in qualitative research: theoretical sampling and case sampling.

Theoretical sampling is very important in qualitative research and requires a great deal of thought on the part of the researcher. The first question to answer is "What is the unit of analysis?" In other words, what do I want to examine? In most traditions of qualitative research, sampling strategies may change as more data are collected. For example, you may initially want to examine the classroom management behaviors of new teachers. In this case, the unit of analysis may be either teacher actions or teacher interactions with students. As you observe teachers and interview them, you may find that the more interesting behaviors occur when the teacher interacts with students of the opposite gender. At this point, the sampling changes from behavior with all students to behavior with students of the opposite gender. After more investigation, you may discover that there is a disconnect between the words the teacher uses and the teacher's nonverbal communication. The sample narrows again. This narrowing or broadening of focus may continue throughout the study, as long as it fits the purpose of the study and can be defended by the researcher.

Case sampling is determining who or what will be part of the study. Random sampling is usually not utilized in qualitative research. Sampling for qualitative research should be purposeful and strategic. In other words, choose a sample that has certain characteristics that fit the purpose of the study. There are several ways to go about this: deviant case sampling, intensity sampling, typical or critical case sampling, and convenience sampling.

As indicated by the name, in **extreme case sampling**, or *deviant case sampling*, the researcher would choose cases that are extreme or dramatically different from the norm in some way. For example, you may want to describe the effects of a school-wide discipline plan on two students with a history of suspensions instead of including two students without a history of behavior issues. For **intensity sampling**, the researcher chooses settings or participants where the unit of study occurs most often. To continue the science lab example, the researcher would choose science classrooms where labs occur frequently with less regard to other characteristics. In **typical case sampling**, the researcher examines the most often occurring situation or participant to give a representative description. In **critical case sampling**, the researcher chooses the situations or participants because of their uniqueness or how important they are to the issue. For example, if the researcher wanted to describe the degree to which parents felt connected to a school, particularly parents whose children rode a bus to and from school, it would be important to include parents who lived quite a distance from the school.

A final sampling method is **convenience sampling**. In this method, the researcher chooses the most efficient and convenient sample available. For example, if you are teaching, your classroom of students would be a convenient sample. This method is usually not very defensible for research purposes; however, it may have to be used in order for a study or a pilot study to be completed.

Researcher Notes. Because qualitative inquiry incorporates a largely emergent design, it is imperative that the researcher document any and all decisions about design and design changes while conducting a study. In qualitative research, the researcher must be meticulous about keeping several types of notes about the research process. These notes can be combined in one place, perhaps written in different colors or in different fonts if using a computer, or they can be kept in a separate file or location. They should be referred to often. These notes also can be considered as data in the analysis process. There are three essential types of researcher notes: field notes, methods notes, and journal notes.

Field notes include information about what is observed in the research setting. This may include observation descriptions, such as a running record of everything that occurred in the observation setting. Field notes may also include data about the situation under observation, such as "Today, the students seemed very restless, and there was a fire drill in the middle of the observation session," or "On my way to interview Mrs. Q, I was told her son had been in an automobile accident yesterday." These notes would also include dates and times of observations, interviews, or document reviews; who is involved; and what is sampled. They may also include ideas that occur while collecting data. For example, you may write, "For the past three days, I've noticed that Mr. X only calls on the girls in the classroom. I wonder if that is significant." Field notes should be included with all information collected while conducting observations, interviews, or document collection.

Each researcher must also keep **method notes**. These are the notes to which the researcher will refer many times during the study and in the writing of the research report in order to identify and defend methodological choices. For example, you should describe all sampling decisions in the method notes. In the previous example of Mr. X, the researcher may write:

> I've noticed for the last three days that Mr. X only calls on girls in the classroom when asking factual questions. When asking open-ended questions, he calls on the boys. I wonder if this is a pattern that he notices or if it is a pattern that continues with different topics. For example, in my observation today, Mr. X asked Courtney if she knew when the Civil War started. He then asked Michelle who the president was during this time. Once the discussion of this time frame was finished, he asked Gary why he thought the South needed to fight the war. I'll need to focus on what types of questions Mr. X asks in class and ask him about this in my interview.

It may be helpful to mark change points in some visible way—a different pen, a highlighter, or a different color font—so that these changes are easy to find when writing the research report. For each change in focus or suggestion about change, it is important to give reasons, because it is very easy to forget the reasoning as research continues over time. It is *imperative* that each researcher maintain meticulous method notes while collecting data and while analyzing data. Make sure to date all entries.

Finally, it may be helpful to maintain a journal with general reflections about the study, including how it is progressing, how the participants are cooperating, what is happening with the question, how a certain interview went, techniques to use next time, and anything else that is relevant. These notes are essentially reflective in nature, but they help to maintain focus and identify strengths and weaknesses in the process. For example, in the study about Mr. X, the researcher may note the following:

> Originally, I planned to collect journals from all of the teachers every time I did observations. The teachers don't seem too thrilled about this and have not been writing much in the journals. I wonder how I can modify this process a bit to make it easier or more meaningful? Or perhaps it is something to do with time. . . . e-mail?

Determining Successive Phases and Logistics of the Inquiry

Conducting qualitative research often requires that researchers and participants work in close proximity. As in most situations involving personal interaction, this

IN THEIR OWN WORDS

Who Are You as a Researcher?

Jean Crockett, University of Florida

As a graduate student I was asked about my philosophy of inquiry, something I'd never thought about before learning qualitative research methods. I was asked questions like these: Who are you as a researcher? Do you tolerate ambiguity by searching for patterns where others see chaos? Are you a sensitive observer who notices details and who analyzes the meaning of things from a variety of perspectives? Are you a good communicator who builds trust, listens well, and writes clearly? I knew who I was as an experienced teacher and school administrator. What I didn't realize was how my own biography could influence my role as a researcher.

The researcher is the instrument in qualitative methods, and I came to understand the importance of recognizing those things that were likely to attract me or to repulse me in the process of collecting and analyzing data. This realization hit particularly hard when I read the transcripts from an inquiry about administrative decision-making in schools and I felt myself grow angry in response to the data. Sometimes I reacted to comments that I thought were trivial or unrealistic, but comments that offended my values incurred a special wrath. "How could she say that? Can't she see the injustice for some children and their families?" I could feel the heat rising on the back of my neck; I wanted to toss the data across the room and yell, "Stupid!" but I didn't. Instead, I put the transcript down and recorded my negative response in my research journal. I let my feelings pour out into my prose and dated the entry. In that way I could express myself yet return to the data more open to the text now that I'd left some of my own subjectivity behind.

Strong feelings, whether positive or negative, can both shape an inquiry and influence its outcomes. So, who are *you* as a researcher? What do you need to be aware of about yourself as you design a qualitative study? There may be no way to abandon our subjectivity, but we can try to manage it by using research journals, by talking with peers, and by checking with participants to ensure that what we conclude is true to our data and not merely a reflection of our own views.

raises ethical issues, and determining phases of the inquiry is important to addressing these issues. Following are several items to think through in the planning process, but this is not an exhaustive list. The important point is to consider the impact of research methods and results on the participants in the study. Do not act without thinking through and addressing ethical issues. This section highlights four issues: researcher entry, use of results, researcher exit, and "going native."

Researcher Entry. How will the researcher gain access to the situations under study? Will she recruit participants, or will she talk with administrators and ask them to recruit participants? When the researcher goes to observe, will she tell the participants why she is there? Will she participate in what is happening (e.g., will she talk with/ help students in the classroom), or will she be a passive observer? Will the participants know that the researcher is observing them? How will she communicate to the parents of the students participating?

Use of Results. Participants should know what the researcher will do with the information collected from interviews or observations. Think this through carefully, because the way that a researcher uses results may have an impact on the information received. If teachers know the research will be used by the administration to make decisions about school policy, they may say very different things in interviews than if the results were going to be used in a thesis project. This brings up an important related point about anonymity. Will participants be named in reports, or will they be anonymous? If anonymous, will they be easily identifiable? What impact will anonymity have on the study's results?

Researcher Exit. How does a researcher know when he has been in a situation long enough? How does he tell educators or students that the research is finished? What will happen next for them and for the research? Do they get to see any of the data or the report or participate in review of it? Most of the answers to these questions are guided by the tradition of qualitative inquiry chosen. However, careful consideration of each of these points, and others that will arise during the study, will make the research more credible and more efficient.

Going Native. In qualitative research, the researcher is the instrument of the study. As the researcher becomes involved in the setting of inquiry, she begins to understand more and more about the participants and their views and ideas. Each researcher must constantly evaluate her focus in conducting the study. There is always the possibility that she gets too close to the situation or becomes inappropriately biased in presentation because of the relationships developed. **Going native** could mean that a study loses its **credibility** and simply becomes a statement of personal opinion that is not valued in the research community.

Identifying the purpose of the research, clarifying the research tradition, determining what sources of data to use, considering how to do the sampling, and working out all of the logistical issues of conducting the study require a tremendous amount of work and planning. Completing these steps allows the researcher to move forward into data management and analysis, described in Chapter 10.

TECHNOLOGY IN RESEARCH

Using Videoconferencing

Videoconferencing over the Internet is rapidly becoming a mainstream technology. It can be tremendously useful for an educational researcher because it can potentially allow access to classrooms and colleagues that would otherwise be impossible to access with limited funds and/or time. For example, videoconferencing could allow researchers to conduct interviews with teachers or colleagues who are all over the country or who have short breaks throughout the day during which they can talk. It could also allow a researcher to conduct a focus group of several educators at a remote location without traveling there. The possibilities are many. Here are short descriptions of several easily accessible options:

Skype

With Skype, you can video chat, share stories, learn a language, hold a meeting. You can use Skype on all devices for video chatting with an individual or with a group. You can video chat and make a call using this app. Skype has cost for the more advance settings.

Advantages: Helps maintain long distance relationships. Useful for conferences. Easy to navigate and use. For the main features, it is free. Can be downloaded on any device.

Disadvantages: Advanced features are not free. International calls cost. There may be problems with calls dropping.

https://www.skype.com/en/

Google Hangouts

Google Hangouts allows you to message or video chat. It is a bit like iPhone messenger on MACs. You have a contact book where you can add individual email addresses, making it fast and easy to connect with someone. You must have a Gmail account to be able to use Google Hangouts. You can video chat with one person, or you can group chat with up to 10 people at once.

Advantages: Free and easy to use. Layout is simple and straightforward. You can share YouTube videos and other videos. Messages are synchronized across devices. File sharing and screen sharing are possible.

Disadvantages: You have to have a Gmail account. Some technical difficulties may occur. Phone app is only for Android users. Runs off Internet connection.

https://hangouts.google.com

Zoom

Zoom offers video conferencing, online meetings, and mobile collaboration. It has a broad and well-structured range of functions, virtual collaboration, online demos, and online trainings. During a meeting, the host can either show his or her entire screen or a selected part. Not only can you video on Zoom, but you can also chat, share files, and invite contacts to meetings. While Zoom does have a free option, there are priced options. Monthly pricing options range from 50 participants to 200 participants.

Advantages: Perfect for business people or large groups. Can talk to multiple individuals. Easy to navigate and understand. Can be used from any device.

Disadvantages: The advanced options cost. If using the app from phone, it may be slow and result in some technical difficulties.

https://zoom.us

(Continued)

(Continued)

Facetime

Facetime is an iPhone app that simply enables you to make video calls. Facetime enables video chats in the same way that Skype and other programs do on your desktop or portable computer. It works the same way as if you were receiving a phone call. The video quality is relatively clear, and the facetime is in real time.

Advantages: Easy to use. You can see the person with whom you are talking. It is built in to all Apple products, so there is no downloading an app. You don't have to have an account and sign in. Facetime gives you the option to use both the front and back cameras while on the phone.

Disadvantages: This is only available on Apple products. If not connected to Wi-Fi, there are some playback issues. While using your phone for other purposes and simultaneously using facetime, the "pause" option may come up and you can no longer see the other person's face.

Facebook Live

Facebook Live is a video streaming app option that lets anyone broadcast from his or her mobile devices or computers straight to their Facebook News Feed. Facebook Live makes it possible for people on your news feed to watch you in real time. Individuals are able to react to your video and leave comments as you are live, or afterwards. The video remains on your Facebook page until you decide to remove it.

Advantages: Easy to use. You can subscribe to other live feeds. It is free to use on a Facebook account. The longer you live stream, the more likely people will discover and share your video.

Disadvantages: You must have the Facebook app installed on your device to be able to use. Facebook live is a one-way video; people are able to watch you live, but you are not able to see them. Can only stay live for up to 90 minutes. There may be technical issues.

Putting It All Together

Reflect on the information provided in the chapter in order to answer the following guiding questions:

1. What is your research question?

   _____

   _____

   _____

2. Is qualitative research the most effective way to examine or answer your research question? Yes/No? Why/Why not?

   _____

   _____

   _____

3. What tradition or domain within qualitative research seems most appropriate for your intended study?

    _____

    _____

    _____

4. Which form of sampling seems most appropriate for your intended study?

    _____

    _____

    _____

5. What types of data will you collect?

    _____

    _____

    _____

Summary

In this chapter, the processes for designing and conducting qualitative research have been described. Overall, a qualitative study begins with a working design that may change during the course of a study. It is very important to consider the following in developing a plan for a study:

1. Determine a focus for the inquiry.

2. Determine fit of paradigm to focus.

3. Determine instrumentation.

4. Determine data collection and recording procedures.

5. Determine successive phases and logistics of the inquiry.

6. Plan data management and analysis procedures.

7. Plan for trustworthiness.

Qualitative research plans typically include reasoned change in specifics, such as sampling, but a consistent focus on the purpose of the inquiry.

There are three basic forms of data in qualitative research: observations, interviews, and document review. There are many forms of observations, ranging from participant observer to onlooker. There are also many forms of interview structures and questions. Interviews can range from having very structured questions and responses to being more conversational. Questions can include from those directed at demographic information to those directed at understanding participant's feelings.

Qualitative research requires continuous documentation of events and analysis decisions. This documentation takes the form of researcher notes, including field notes, method notes, and journals. Many notes become data used in data analysis.

Discussion Questions

1. What is the difference between qualitative research and nonexperimental, quantitative descriptive research?

2. Name and describe three traditions of qualitative research.

3. Describe how the role of an observer would be different with full participant observation than with onlooker observation.

4. What are the advantages and disadvantages of an informal conversational interview?

5. Why are researcher notes, particularly method notes, so important in qualitative research?

Your Research Project in Action

Complete the following table to help plan the logistics of your study:

Logistics Item	Description/Explanation	Complete?
Who will participate in the study?		
How many participants will I study?		
How will I find these participants?		
How will I gain access to these participants and their environment?		
How will I obtain permission to collect data from participants?		
When will I begin the study?		
When will I conduct interviews, observations, and document reviews?		
What materials will I need for data collection (e.g., computers, paper, audio recorder, other researchers)?		

Logistics Item	Description/Explanation	Complete?
Where will data be collected?		
How will I get to the study site?		
Will I provide participation incentives for participants?		
When do I anticipate being finished?		
Will participant responses/ behaviors be anonymous in my study?		
Who will know the specifics about the study?		
With whom will I work to complete the study?		
With whom will I share the results of the study?		
How much will my research study cost?		

Further Reading

Creswell, J. W., & Poth, C. N. (2017). *Qualitative inquiry and research design: Choosing among five approaches* (4th ed.). Thousand Oaks, CA: Sage.

The authors "explore the philosophical underpinnings, history, and key elements of each of five qualitative inquiry approaches: narrative research, phenomenology, grounded theory, ethnography, and case study" (from the publisher). Creswell and Poth clarify the idea of conceptual framework and how it impacts qualitative research. They also provide a description of the steps required by each approach and its subgroups. This book is helpful in determining the appropriate tradition and methods related to research questions.

References

Fraenkel, J. R., Wallen, N. E., & Hyun, H. H. (2015). *How to design and evaluate research in education* (9th ed.). New York: McGraw-Hill.

Marshall, C., & Rossman, G. B. (2016). *Designing qualitative research* (6th ed.). Thousand Oaks, CA: Sage.

Patton, M. Q. (2015). *Qualitative research & evaluation methods* (4th ed.). Thousand Oaks, CA: Sage.

Literature Examples

Carey, R. L. (2018). "What am I gonna be losing?" School culture and the family-based college-going dilemmas of Black and Latino adolescent boys. *Education and Urban Society, 50*(3), 246–273.

Ozturk, Z., Dooley, C. M., & Welch, M. (2018). Finding the hook: Computer science education in elementary contexts. *Journal of Research on Technology in Education, 50*(2), 149–163, DOI: 10.1080/15391523.2018.1431573

Pressley, T., Roehrig, A. D., & Turner, J. E. (2018). Elementary teachers' perceptions of a reformed teacher-evaluation system. *The Teacher Educator, 53*(1), 21–43, DOI: 10.1080/08878730.2017.1391362

Weiss, M. P., & Lloyd, J. W. (2002). Congruence between roles and actions of secondary special educators in co-taught and special education settings. *The Journal of Special Education, 36,* 58–68.

Designing and Conducting Descriptive Research

A s mentioned in Chapter 1, descriptive research is used to describe the features of or provide a picture of a condition or phenomenon. Researchers who conduct descriptive research do not manipulate the subject of study in order to determine cause and effect. As such, the work is considered nonexperimental. Descriptive research is important when research questions fundamentally take the form of "What is going on here?" The "here" in this statement may be a classroom context, a social program, a teacher or student's mind, a cultural group meeting, or a school district office. Although qualitative research is also descriptive in nature and purpose, this chapter highlights three quantitative types of descriptive research often used in education: basic (quantitative) descriptive research, correlational research, and causal comparative research.

Types of Quantitative Descriptive Research

Basic Descriptive

The purpose of basic (quantitative) descriptive research (from here simply referred to as *descriptive research*) is to understand features of or provide a picture of a condition or phenomenon, such as educator beliefs about inclusion or student perceptions of peer pressure, using quantitative data. Descriptive research methods typically rely on responses of participants to specific written (survey) or interview questions. That is, in descriptive research in the field of education, the researcher usually creates and administers a written or electronic survey/questionnaire or conducts interviews; documents responses; analyzes the data; and describes the nature of participant attitudes, beliefs, or behaviors based on the responses. Descriptive research results later may be the basis for additional comparisons or experimentation. Descriptive research yields quantitative outcomes such as tally frequencies, percentages, and mean scores.

Read through the following journal excerpt from Kotrlik and Redmann (2005) as an example of the way that your research might be described if you conduct descriptive research. Notice that the researchers explained their purpose and objectives, noted the variables and population, and then detailed the measurement system.

The purpose was to determine the extent of technology integration in instruction by ABE teachers in programs operated by public school systems. The objectives were to determine (a) the extent to which technology has been integrated into the teaching-learning process based on the four levels of the Kotrlik-Redmann Technology Integration Model (© 2002); (b) the magnitude of barriers that may prevent teachers from integrating technology into the teaching/learning process; (c) the technology anxiety of teachers; (d) teachers' perceptions of their teaching effectiveness; (e) the sources of technology training and types of technology used by teachers; and (f) whether selected variables explain a significant proportion of the variance in advanced technology integration scores. The potential explanatory variables used in this analysis were the number of technology training sources used, barriers to technology integration, teachers' technology anxiety level, perceived teaching effectiveness, and six types of technology available for use by the teacher in instruction. For this study, technology was defined as "employing the Internet, computers, CDROMs, interactive media, satellites, teleconferencing, and other technological means to support, enhance, inspire and create learning." . . .

The population included 311 ABE teachers employed by public secondary school systems in Louisiana as listed in the directory of ABE teachers obtained from the Louisiana Department of Education. These teachers work with learners in ABE programs to obtain the GED diploma . . . .

A complete listing of the population was obtained by securing a list of ABE teachers from every public school system in the state. To determine the random sample size needed for this study, Cochran's (1977) sample size formula was used. Based on an alpha level of .05, a standard error estimate of .03, and the primary variables reported on a 5-point scale, a minimum returned sample size of 85 was required. Because a response rate of approximately 50% was anticipated, a research sample size of 172 was used for this study . . . .

The instrument was based on the Kotrlik-Redmann Technology Integration Model (2002) . . .

The instrument contained three multi-item scales: the Technology Integration Scale (which included four subscales, namely, Exploration, Experimentation, Adoption, and Advanced Integration), the Barriers to the Integration of Technology Scale, and the Perceived Teaching Effectiveness Scale. In addition, several questions and items were used to collect data on personal and demographic variables such as gender, age, years teaching experience, sources of technology training, types of technology available for the teachers' use, and level of technology anxiety. An expert panel of university faculty and doctoral-level graduate students with expertise in andragogy, instrument design, research methodology, electronic (e)-learning, and technology integration evaluated the face and content validity of the instrument. The instrument was field tested with 29 teachers. (pp. 207–209)

Correlational

The purpose of **correlational research** is to describe or analyze relationships between variables, conditions, or events, any of which may be reported attitudes, beliefs, or behaviors (Salkind, 2016). Correlational research, then, provides an indication of whether or to what degree two or more variables are related or how an outcome, behavior, or event might be predicted by other information, beliefs, behaviors, or events (Gall et al., 2006). Correlational research attempts to answer the broad question: What is the magnitude or degree of relationship? As with causal comparative research, which we will describe next, the researcher's purpose is to investigate relationships, not true causality. For instance, a researcher may conduct correlational research to investigate the relationship between teacher access to technology and teacher attitudes toward the use of assistive technology for students with disabilities. A researcher could also attempt to predict differences in student performance based on variables such as gender and socioeconomic status.

Correlational research often relies on data collected through surveys/questionnaires, rating scales or interviews, similar to that used in descriptive research. Correlational research also may include data from existing or extant databases found at a school, at an agency, or in other public records. Correlational research allows a researcher to explore relationships among a greater number of variables at one time than causal comparative research. A researcher could, for example, explore the relationships among gender, ethnicity, number of Advanced Placement courses taken in high school, and SAT scores and college acceptance rates or even college performance measures such as GPA. Analyses typically yield an index of the strength of relationships called a **correlation coefficient**. Because causality is not measured, caution is required in interpreting results.

Read through the following excerpts from a correlational study by Wood and Gabas (2017) as an example of the way that your research might be described if you conduct this type of research. Examine how the questions are aligned with the sample and data sources in this design.

. . . the current study aimed to address the questions:

(1) What are the attitudes of Spanish-speaking ELs towards recreational and academic reading?

(2) Are there differences between groups of children by grade (kindergarten and first grade) or gender in their attitudes and interest in reading?

(3) Is there a significant relationship between ELs' attitudes regarding reading and their performance on standardized language and literacy assessments? . . .

The subsample for the current study was a convenience sample and included participants from the larger intervention development project at school sites that agreed to invite participation in the reading survey prior to beginning the intervention. In the context of this study, eligible participants were those who were classified as Spanish-speaking ELs as children who were exposed to and used Spanish at home, to varying degrees . . .

The *Elementary Reading Attitude Survey (ERAS)* (McKenna and Kear 1990) is a norm-referenced questionnaire that measures the reading attitude of students in elementary school. The ERAS consists of 20 questions related to attitude towards recreational reading and attitude towards academic reading . . .

The *Woodcock Reading Mastery Tests, Third Edition (WRMT-III)* (2011) letter identification, phonological awareness and rapid automatic naming subtests were administered in the fall of the school year . . .

The *Peabody Picture Vocabulary Test-4*, PPVT-4 (Dunn and Dunn 2007) is an untimed, norm-referenced, individually administered measure of receptive vocabulary (normed for individuals 2- to 90-years-old) . . . (pp. 412–416)

Causal Comparative

Causal comparative research attempts to broadly answer the question: Is there a causal relationship? That said, "causality" is perhaps misleading, since with this design researchers do not have control over independent variables as in experimental research. Thus, researchers test the relationship of an independent variable and a dependent variable, or the "effect" of the independent variable on the dependent variable (Mills & Gay, 2015). For example, a researcher may study the relationship between teacher experience and attitudes toward inclusion. In the research design, a researcher selects an independent variable (e.g., years of experience among high school teachers), identifies the sample, and collects survey responses or information from an existing database (dependent variable). The researcher then compares responses by years of experience and draws causal inferences.

By contrast to basic descriptive and correlational research, the purpose of causal comparative research is to identify potential cause-and-effect relationships between targeted groups of individuals in whom an independent variable (i.e., causal factor) is absent or present, or present at several levels, and a dependent variable (i.e., effect factor). Like correlational research, variables are not manipulated, but a study can provide information on which to base future experimental research. The independent variable is not a treatment or intervention, as in experimental or quasi-experimental research. That is, the researcher may attempt to determine if the groups are different in terms of their relationship to the dependent variable (Gall, Gall, and Borg, 2006). Here's another more detailed example: a researcher might explore the relationship of gender (independent variable) and performance on a computer competency test (dependent variable). Educational researchers also might be interested in exploring the relationship of age, ethnicity, and parent education levels to various effect variables. The independent variable could translate to categorical data that are nominal (e.g., male or female; elementary, middle, or high school teacher). In educational research, an independent variable may also translate to ordinal level data (e.g., new, experienced, veteran teacher) or ratio level data (e.g., 0, 1–3, 4–10, or 11+ years of experience), depending on a questionnaire item.

Some researchers and writers have suggested that causal comparative designs can include ex post facto control group studies. That is, a researcher would compare the effects of an independent variable after the fact instead of intentionally manipulating the variable or assigning participants ahead of time (Mills & Gay, 2015). For example, a researcher could compare the differential effects of a new reading curriculum on students from two classes, one that receives the new curriculum and one that does not. The dependent variable might be year-end state reading test scores. This example more clearly illustrates the potentially misleading nature of causal comparative research, since the variables were not controlled ahead of time. You could, however, attempt to control participant variables by ensuring that you have groups of students similar in terms of performance or by statistically controlling for initial differences in group performance.

Read the following excerpt from a causal comparative study by Porfeli, Wang, Audette, McColl, and Algozzine (2009) as an example of the way that your research might be described if you conduct causal comparative research. Look carefully at the research questions and how they are related/connected to the design, variables, and data sources.

We were interested in the issue of equity and its effects on the chronic and intractable achievement gap observed in America's schools. Two research questions focused our research:

Research Question 1: To what extent do school, student, and community characteristics and achievement vary across elementary schools in a large urban school district?

Research Question 2: To what extent do school, student, and community characteristics predict achievement in elementary schools in a large urban school district? . . .

We described and evaluated the influence of school, student, and community demographics on academic achievement. We documented community capital and distributions for students with disabilities as well as for academically gifted students (i.e., those who demonstrate or have the potential to demonstrate outstanding intellectual aptitude and specific academic ability) and used them to predict achievement . . . .

Data were available from public Web-based sources maintained by the school district to create indicators of *community capital* (e.g., the percent of the children receiving free and reduced lunch within a school), *special education concentration* (the percent of children with an "academically gifted" classification and the percent of children with a disability), and *academic achievement* (the percent of students earning passing scores on end-of-grade standardized academic achievement tests). Information pertaining to the quality of life of the communities surrounding each school was also available from a study conducted by Metropolitan Studies Group (2004) . . .

The nature of this causal-comparative (*ex post facto*) archival research allows us to document existing differences among the participating schools and to explore the cause, or reason, for them. Since professionals and policy makers are mostly interested in predicting school success in terms of academic achievement, we used *academic achievement* as the dependent variable for data analysis. (pp. 75–80)

Each of the three types of descriptive research requires that you have an in-depth knowledge of the area of study. Each type may utilize data from a questionnaire or interview. The most significant differences are in the purpose of the research, the potential use of existing databases in causal comparative and correlational research, and what you do with the data (i.e., your analyses and the outcomes they may yield). Table 7.1 provides a simple comparison of the three types of descriptive research.

The next part of this chapter outlines steps for designing and conducting descriptive research projects, primarily basic descriptive and correlational. Unless you are using data from an existing database, descriptive research may rely on data obtained through administering a survey or questionnaire. Therefore, you need to understand survey methods, design components, and the importance of sampling. After a discussion of those topics, you will learn about accessing extant databases.

Survey Methods

Everyone has probably participated in a survey at some time. Survey methods are generally used to measure attitudes, decisions, needs, behavior, lifestyles, affiliations, and/or demographics of the sample chosen. You can design surveys and choose samples to measure and describe characteristics or constructs in a variety of ways and from a

TABLE 7.1 ● Comparison of Descriptive, Correlational, and Causal Comparative Research		
	Descriptive	**Correlational**	**Causal Comparative**
Purposes	• To describe features of or provide a broad picture of a condition or phenomenon	• To describe/analyze relationships between variables, conditions, or events	• To explore the relationship between causal factor and effect factor
Characteristics	• Gets information from or opinions of people. • May be the basis for comparisons or experimentation. • Provides quantitative, statistical results such as mean. • No manipulation of variable(s) or experimentation occurs.	• Provides indication of how two or more variables are related. • Provides indication of how an outcome or event might be predicted by other information or events. • Provides quantitative index of strength of relationships (correlation coefficient). • Does not indicate cause and effect.	• Provides indication of how variables are related. • Causality is suggested. • May be ex post facto research.
Data collection methods	• Survey using mail or electronic questionnaire • Phone or person-to-person interview	• Survey using mail or electronic questionnaire • Phone or person-to-person interview • School/district/state records • Other existing databases	• Survey using mail or electronic questionnaire • Phone or person-to-person interview • School/district/state records • Other existing databases
Examples	• Survey of literacy practices among high school teachers • Parent interviews regarding year-round schooling	• Examination of relationship between literacy practices among high school teachers and student performance on state tests • Analysis of relationship between parent views on year-round schooling and growth of private school enrolments	• Exploration of relationship between gender and computer competency test scores among seventh graders • Investigation of relationship of teacher experience and attitudes toward inclusion

variety of populations. You can also use those data for descriptive purposes as well as for analyzing the relationships among the constructs, as in correlational designs. **Survey methods** include the use of interviews or completion of questionnaires that yield data from respondents. These data are then analyzed for specific responses to the research questions. Generally, the information is gathered from a large group of participants, unlike in qualitative studies. Let's take a look at designing a survey.

Survey Design

There are several important elements of survey design (see Figure 7.1). You may work simultaneously on more than one element or work on one element and then go back to another to revise it after having thought more thoroughly about the design. In other words, the process is not necessarily linear.

Perhaps the most important determinant of survey design is your information needs or, more specifically, your research questions. What do you want to know about a group? This may begin as a general statement such as "What are the attitudes of general education teachers toward inclusion?" but in order to develop a detailed plan, the specifics of this question must be determined. For example, *attitudes about inclusion* may include how a teacher feels about students with disabilities, how she feels about working with other teachers, and whether she believes including students with disabilities affects the education of students without disabilities. Will the survey address all of these topics?

Once the specific information needs are determined, you can more thoughtfully select your sample. Who should be included in the survey? What do I know about these people? What level of reading and writing skills do they have? How large should my sample be? Can I get lists of individuals with certain characteristics (e.g., lists of elementary school teachers in a state)? Are these individuals in a certain geographic area, or are they widely dispersed? The number of questions is potentially quite large. However, the decisions you make about a sample should be guided by your research questions.

Developing effective questions or survey items is clearly a central element of survey design. What types of questions will you ask? What types of response modes will you use? Should your response options be structured or unstructured? What types of data

---

FIGURE 7.1 ● Dimensions of Survey Design

- Determine your information needs.
- Select your sample.
- Design your instrument and create your questions/items.
- Determine how you will collect data.
- Plan for how you will analyze the data.

do you want—nominal, ordinal, interval, or ratio? What topics will you address? How will you make sure the questions and responses are clear to the participants?

While you determine the form of instrumentation, you will also need to decide how to collect the data. How will you obtain information from this sample? Will you use personal or phone interviews? If so, who will do the interviewing? How will the interviews be set up? If you decide on self-administered questionnaires, how will the questionnaires be distributed? Mail or online? What will you do about nonresponse? What level of nonresponse will you tolerate?

Finally, you must plan for analyzing the data once you have collected it. What types of analyses will you conduct? How will you use the data? What type of report will you generate? How will you use the information, and what value will the information have? These questions will be addressed in greater detail in Chapter 11, but by beginning to think about your analysis in advance, you can create better instrument items and formats that will make analyzing the data much easier.

As with all types of research, elements of survey design are driven by the clear statement of your research question. Given that you already know how to write good research questions (from Chapter 2), begin to think about designing your instrument (creating a written questionnaire or interview questions), including question/item formats and the types of data they will yield. Also, particularly in the following section, recall the importance of reliability and validity (from Chapter 4).

Creating Questions/Items

In descriptive research, questions and items are designed to yield information for the researcher about the reality being studied. According to Alreck and Settle (2004), good questions have the following attributes: (a) focus, (b) brevity, (c) clarity, (d) vocabulary, and (e) grammar. The first step in creating questions is to define what you want. What variables are you are interested in studying? How do you want to analyze these variables? This is the time to get specific. If you want to understand the attitudes of educators toward students who have differing racial backgrounds, what variables are included in the concept of "attitude"? Should you ask a question about whether the educator has ever taught students from various racial backgrounds? Should you ask a question about types of behaviors the students might exhibit? Should you ask a question about how the participants define various racial backgrounds?

Next, if possible, try to have focus group discussions, even if they are small ones. To extend our example of educators and students from various racial backgrounds, you might want to gather a few teachers and administrators to talk with them about what you see as important questions related to the topic. For example, you may want to ask a question about how often an educator interacts with students from various racial backgrounds. The educators may say that it is more applicable to ask about periods of time, or that time is not as important as the number of students in a school.

Question and Response Formats

Once you decide on the topics and objectives for the questions/items, you must determine the best format for the responses. Essentially, there are two options: structured responses and unstructured responses. When you include options for responses, they are called **structured responses**. **Unstructured responses**, on the other hand, are open-ended and require respondents to create answers. There are a couple of factors to consider in choosing structured or unstructured responses. First, how do you want to compare the data you collect? Structured responses provide you with similar data across respondents. Unstructured responses may yield the data you were anticipating or responses that do not make much sense; these data are usually in the form of words that may be open to interpretation.

If you decide to include questions with structured responses, you must determine the type of data you are interested in collecting. There are four types of data, as described in Chapter 5: nominal, ordinal, interval, and ratio. For our purposes here, let's put these types into the context of questionnaire items.

Nominal data are arranged by unordered groups. For example, the question "What is your favorite color?" puts people in groups by color but does not order them in any way. "Are you male or female?" also puts respondents in groups without order.

Ordinal data places responses in a certain order or rank, but this order does not have equal intervals between items. For example, a question such as "How would you rate your fitness level—excellent, good, fair, or poor?" asks a respondent to describe his fitness level along a continuum. This continuum includes descriptors that are ordered in some fashion. With ordinal data, you can compare answers to the same question across groups, or you can compare answers from comparable samples over time (Fowler, 2013). Interval data are numeric and have equal intervals between values, but the range does not have to contain a zero value. In surveys, interval data are obtained with linear, numeric scales. For example, an item might read, "Rate the following items on a scale of 1 (*unimportant*) to 5 (*extremely important*)." You may use most descriptive statistics with interval data (i.e., mean, median, mode).

Finally, ratio data have the characteristics of interval data, but the equal intervals are related by ratios. For example, someone who weighs 40 pounds is twice as heavy as someone who weighs 20 pounds. Ratio data also have an absolute zero, where no value of the characteristic exists. There are no limitations on statistical operations with ratio data; however, few items (other than age) lend themselves to measurement by this data type.

So you see, asking the right questions will enable you to get the type of data that you can manipulate in the analysis that you want to perform. For example, if you want to be able to say that, on average, elementary teachers in a certain school district have 8.5 years of teaching experience, and you format the question like this,

How many years have you taught classes in the elementary (K–5) grades?

_____ 0–3 years

_____ 4–5 years

_____ 6–10 years

_____ More than 10 years

[Y]ou will not get the data that you want because these are ordinal data. You will be able to report the frequency of responses in each category and perhaps compare responses from elementary and high school teachers related to frequency, but you will not be able to generate an average number of years of teaching experience.

Categorical Questions. **Categorical questions** require a respondent to put the answer into a predetermined category. Examples include questions such as "How did you first learn about our business?" with a list such as newspaper, television, and radio. Or a question could be "What is the best way for you to receive further information?" followed by a list including e-mail, mail, and telephone. According to Alreck and Settle (2004), questions that include categorical responses should have the following characteristics:

- The categories used must be all-inclusive and mutually exclusive, and there should be more variance between categories than within.

- The upper limit is usually about six to eight categories per question.

- If you have doubts about categories, use more that are narrow in focus than fewer with broad focus, because more focused categories can be combined later to create broader categories.

Categorical questions allow you to identify important characteristics about a sample and can be used to describe the sample in relation to other variables. For example, if you ask respondents to indicate whether they are male or female, you can then identify how each of the females and males responded to further questions. You can also set up questions that would allow multiple responses, such as the question about the best way to receive further information above.

Scales. Many of the items included in surveys use scales to help respondents place their answers on a continuum. **Scales** (scaled items) allow you to organize and perhaps more easily later analyze the data using statistics. To compare responses across questions, scales must utilize the same continuum (e.g., *always, sometimes, rarely, never*). There are many types of scales for use by researchers. Following are descriptions of three: Likert scale, verbal frequency scale, and linear numeric scale. For descriptions of other types of scales, see Alreck and Settle (2004).

Likert scale: In a **Likert scale**, participants respond to statements with varying degrees of agreement or disagreement. One example is the rating form used to get feedback about college courses. One question is usually "The workload for this course was appropriate," and the respondent indicates *strongly agree, somewhat agree, somewhat disagree*, or *strongly disagree*. This scale allows you to assess someone's opinion, but it may be confusing for the respondent when negative statements are used.

Verbal frequency scale: A **verbal frequency scale** is similar to the Likert scale in that it is relatively easy for the respondent to use. The difference is that the respondent is asked to rate how often something occurs along a continuum. For example, a question might be "The student follows directions," and the options may be *always, sometimes, never*. This type of scale, as with the Likert scale, gives a broad measure of the participant's response to a statement.

Linear, numeric scale: You should use a **linear numeric scale** "when items are to be judged on a single dimension and arrayed on a scale with equal intervals" (Alreck & Settle, 2004, p. 443). Most examples include rating a question or statement on a scale of 1 (*strongly agree*) to 5 (*strongly disagree*). Another example is to rate levels of exertion during exercise from 1 (*no exertion*) to 10 (*complete fatigue*). Using a linear numeric scale allows you to convert the data to numbers easily and use statistics to describe and make statements about the included sample. It is best to label the extremes of the continuum that you use in this scale (e.g., *agree/disagree, important/unimportant*), but it may be best to leave out the intermediate descriptors.

Question Reliability

In creating a written or interview questionnaire, it is important that your data are reliable, meaning that you would get similar responses from individuals if you asked the questions on multiple occasions. Fowler (2013) described three general ways to address question reliability:

1. Make sure that the researcher's side of the process is entirely scripted. In other words, script how directions are to be delivered, how questions are to be administered, and how respondents are to be probed or redirected with regard to those questions.

2. Make sure that each question means very close to the same thing to each respondent.

3. Make sure that the kinds of answers that constitute an appropriate response are communicated consistently. In other words, frame the questions in such a way that the respondent knows how to answer appropriately.

If you address these three items, you will increase the reliability of your survey instrument.

Question Validity

Creating questions with validity (i.e., construct validity) means that your questions ask about what you are trying to understand. The questions will also yield the data that you want. Generally, responses to questions are inaccurate and invalid because (a) respondents do not understand the question, (b) they do not know the answer, (c) they cannot recall the answer, or (d) they do not want to report the answer. You can minimize these problems by having a single focus for your question and by using terms that are either defined for respondents or are known by them. You can also pilot your questions with respondents not from your sample. Additionally, you could try to minimize respondents' sense of being judged about sensitive issues by using a self-administered survey. For subjective questions, you might want to ask a similar question multiple times and compile the answers into a scale score or response.

Moreover, good questions or survey items enable the researcher to better match responses to just what it is that you are trying to measure (Fowler, 2013). In other words, good questions do not introduce bias. Fowler suggested that researchers must be careful not to introduce bias and error unintentionally into questions by overemphasizing certain topics or including leading questions, loaded questions, and ambiguously worded questions.

In summary, to create good questions, you must consider what kinds of questions you will ask and how to structure them. Questions need to be reliable and valid. It is generally easier to create questions with unstructured responses because you do not have to develop the responses. However, by using unstructured responses, you often sacrifice comparable data, and you may introduce bias and error into the survey by having to interpret responses. That is not to say that a few questions with unstructured responses would not provide quality information; you just must be deliberate in your choice to use this response type. You also need to be sure that your questions yield data that you can analyze relatively easily.

Checking Your Survey Instrument

After you have written a draft of your questions, submit the draft to critical review. Critical review may mean submitting the questions to the participants in a focus group, submitting the questions to professionals or other survey researchers in the field, or submitting the questions to your doctoral or master-level committee. Whatever the most appropriate review source, submit the questions for feedback, particularly with regard to clarity of wording for items and validity of the constructs you are trying to measure with your instrument items.

It is also recommended that you field test the instrument. In the Kotrlik and Redmann (2005) excerpt earlier in this chapter, the researchers did just that. Conduct the interview or administer the questionnaire to people similar to those in your target population and get their feedback. You want to find out if the instrument is easy to administer, if more guidance or clarity is needed in certain areas, or if questions are understandable. It is critical that the instrument is easy to use and is understandable to bolster reliability and validity.

Selecting Your Sample

Your research question(s) will guide your sample selection. From the Kotrlik and Redmann (2005) excerpt, you should be able to see that in action. For example, do you want to describe the results of high-stakes testing for students with disabilities who received accommodations versus those who did not receive accommodations? If that is the case, you would sample both those who received accommodations and those who did not. Are you interested in describing the opinions of parents about year-round schools? In that case, you would sample parents whose children attend year-round schools and those who do not. The type of information you need, resources available, and your purpose in conducting the survey will determine the best way for you to choose your sample. There are three basic alternatives to consider: random sampling, stratified sampling, and cluster sampling.

Random Sampling. Random sampling is most often used when substantial resources are available and the purpose of the survey is to describe a population as accurately as possible. In random sampling, any individual in a population has an equal chance to be chosen to participate. For example, if you wanted to obtain information from elementary teachers in a certain state, you would have to be able to obtain a list of all of those teachers (and contact information) and randomly choose from that list of possible participants. If you could not obtain that list, but you could obtain a list from a local school district, you would be using a **convenience sample**, which is a sample of participants who happen to be readily accessible to the researcher. This is acceptable. Just be aware of (and make certain you make sure your readers are later aware of) the limitations of generalizing your results to the larger population.

Stratified Sampling. In **stratified sampling**, one creates subgroups in a sample to guarantee their representation. In other words, in a sample of teachers, you may want to ensure that a certain percentage of each racial subgroup is included. To do that, you would determine the number of individuals of each race included (e.g., in a sample of 100 teachers, based on demographics, 12 would be Asian, 16 Hispanic, 23 African American, and 49 Caucasian). From the possible sample, you would choose these numbers of participants randomly from the pool of participants in a certain racial group. This guarantees representation of certain groups in the sample, but it does not guarantee random sampling and, thus, increases the chance of sampling error.

Clustered Sampling. **Clustered sampling** involves choosing certain physical or geographic areas and identifying a certain number of units to be chosen from each area. For example, if you were interested in sampling high school teachers in a school district and you wanted to make sure that you included teachers from cities as well as from rural areas, you would designate areas within a county as either city or rural areas and choose a certain number of participants from the different areas. You could also designate areas within a city as predominantly poor or affluent and then sample from each cluster. Clustering allows you to choose characteristics of certain areas to conduct your sampling.

Conducting Descriptive Research

Once you have determined your research questions, created your survey items, and targeted your sample, you must determine the best way to collect the data. While you may certainly consider this decision earlier, you really need a thorough understanding of what you hope to accomplish before you can make the final decision as to the best way to go about it. Hence, as noted, the survey design process is not necessarily linear.

According to Fowler (2013), how you collect data is related to the following:

- The way the sample is drawn
- Characteristics of population (e.g., reading/writing skills, computer access, ease of contact)
- The question form you choose

- The question content you include
- The response rate you hope to obtain
- How much the different modes of data collection cost
- The facilities available for data collection
- The length of time you will collect data

Most of these items on Fowler's list are self-explanatory. For example, if you choose a sample that is dispersed across the United States, it would be very costly to do personal interviews. If your sample has limited reading and writing skills, a paper survey of unstructured questions will be very difficult for respondents to complete. If you include questions that may be private or controversial, such as those pertaining to sexual behavior or medical history, you may only get a reasonable response rate through a self-administered questionnaire.

Technology may provide helpful ways to collect data from surveys. Improvements in computer technology and an increased online presence have made online questionnaires an option in addition to questionnaires administered by phone or sent through the mail. Other options are also available, depending upon your ingenuity and access to resources. The focus of your decision should be how best to reach the sample that you have chosen. Interviewing is an option too.

Interview

An interview is an opportunity for you to get information about beliefs, perspectives, and views from the participant. As described in Chapter 6, there are a variety of interview techniques. In quantitative descriptive research, however, researchers use either a standardized open-ended interview or a closed, fixed-response interview. Each has a unique purpose, as well as strengths and weaknesses. They may be used individually or in combination.

A standardized, open-ended interview is one in which you have already determined the specific questions that are to be asked but the responses can vary by individual. In other words, the questions are set up to require more than one-word answers and may allow the participant to take the response into an area that the researcher did not consider. This type of interview also allows for some standardization across researchers or situations and reduces some issues of bias.

In a closed, fixed-response interview, you develop the questions and the alternative responses for the participant in advance. The participant then just chooses the most suitable response. This type of interview has the advantage of being efficient and standard across researchers and participants.

You can conduct interviews over the phone or in person. In either case, interviewing is an important method of data collection in descriptive research, but it requires skill. You should practice conducting interviews before beginning research in order to avoid practices that increase bias, decrease participant willingness to respond, or predetermine outcomes.

Nonresponse

Although you may think that addressing **nonresponse** may be more appropriate after data are analyzed (i.e., in conjunction with the concepts and activities included in Chapter 11 on analyzing and interpreting descriptive research), it is wise to be proactive and avoid some mistakes that may lead to nonresponse by survey participants. The Kotrlik and Redmann (2005) excerpt is a good example of planning ahead for potential nonresponse. That noted, participant nonresponse can occur for at least three reasons: (a) participants are not given a chance to participate (i.e., not chosen), (b) participants are given a chance and refuse to participate, and (c) participants are given a chance to respond and cannot (e.g., cannot read a written survey) (Fowler, 2013). Therefore, since nonresponse from participants may completely skew the chosen sample, introduce significant levels of bias, or lead to poor external validity, your job is to eliminate as many of these problems as possible.

First, you need to consider access. If you decide to use personal interviews, how will you schedule them? When will you schedule them? Participants who work all day will not be able to participate in interviews that are conducted during work hours unless something is set up through their employer. If telephone interviews are used, you must verify that your sample has access to telephones. If you decide to use the Internet, you must make sure that your sample has access to the Internet or that you provide that access.

Second, you should consider motivation. If a participant receives a survey in the mail with little information about the survey and its purpose, the participant likely will have little motivation to complete it. If the interview you conduct is about a politically charged issue and the participant will be somehow identifiable, that participant

IN THEIR OWN WORDS

Pamela A. Boudah, MSEd

As I thought about completing my master's thesis, these are some bits of advice I would give to graduate students engaged in doing descriptive research, particularly research involving a questionnaire:

- Be realistic about what you can do. This is a master's project.

- Try to address a situation or research question that is applicable to the real world. It will make the work more meaningful and enjoyable.

- Create distinct sections in your questionnaire. This will make coding easier for you afterwards.

- Provide an incentive for respondents. Even something small is better than nothing for a respondent's time.

- If you use a paper copy of your questionnaire, print it on colored paper. It will stand out in a stack of other papers and therefore help you get a better response rate.

- Pilot your survey with a variety of people from your target population. This will give you great feedback, particularly in regard to how well respondents understand the questions.

may not want to respond. If a survey or interview includes topics that are not socially rewarding/acceptable, participants may not want to participate. On the other hand, if a survey is directly related to issues that are of interest to the participant or if there is some reward for participating, more people will choose to respond.

Finally, you must consider costs. Costs include respondents' time and energy. If a survey includes many questions and all of them are open-ended, requiring quite a bit of writing, participants may not want to respond. If interviews will take an hour or more, participants may not want to respond. However, questions that are easy to respond to and interviews that allow participants to provide information in an efficient fashion will increase response rates.

Providing an incentive, such as a small amount of money, a gift certificate, or even just a pencil, increases your costs but often will increase response rates. You also may want to ask potential participants to field test your questionnaire or interview. Ultimately, you need to develop a thorough understanding of your sample and the best options to gather data.

Accessing Extant Databases

As mentioned at the outset of the chapter, (quantitative) descriptive research can be divided into three major categories, basic descriptive, correlational, and causal comparative. Descriptive research often utilizes written questionnaires or interviews as data sources in order to describe features of or provide a broad picture of a condition or phenomenon, such as teacher beliefs about inclusion or student perceptions of peer pressure. Causal comparative and correlational research may use questionnaires or interviews as data sources in order to describe or analyze relationships between variables, conditions, or events, any of which may be reported attitudes, beliefs, or behaviors. While the researcher may utilize surveys to conduct a descriptive, causal comparative, or correlational investigation, causal comparative and correlational research may also utilize extant databases for information from which to look at relationships among variables.

An **extant database** contains data already collected by others. The data might consist of grades and attendance reports saved by a school or district over time. The database could be larger, including grades, attendance reports, office referrals, and state test scores for students in an entire school or district. The database could even be larger than that, including demographic data, student performance data, socioeconomic data, expenditures, and other figures for a state or a nation. District and state data, as well as other data, including number of and academic performance data of students with disabilities and students for whom English is a second language, are public records and are readily available through one or more state or national sources. In the earlier excerpt of a study by Porfeli et al. (2009) of student achievement in an urban setting, you can read about the extant databases that they used.

For example, the National Center for Educational Statistics (nces.ed.gov) provides easy access to state, district, and individual school profiles that include, for instance, data on per pupil expenditures, teacher/student ratios, National Assessment of Educational Progress (NAEP) scores, and number of students receiving free and reduced-price lunch. With just a few clicks on your computer, you can access a lot of data that may be of considerable interest and, with proper analysis, enable you to correlate variables that address your research questions.

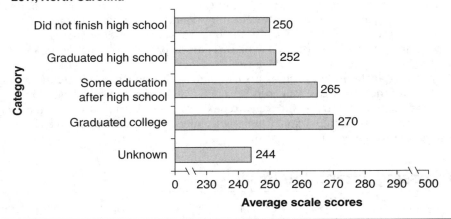

FIGURE 7.2 ● Sample Output From NAEP Database

Average scale scores for Grade 8 reading, by Parental education level, from 2 questions [PARED] for jurisdiction: 2017
2017, North Carolina

Source: National Assessment of Educational Progress (2017).

The NAEP database (www.nationsreportcard.gov) reports information for the entire nation and specific geographic regions. It includes students drawn from both public and nonpublic schools and reports results for student achievement [in] Grades 4, 8, and 12. You can look at subject-area-specific test results as well. The researcher can create custom data searches by several variables, using the Data Explorer feature under the Data Tools tab, and download results into chart or table formats. For instance, to look at the NAEP eighth-grade reading scores (variable 1) for students learning English as a second language (variable 2) by parent education level (variable 3) in the state of North Carolina, the database generated the output in Figure 7.2 in a matter of seconds.

In terms of causal comparative and correlational research, you could then statistically analyze the data to look at potential relationships. Analysis of causal comparative and correlational research will be discussed in greater detail in Chapter 11, but for now understand that, besides creating your own databases through administering a questionnaire or interview, you can very easily access information from many extant databases to answer your research questions.

Mixed Methods Research

As you read in Chapter 1, some research studies include questions that are best answered using mixed methods research. In short, mixed methods research typically either employs experimental and descriptive designs, or qualitative and at least one type of descriptive research design. It is not uncommon for researchers to use mixed methods, but normally, one design will be the primary focus of the research. Still, as we have said throughout the book, it all depends on what questions you are asking.

For instance, Boudah (2018) evaluated the effects of an intensive reading intervention on the performance of 237 low-achieving middle school students. Primarily, the research utilized quasi-experimental methods and large group statistical analyses. Secondarily, however, the research utilized descriptive methods to address questions regarding student performance by school and by teacher. Frazier and Trekles (2018) posed the following research questions in their study of technology implementation in elementary classrooms:

1. How do elementary teachers anticipate and actually use iPads in the classroom over the course of the first year of 1:1 implementation?

2. What issues arise in elementary schools during Year 1 of 1:1 iPad adoption?

3. What do elementary teachers perceive are the benefits and challenges of using iPads in classrooms?

4. How do elementary teachers' perceptions change throughout the first year of 1:1 iPad implementation? (p. 464)

Can you guess which methods they used? If you thought qualitative and quantitative descriptive methods, you are correct. In fact, the researchers reported:

Quantitative data were collected from the survey items as well as qualitative data from the focus groups. While the survey focused primarily on self-reported data, the purpose of the study was to gather teacher perceptions, as well as their insights of how they did and did not use the iPads over the course of the school year during Year 1 of 1:1 adoption. (p. 470)

Researcher Notes

While conducting any kind of field-based research (e.g., descriptive observations of identified behaviors or in-person interviews, as opposed to analysis of an extant database or online questionnaire), you should keep field notes about what you observe in participants or your reflections during the research process. For example, field notes may include a running record of events that occurred during an interview that you think might affect the results, particularly when validity may be an issue. Notes may address the situation under observation such as "Today, the students seemed very restless, and there was a fire drill in the middle of class," or "On my way to interview Mrs. Q, I was told her son had been in an automobile accident yesterday." These notes would also include dates and times of observations or interviews, as well as who was involved. They may also include ideas or questions you have while collecting data. For example, you may write, "While waiting to talk to Mr. S, I noticed that he only called on the girls in the classroom. I wonder if that is significant?" Field notes can be combined in one place, or they can be kept separately and referred to during analysis and interpretation of results of experimental, qualitative, or descriptive research. Analyzing and interpreting mixed methods research will be discussed in more detail in Chapter 11.

TECHNOLOGY IN RESEARCH

SurveyMonkey

Many researchers are now using online surveys to gather data from participants. Participants find online participation easy and acceptable, as long as the site is secure. One tool with growing popularity is SurveyMonkey. SurveyMonkey can be used to develop and administer a survey, as well as to collect and analyze data. This online tool is used by many businesses, public and private organizations, and educational institutions such as universities and schools. According to the website, the most popular uses include "customer feedback, employee reviews, marketing research, popular opinion, event attendance and guest preferences, course evaluations, and thesis research." Researchers can use the basic features for free or access more advanced features for a small fee. You can find more information or try the product at surveymonkey.com.

Putting It All Together

As in previous chapters, this section presents you with several examples of research questions, along with possible related research designs, samples, and instrument/data sources. Again, the purpose is to help you to see how the elements of a research design are interconnected. Look at Table 7.2. Each row includes a question and possible associated design, sample, and data sources; however, some cells are left empty for you to fill in.

TABLE 7.2 ● Example Questions With Associated Research Design Elements

Research Question	Design	Sample	Data Sources
What are the literacy practices among high school teachers in district X?	Descriptive	Stratified sample of 100 teachers across the district high schools	
What is the relationship between the literacy practices of high school teachers and student performance on state reading tests?	Correlational	Stratified sample of 100 teachers across the district high schools	
What is the relationship of gender and computer competency test scores of seventh graders?	Causal comparative	Random sample of seventh graders at a middle school	
What are the views of parents toward year-round schooling?		Convenience sample of parents in car pool lane and from school directory at two schools	Personal and phone interviews
What is the relationship of parent demographics with their views of year-round schooling?		Random sample of parents in directory at two schools	Phone interviews and school district database
What is the relationship between teachers' experience and their attitudes toward inclusion?		Convenience sample of high school teachers	Mailed questionnaire

The example questions in Table 7.2 also illustrate the differences in questions and data sources that may be associated with descriptive, correlational, and causal comparative research. You will also notice that the research topic is similar in rows 1 and 2 and in rows 4 and 5 of the table, but the questions, design, sample, and data sources may be different. Again, these examples illustrate how your questions lead you in making the important decisions about the connectedness of the rest of your research design. Can you figure out which data sources could be used in rows 1–3 and what kinds of designs are illustrated in rows 4–6?

In row 1, the best data source might be a mailed questionnaire; this would certainly be the most efficient option. In row 2, a good data source may also be a mailed questionnaire, but you would likely have to access state test scores from the district database. In row 3, a district database would also need to be accessed. In row 4, the research question, as well as the sample described and data sources, suggest a basic descriptive study, whereas in row 5, those pieces of information suggest correlational research and, in row 6, causal comparative research.

Summary

As in all types of research, it is very important that you determine your purpose at the outset of your work. In descriptive research, as well as in correlational or causal comparative research, clarifying the purpose of your study will guide you in all phases of the research process. In descriptive, correlational, or causal comparative research, you must write good questions, select a proper sample, create a reliable and valid instrument or target a useful extant database, and then carry out appropriate methods of data collection. Moreover, it is important to understand the type of data you want to collect so that you can later carry out a suitable analysis plan. Analysis procedures for descriptive research are discussed in Chapter 11.

Discussion Questions

1. What are some similarities and differences among basic descriptive, correlational, and causal comparative research?
2. What kind of information might best lend itself to a categorical question, and what kind of information might best lend itself to a scaled item on a questionnaire?
3. Name one situation in which a stratified sample might be helpful to you.
4. Under what conditions might you choose to conduct a personal interview, and under what conditions might you choose to administer a written or online questionnaire to collect descriptive data?

Your Research Project in Action

1. Restate your research question.

2. What type of sampling will you select for your research project?

   _____

   _____

3. Why is your choice of sampling appropriate for answering your question?

   _____

   _____

4. Identify five questions/items you could include on a survey that might address a research question of interest to you.

   A. _____

   _____

   B. _____

   _____

   C. _____

   _____

   D. _____

   _____

   E. _____

   _____

5. What scale(s) is (are) the most appropriate for your previous five questions?

   _____

   _____

6. How might categorical questions be appropriate in your survey?

   _____

   _____

7. How will you ensure construct validity in your questions?

   _____

   _____

8. How will you ensure access to your participants?

   _____

   _____

9. How do you plan to address nonresponse in your research project?

   _____

   _____

Further Reading

Salkind, N. J. (2016). *Exploring research* (7th ed.). London: Pearson.

 This book provides an overview for conducting and writing research studies, particularly in the social and behavioral sciences. The author focuses on the data collection and analysis process and what those data signify. An introduction to the software program, SPSS, is also provided. Steps for creating a professional written product are included for quick reference. In addition, the book highlights the importance of research in relation to several different fields of study and how that research has helped advance those fields.

References

Alreck, P. L., & Settle, R. B. (2004). *Survey research handbook* (3rd ed.). New York: McGraw-Hill/Irwin.

Fowler, F. J. (2013). *Survey research methods* (5th ed.). Thousand Oaks, CA: Sage.

Gall, M. D., Gall, J. P., & Borg, W. R. (2006). *Educational research: An introduction* (8th ed.). Boston: Allyn & Bacon.

Mills, G. E., & Gay, L. R. (2015). *Educational research: Competencies for analysis and applications* (11th ed.). London: Pearson.

Salkind, N. J. (2016). *Exploring research* (7th ed.). London: Pearson.

Literature Examples

Boudah, D. J. (2018). Evaluation of intensive reading strategies intervention for low-performing adolescents with and without learning disabilities. *Insights into Learning Disabilities*, 15(2), 149–159.

Frazier, D. K., & Trekles, A. M. (2018). Elementary 1:1 iPad implementation: Successes and struggles during the first year. *Journal of Educational Technology, 46*(4), 463–484.

Kotrlik, J. W., & Redmann, D. H. (2005). Extent of technology integration in instruction by adult basic education teachers. *Adult Education Quarterly, 55*(3), 200–219.

Porfeli, E., Wang, C., Audette, R., McColl, A., & Algozzine, B. (2009). Influence of social and community capital on student achievement in a large urban school district. *Education and Urban Society, 42*(1), 72–95.

Wood, C. L., & Gabas, C. M. (2017). Young Spanish-English speaking children's reading attitudes in relation to language skills. *Educational Research, 59*(4), 408–425. DOI: 10.1080/00131881.2017.1373028

8

Creating a
Research Proposal

The Purpose of a Research Proposal

Your understanding of the information and concepts presented in the first seven chapters of this book has prepared you to write a research proposal. Given the sequential nature of this guidebook to carrying out a research project from start to finish, you will now be presented with a series of steps to complete a research proposal, prior to chapters that discuss analyzing and interpreting your research data. To begin, let's answer three basic questions: What is a research proposal? What are the parts of a research proposal? What does a research proposal look like?

What Is a Research Proposal?

Most simply, a **research proposal** is a written rationale and plan for conducting research. A researcher typically creates a proposal prior to conducting formal research, whether the research is to be done as part of the requirements of a graduate school program or professional responsibilities, or the proposal is part of an application for grant funding. Educators who conduct research in their classrooms, schools, or other related settings may or may not be required to write a written proposal. Nonetheless, writing a proposal is valuable for helping education researchers think through their purpose and methods, as well as giving other stakeholders a document they can use to provide feedback to the researcher before the actual work begins.

What Are the Parts of a Research Proposal?

A research proposal typically includes three key parts:

1. A description of the problem or phenomena to be investigated

2. A review of relevant literature

3. A section on research methods, which would include information on design, procedures, and potential analyses

A list of references and appendixes would likely be attached also. Not coincidentally, these three parts of the proposal would most likely form the basis for the first three chapters of a graduate program thesis or dissertation, followed by the completed results and discussion. You should already be familiar with these three parts from previous chapters in this book and perhaps from other coursework as well. Following is a brief review of the first two parts, followed by a more extensive discussion of the critical aspects of design, procedures, and analysis.

What Does a Research Proposal Look Like?

Within the framework of the three major parts of a proposal, some variance is appropriate depending on the type of research proposed. That is, the titles of the parts or sections may be a little different, depending on whether your proposed research is descriptive (e.g., based on a survey, factor analysis, or qualitative investigation) or experimental (e.g., pretest-posttest comparison, single-subject, or multivariate analysis). It also may vary depending on the requirements of your university (if you are writing for a major project, thesis, or dissertation) or of a funding agency (if you are writing a grant proposal).

Figure 8.1 illustrates the table of contents from a dissertation proposal. You will note that the major headings are pretty self-explanatory, and they generally follow the format and parts mentioned earlier. That is, the methods are divided into more than one section, and an additional section is devoted to expected outcomes. The methods information regarding design, procedures, and potential analyses is detailed across sections 3.0, 4.0, and 5.0, rather than simply placed in one section. The last major section, titled "Expected Outcomes," was additionally required as part of this graduate proposal. Including such a section is not a bad idea, since it prompts the researcher to project the value of the research, as well as tie the research methods and procedures back to the originally stated problem. Later in this chapter, you will read narrative excerpts from another dissertation proposal, following a brief

---

FIGURE 8.1 ● Sample Table of Contents for a Research Proposal

TABLE OF CONTENTS

review of what is included in the problem identification and literature review sections, as well as what is involved in identifying and stating a research question. Following that, we will describe the method portions of the proposal.

Identifying a Problem

As you have learned, the process of conducting research begins with identifying a problem. In Chapter 2, you learned about the nature of a research problem, where you might get ideas for a problem to investigate, and the importance of narrowing down or focusing on a particular problem to address. A research problem or phenomenon (as it might be called in many forms of qualitative research) is the topic you would like to address, investigate, or study, whether descriptively or experimentally. It is the reason or interest for engaging in your research. Carefully defining a problem is particularly critical for designing and implementing effective experimental interventions.

Investigating and Identifying Relevant Literature

Searching, identifying, and analyzing relevant literature was previously addressed in Chapters 2 and 3, but now you should focus primarily on two of the reasons for conducting a literature review: (a) to pinpoint an area of further study, and (b) to provide a rationale/background for study.

As noted earlier, if you are interested in a particular topic, a literature review may simply reveal that little or no research exists on your topic. In one example from Chapter 2, you may recall that if you reviewed the literature on the outcomes of learning strategies, you would find quite a bit, but if you reviewed test-taking strategies in particular, you would find very little. Such limited existing research would add to the importance of conducting research on test-taking strategies. You might also discover that little research exists on your topic specifically with regard to a population of interest to you; for example, adolescents. Therefore, a literature review not only provides you with an opportunity to review the existing literature on a given topic but also a chance to create support or a rationale for engaging in a particular area of proposed research. Such persuasive information may be valuable in a proposal. Follow the guidelines in Chapters 2 and 3 for conducting a literature review in conjunction with your research proposal.

Identifying a Research Question

Tentative research questions are often written prior to conducting a literature review. After conducting a literature review, however, you should be in a much better position to write specific research questions, based on your knowledge about previous research or where gaps may exist in previous studies.

From Chapter 2, you will recall that a research question is a way of expressing your interest in a problem or phenomenon and that you may have more than one research question, depending on the complexity and breadth of your proposed work. It was suggested that the characteristics of a good research question are that it is clear and specific, refers to the problem or phenomena, reflects an intervention in experimental work, and notes the target population or participants. You have learned that a research hypothesis follows a research question and that sometimes a question can be directional and include a null hypothesis as well.

By taking the time to think through and write good questions and hypotheses (when appropriate to the method), you provide direction and a link to the next section of your proposal, the research design and method.

Identifying a Research Design and Method

The good research questions and hypotheses that you write will foreshadow important parts of your research design and method. Take another look at two questions and hypotheses first presented in Chapter 2.

> *Question*: Do students in Algebra I classes who engage in the XYZ curriculum perform significantly differently on state tests than students who do not participate in that curriculum?

> *Possible hypothesis*: Students who participate in the XYZ curriculum in Algebra I classes will perform significantly differently on state achievement tests than students who do not participate in that curriculum.

> *Question*: Do general education and special education teachers evaluate student homework differently, based on five criteria?

> *Possible hypothesis*: General education and special education teachers evaluate student homework significantly differently on each of five given criteria.

Not only is the problem noted in the questions and addressed in the hypotheses, but the method is clearly foreshadowed. That is, in each case, the participants and variables are noted. In the first question, the participants are Algebra I students, and the second includes general and special education teachers. Regarding measured variables, the first question states that the difference in performance will be measured by the state test. In the second question, the difference will be measured based on some set of criteria. In the question about Algebra I students, an intervention variable is mentioned also (the XYZ curriculum).

In the next section of this chapter, you will learn about decisions that you need to make about research design and important features or concepts of your method. Additional decisions need to be made with regard to topics addressed in Chapters 5, 6, and 7 on designing and conducting research also, namely your purpose and objectives and identification of variables and data sources.

What Is Your Purpose and What Are Your Objectives?

Your research design is directly related to the purpose and objectives of your research. Whether your research is qualitative, descriptive (quantitative), or experimental, you should have a pretty good idea of your purpose and at least some of your related objectives after you have found your topic, looked at the literature, and written at least one research question. That is, if your research question was something like *What is the nature of teacher attrition in rural schools?* or *Why do rural schools have such a hard time keeping good teachers?* your research will be descriptive. From that point, you would need to decide whether you wanted to investigate this phenomenon qualitatively or perhaps through a survey and/or interviews. If you opted for a qualitative study, your objectives might be to understand better the stresses and other factors that contribute to teacher decisions to leave rural schools. You may have other, related objectives as well, such as to understand the connection between a rural school and the community in which the school is located.

If, on the other hand, you reviewed the literature and decided you wanted to answer a question such as in our earlier example, *Do students in Algebra I classes who engage in the XYZ curriculum perform significantly differently on state tests than students who do not?* you would clearly be headed for an experimental design. Certainly, then, your objective would be to experimentally test your hypothesis: *Students who participate in the XYZ curriculum in Algebra I classes will perform significantly differently on state achievement tests than students who do not participate in that curriculum.* In addition, your objectives might include looking at the performance of various student subgroups in response to the XYZ curriculum.

Having read these points about purpose and objectives, you may wonder if purpose and objectives can precede identification of specific research questions. The simple answer is yes. Certainly, as noted in an earlier chapter, researchers often come to research activities with interests in a topic that underlie purpose and lead to initial research questions. Therefore, it may well be that it is easier or more sensible to decide on your purpose and objectives before writing your formal research questions.

What Variables Do You Want to Investigate?

As said before, your research question foreshadows your method, including variables that you may wish to address. Variables, sometimes called factors, are the changeable parts of studies that researchers may want to manipulate or measure. Thus, they are discussed in the context of experimental research and quantitative descriptive studies and rarely, if ever, in qualitative or naturalistic research. So, for example, if your experimental research question is *Do students in Algebra I classes who engage in the XYZ curriculum perform significantly differently on state tests than students who do not?* you have identified your independent variable and your dependent variable. An independent variable is the intervention or what may be called the treatment. It is the conditions created by the researcher in an effort to create a result. In the example, engagement in or learning the XYZ curriculum is the independent variable. A dependent variable is the outcome of the intervention, measured in some way. If an independent variable is deemed the cause, a dependent variable is the effect or result. In the example, student performance is the dependent variable, as measured by the state test scores. To keep the two terms straight, you could think of it this way: in this example, the scores *depend* on the implementation of the independent variable.

What Data Will You Collect?

Experimental Study. In an experimental study, after making decisions about your variables and before launching an intervention, you also need to consider the question "How will I measure the outcomes (dependent variable) of the intervention (independent variable)?" or perhaps even "How will I know if my intervention has been successful?"

Review and consider the data collection methods discussed in Chapter 5, including the sample tools. You must determine the instruments or tools you will use, as well as how and when you will use them and to whom you will administer the instruments. This all needs to be documented in your research proposal. You may need to create a measurement instrument to capture a behavior that you wish to observe, or perhaps you will never have to administer an instrument but can rely on permanent records, such as state test scores. Salkind (2016) suggested the following:

- When you select a dependent variable, try to find measures that have been used before and in which validity and reliability have already been established.

- If you are using a test, be sure to get the latest version and that its norms match those of your participants.

- If a given test administration requires special training, be sure to consider the time, effort, and expense that may be involved.

You can find information about many widely used tests online at the Buros Institute (marketplace.unl.edu/buros/) and the Educational Testing Service (www.ets.org).

Qualitative Study. If you are proposing a qualitative study, then let's go back to our example investigation of teacher attrition in rural schools. In this case, your data might come from interviews with teachers, administrators, parents, students, and local residents. You might also look at salary scales in the school district and elsewhere, in addition to other permanent records. You could spend time observing the nature of the buildings and interactions among people in them.

Quantitative Description. As an alternative, you could choose to investigate the problem of teacher attrition in rural schools through quantitative description. It would make sense to collect school district data on teacher attrition, including demographic data, and then formally interview or survey teachers in one or more rural districts (those who have stayed and those who have not) in order to try to correlate certain teacher and district characteristics or variables with attrition.

Mixed Data Sources. You may design a study that includes mixed data sources, such as quantitative data from state tests as well as interviews or naturalistic observations of students who participate in the XYZ curriculum. It may help you to **triangulate** your analysis, a concept introduced in Chapter 6, if doing so is manageable.

For more information on experimental, qualitative, and descriptive research designs, be sure to refer to Chapters 5, 6, and 7. You will have to apply your understanding of the information in those chapters when preparing your research proposal.

Identifying Research Procedures and Plans

In this section, you will learn about some of the critical "nuts and bolts" to consider in a research proposal and that you certainly need to respond to in your study. These details include who will participate; how your study will take place; when, where, and how you will collect data; and potential costs of the study.

Who Will Participate in Your Study?

Decisions about who will participate in your study are critical. First of all, let's make sure to review your understanding of a couple of basic terms. A **participant** is a person from whom you collect data, whether the data are interview responses, observations, test scores, or something else. A population is the larger group of people to whom you wish to generalize, apply, or relate the results of your research. The concept of population is more applicable to experimental and quantitative descriptive research.

At this point, you certainly have some target group in mind for your study, based on your research question(s). Your target group may be high school algebra students, general and special education teachers, or rural educators, for example. Your goal is to find participants that have characteristics similar to those of your target population. This is particularly important with experimental research and quantitative forms of descriptive research. Without such a match, you will not be able to make any valid claims about the applicability or generalizability of your results to the larger experimental or descriptive population of interest. For instance, if you were to study the behavior of students in elementary settings, the findings would have, at best, limited meaning or generalizability for middle or high school students. Thus, as you think about who should be included in your study, you must consider two key activities that enhance potential generalizability: sampling and recruiting.

As noted earlier in the book, sampling is the selection of participants for a study. There are many procedures for sampling, including forms of probability sampling and nonprobability sampling. The most notable type of probability sampling is random sampling. The most common form of nonprobability sampling is convenience sampling. McMillan (2015) as well as others has written extensively about the pros and cons of each form of sampling. You need to think about how you will sample participants from your target population and include that plan in your research proposal. You may also want to refer back to the Chapter 3 discussion on analyzing literature and take another look at the section on what to look for in the description of participants.

Once you decide on your sample, your research proposal needs to include a plan for recruiting participants. **Recruiting** is the process by which you target, inform, and secure the commitment of participants to be included in your study. For starters, you may be wondering where to look and ask. Certainly, local schools, agencies, civic groups, professional organizations, and parent organizations are a few places to consider. For the sake of convenience, local may be better, but if, for example, you are situated at a research university located in a relatively small community, the schools may be "researched out." That is, you may find it more difficult to locate willing participants in schools where a great deal of research has already taken place in recent years.

So, let's say you have a target group of students at a certain school. You will likely need to get permission from the administration to recruit students and their parents.

In a later section of this chapter, you will learn about securing voluntary consent and, in particular, the protection of human research participants. For the sake of discussion now, let's just say that you will need to address consent by providing information about your study and consent forms for participant signature. In your proposal, you likely will need to provide a copy of your participant information and consent forms, as well as a letter of support for the study from an administrator or authority at the school, district, or agency where data will be collected.

Where Will the Study Take Place?
Where and How Will the Data Be Collected?

Let's say you have proposed to study the performance of algebra students in response to the XYZ curriculum. You may have a school in mind, whether it be one where you currently work or another. After you have approached the administration and secured their support, think about where you anticipate introducing the experimental intervention and collecting the data. Most likely, you will introduce this in a classroom or several classrooms. Still, not all data collection may take place there. You might collect some observational data there, but dependent on your design and objectives, you might administer some performance tests outside the classroom, maybe after school in another location. You also may need to collect some data from permanent files elsewhere in the school, such as previous state test scores. You may want to think about and plan for simple ways of collecting the data, such as using protocol sheets.

If you were conducting a descriptive study on the homework evaluation practices of general and special education teachers, on the other hand, you would need to think about place as well as time to conduct interviews. If you administered a written survey, you might just need to get addresses and mail or e-mail the surveys. If you were conducting phone or face-to-face interviews, you would clearly want an uninterrupted place at school or elsewhere. Again, think about and plan for simple ways of collecting the descriptive data, such as using consistent, standardized, protocol sheets. You will need to document these decisions in your research proposal.

How Will the Intervention Be Implemented?

If you are conducting experimental research, some of your most important decisions will concern how to conduct the intervention, including answers to these questions: Who will provide or administer the intervention? How often, how long, and under what conditions will the intervention occur (e.g., during class discussions, during lecture or small-group work, as a review before a test)? Clearly, if part of your purpose for the research is to address a need or problem, you want to flesh out your plan to conduct the intervention. Moreover, if you want the research to be generalizable and, ultimately, shared with others with similar problems, you want to document your procedures well. You may find it helpful to refer again to the Chapter 3 discussion of what to look for in the description of research procedures. That chapter included this exemplary description:

> . . . instructors administered a sentence construction probe at the end of each session. Instructors handed out a sentence construction probe to students and said, "I will give you 1 min to write as many complete sentences as you can.

Work quickly and accurately. Do you have any questions?" Instructors answered any questions and read any words requested by students. Students were told to pick up their pens or pencils and begin. A countdown timer was started. At the end of 1 min, sentence construction probes were collected and no feedback was given. Sentence construction probes had 10 unique picture-word prompts displayed across two pages. The pictures on sentence construction probes were not used during intervention (i.e., no overlap between probes and intervention materials). The pictures were approximately 4 cm by 4 cm with two to three words accompanying each picture. Three lines to the right of each picture-word prompt provided space for student responses. Figure 1 shows examples of picture-word prompts and formatting of probes (Datchuk, 2017, p. 65).

For the purposes of a research proposal, you will, of course, be writing in the future tense, but it bears mentioning that when you later conduct your research, you should note any modifications to your procedures so that when you complete your final report, thesis, or dissertation document, you can be clear.

What Instruments Need to Be Created or Acquired?

We previously noted that the measurement of some dependent variables may require specific instruments or tests that you have to create or acquire. You need to think carefully about this possibility, and document your decisions in the proposal. If you are conducting descriptive research, whether nonexperimental/quantitative or qualitative, such decisions are equally important to document in your proposal.

When Will the Study Take Place?

It may be very helpful, if not required, for you to draft a timeline for conducting your study. Include the activities associated with research design and method, as well as procedures and plans. To communicate your timeline clearly to your readers (e.g., committee or reviewers), create a table or spreadsheet with the activities and dates for conducting the activities. Table 8.1 is a sample study timeline.

What Will the Study Cost?

For the sake of a thesis or dissertation, you may not have to outline a detailed budget, although for a research grant proposal you will. You will read about a few other differences between a grant proposal and a thesis or dissertation proposal a little later in this chapter. For the time being, let's say you are writing a thesis or dissertation proposal for your university. At a minimum, you should consider whether and what costs may be associated with your proposed research activities. If you are conducting a mail survey, you at least have to consider the cost of postage. If you have to drive a distance to record interviews or observe participants, you will likely have gas costs. If you have to acquire a particular test, it may cost you something as well. If you want to offer a participation stipend or incentive to teachers, students, or others, you should budget that also. These are just a few examples to consider.

TABLE 8.1 ● Sample Study Timeline

XYZ Research Study

Timeline and Milestones Chart

(+ = continuing work; * = milestone to be reached)

	Aug	Sep	Oct	Nov	Dec	Jan	Feb	Mar	Apr	May	Jun	Jul
Obj. 1: To design a system of care for students with LD and E/BD with schools and advisors	+	+	*									
Obj. 2: To train and support teachers in implementation of learning strategies and behavioral support techniques			+	+	+	+	*					
Obj. 3: To develop and implement a program of career and extracurricular activities exploration			+	+	+	+	+	+	+	*		
Obj. 4: To develop and implement a program of individualized coaching/mentoring			+	+	+	+	+	+	+	*		
Obj. 5: To develop and implement a MOST Team to support individual students with mild disabilities			+	+	+	+	+	+	+	*		
Obj. 6: To evaluate the model in terms of academic, behavioral and social, and systemic effects on participants	+	+	+	+	+	+	+	+	+	+	+	+
Obj. 7: To disseminate information and materials to schools, agencies, and other audiences								+	+	+	+	+

This section of the chapter has highlighted some of the important decisions regarding research procedures and plans that you need to consider in your proposal. For further information on experimental and descriptive research designs, be sure to refer back to Chapters 5, 6, and 7.

Identifying Potential Analyses

As already noted, the goal of this chapter is to walk you through the process for developing a research proposal, regardless of the type of research that you may propose. The data you plan to collect may take several forms. Therefore, you will need to identify potential ways of analyzing the data, as well as how you might display them. Although this book is not a substitute for taking research methods as well as statistics courses, it contains separate chapters that will highlight ways of analyzing and interpreting experimental data, qualitative findings, and quantitative descriptive research. The next part of the chapter will briefly highlight statistical analysis and then discuss descriptive research analysis that uses qualitative methodology.

What Statistics or Qualitative Procedures Will You Use?

Once more, let's go back to the experimental research example regarding an algebra curriculum and the question, *Do students in Algebra I classes who engage in the XYZ curriculum perform significantly differently on state tests than students who do not?* Since you understand what the independent and dependent variables (or factors) are, based on our earlier discussion, you now need to decide how many levels of each variable you propose to study. Next, you will need to consider which statistic you will use for initial analysis, as well as any other statistic you might want to use for follow-up analysis. In this example regarding the algebra curriculum, you know that you are going to compare mean performance on the dependent variable for two groups, at least initially. Therefore, in your proposal, you would probably opt to suggest conducting an analysis of variance.

If you supposed that another possible factor might covary with results, such as math aptitude, you might run an analysis of covariance. If you wanted to include other variables, such as age, socioeconomic status, gender, or previous teachers, in your analysis in order to look at interaction effects, you would probably choose to run a multivariate analysis of variance. In your proposal, you would stipulate what the other variables were and how many levels of each you planned to investigate; for example, two levels of gender within the two groups (experimental and comparison).

The information in this brief example may be a bit much for some of you to consider at this point, particularly without one or more previous research methods or statistics classes. Referring to Chapter 9 for further explanation and more examples may be helpful. You are also encouraged to access other resources such as Gall, Gall, and Borg (2006) and, of course, your university statistics professor.

For interviews that contain transcribed comments, you might plan to use constant comparative or grounded theory methods (e.g., Corbin & Strauss, 2014) for analysis. You should detail how you intend to either use qualitative analysis software or hand sort information and comments in topical categories in order to analyze patterns that exist within or between categories. A similar plan of analysis also would be reasonable for observational field notes, or written commentaries made in a log. Remember that qualitative analyses are described in greater detail in Chapter 10. In addition to Corbin and Strauss (2014), other excellent resources for qualitative analyses are Lincoln & Guba (1985), Patton, (2015), and of course, your qualitative methods professor.

You may also decide to propose mixed methods of analysis that include statistical as well as qualitative analysis, depending on your research questions and data collected. If this approach is warranted as well as feasible for you, it is an excellent way to provide a strong, triangulated analysis of your data.

What Is the Expected Outcome or Importance of the Study?

Sometimes a research proposal will include a closing section that includes that researcher's thoughts on the expected outcomes and/or importance of the study. In this section of your proposal, you have an opportunity to project the outcomes of your analyses, as well as how and why this research will be important to your area of education or the larger field of education. While you won't predict exact statistical outcomes, you can discuss the direction of results you expect. If the inquiry is qualitative, you may project the themes you expect to emerge from the data. Whatever your specific area of interest, you can also discuss why and how you expect the results to be important, and tie your expected results back to your literature review and research question(s).

Protection of Human Participants

Earlier in this chapter, in the discussion of sampling, you briefly read about the protection of research participants. Prior to initiating your research, and typically as a part of any research proposal in which new data will be collected on individuals, information and consent forms must be designed to ensure the protection of those involved. If school-aged students are to be involved, written consent from parents must be obtained in addition to student assent. If participants only include teachers, then you need to design content forms them as well. If you are at a university, your institution typically has a human subjects/participants review board that sets standards and requirements for information and consent forms, which must be created and received prior to data collection.

Often you will need to follow a process for approval of your research from the human participants committee prior to receiving approval of your entire research proposal from your thesis or other project oversight committee. Thus, it is helpful to know a little bit about the information that the human participants committee is looking for. While the committee will want to understand your proposed research, they are most interested in information about protection from harm, informed and voluntary consent, confidentiality, and data storage.

Protection From Harm. To ensure protection from harm, you need to include specific information about what you are going to do in your research and what, if any, risks are posed to the participants. Particularly in research with children, you want to assure the committee and the participants that in no way will participants ever be exposed to risk of physical or emotional harm, and that the study will not negatively affect their educational performance. To ensure informed and voluntary consent, you will need to provide information to the participants about what they are expected to do or provide in the study; this must be written in the language required by your university, which will stress that participation is strictly voluntary and without coercion.

Confidentiality. To ensure confidentiality, you need to provide information to the human participants committee and in the participant's letter of informed consent about how you will keep any information about participants private. This often includes promises of anonymity with regard to reporting the results of the study (e.g., specific names will not be attached or associated with any data reported or disseminated). You should tell the human participants committee and the participants how and where the data will be stored to ensure confidentiality. Finally, information and consent forms should include names and phone numbers for participants and/or parents to contact if they have questions or concerns. You may need to create several drafts in order to get forms approved. Refer to Figures 8.2 and 8.3 for sample parent and student information and consent forms.

Eventually, once your research is approved by your human research participants committee and your thesis or dissertation committee, you'll want to set dates for printing, distributing, and collecting the signed forms. In addition, you may want to buy a bag of candy or something to distribute to participants as an incentive for returning the signed forms.

Pilot Testing

Having identified a problem to research, relevant literature, research questions, a design and method, plan and procedures, as well as potential analyses, you may decide to run a pilot test of your study with a smaller sample of participants and/or a smaller number of variables and questions. Your research advisor may suggest that you do this, particularly if your problem, question(s), and/or method is not well defined. Also, if you have the time and opportunity, you may decide to do so to clarify things for yourself. If you do conduct a pilot study, you should use procedures closely defined as those in your original proposal. That way, you should have the opportunity to learn as much as possible about your research problem or phenomenon, questions, and how you might need to revise your methods and procedures.

Putting It All Together

As you read at the beginning of this chapter, a research proposal typically includes the following:

- Description of the problem or phenomena to be investigated

- Review of relevant literature

- Section(s) on research methods, which would include information on design, procedures, and potential analyses

- List of references and appendixes

FIGURE 8.2 ● Parent Information and Consent

PARENT INFORMATION About Research of Reading Strategy

The University of ABC supports the practice of protection for individuals participating in research. The following information is provided so that you can decide whether you wish your son/daughter to participate in a study being conducted at his/her school that has been approved by the school. You should be aware that even if you agree to participate, you are free to withdraw your consent at any time without fear of future prejudice against you or your child.

Over the next six to eight weeks, one of your son's/daughter's teachers will be participating in a research study that will include approximately 20 students. The purpose of the study is to evaluate a new instructional strategy to help students better understand what they read. If you agree to allow your child to participate in this study, your son/daughter will participate in classes as he/she normally would. For approximately 15 minutes each day, teachers will teach a strategy to better understand what students read in textbooks. After learning the strategy, your son's/daughter will provide written and verbal explanations of what he/she has understood about information presented. The responses your son/daughter gives, information from standardized tests that he/she has taken, and other descriptive information (such as age, gender, and race) will be gathered from school records and integrated. From this analysis, I will be able to determine the effects of the new strategy. Please be assured that confidentiality will be maintained throughout the study. Your son's/daughter's name, as well as the names of other students, will never be given to anyone, nor will any names be associated in any way with the research findings. All written responses and notes from responses will be securely stored in Intelligence Hall at UABC and destroyed at the conclusion of the project.

Your son's/daughter's participation is requested but is strictly voluntary. Participation will have no negative effect on your son's/daughter's school program. Feel free to call me at the phone number listed below if you have any questions. I appreciate your cooperation very much and hope that you will participate in the project. <u>Please sign both, identical orange and white copies. Return the white copy to your son's/daughter's teacher and keep the orange copy for your reference.</u>

Sincerely,
Daniel J. Boudah, PhD
Principal Investigator
555-1221

_____

_____

_____

FIGURE 8.3 ● Student Information and Assent

STUDENT INFORMATION About Research of Reading Strategy

The University of ABC protects people who participate in research. We are inviting you to be included in a study being conducted at your school and approved by the school. Even if you agree to be in the study, you are free to stop being in the study at any time. Participating or not participating will not affect the help you receive at school.

Over the next six to eight weeks, one of your teachers will be included in a research study to help you and about 20 other students. The purpose of the study is to test a strategy to help you better understand what you read. If you agree to be in this study, you will be in classes as you normally would. For about 15 minutes each day, teachers will teach you a strategy to understand better what you read in textbooks. After you learn the strategy, you will talk and write about what you understood about what you read. Your answers, along with information from tests that you have taken, and other information, such as age, gender, and race, will be gathered from school records and analyzed. From this analysis, I will be able to decide if the new strategy really worked. Your privacy is important. Please know that your name, as well as the names of other students, will never be given to anyone, nor will any names be used in any way with the research findings. All written and spoken answers will be locked up at Intelligence Hall at UABC and destroyed when the project is over.

Your parents may have given their permission, but you still do not have to be in the study. Whether you are in the study or not, it will not affect your grades or school program in any bad way. Feel free to call me at the phone number listed if you have any questions. I appreciate your help very much and hope that you will be in the study. <u>Please sign both orange and white copies (they say the same thing). Return the white copy to your teacher and keep the orange copy for yourself.</u>

Sincerely,
Daniel J. Boudah, PhD
Principal Investigator
555-1221

_____

_____

_____

STUDENT ASSENT

This research study has been reviewed and approved by the Human Research Participants Review Board at the University of ABC. If you have any questions regarding your rights, you can also contact Dr. I. M. Smart, Chair, Human Research Participants Review Board at 555-3454 or chair@abc.edu. All notes and tapes will be locked up at Intelligence Hall at UBC and destroyed when the project is over. Thank you for helping us with this important research; it should help teachers to teach you better and help you to be a better learner now and in the future.

I have read the information about the research that is being conducted by researchers from the University of ABC at my school. I have had all my questions answered, and I voluntarily assent to be in the study, including permission for researchers from UABC to look at my school records only for information such as test scores and other information such as age, gender, and race. I understand that all information about me will be private and that the published findings will in no way use my name or identify me. Even though I am volunteering to be in the study, I am free to stop being in the study at any time.

Check one of the two sentences below:

☐   I agree to participate in this study.

☐   I choose not to participate in this study.

Student signature: _____   Date: _____
Student name: _____
Teacher name: _____   School: _____

IN THEIR OWN WORDS

Tamara Nimkoff, upon completing her PhD

The research proposal serves the dual purpose of trial run for your upcoming study and sales pitch to your committee. The proposal may be the first time that you articulate the full scope of your research plan from topic to methods. Use it to develop your own understanding and development of your topic and as a blueprint for what the final dissertation document will look like. As research progresses, it has a way of taking on a life of its own. Coming back to the proposal can keep you on course and grounded within the scope of your topic. That being said, I don't know anyone whose study proposal was a perfect foretelling of the actual research to come. It's not so much a contract of details and fine print with your committee as a contract of intention and scope. That's where the proposal as sales pitch comes in. The proposal serves as the first piece of evidence to your committee that you know what you are doing and where you are going. It's also the point where you sell them on the "so what"—why what you are planning to do is important. Don't hesitate to get specific feedback from your advisor and anyone else you can find (friends, family, coworkers) about the degree to which your proposal reflects a person who knows what she is doing and why. It will build confidence in yourself and your committee regarding the project to come.

You also learned that the titles of the parts (often called chapters) may be a little different, depending on whether your proposed research is descriptive or experimental, on the requirements of your university, on whether you are writing a thesis or dissertation, and on the requirements of a funding agency to which you may be submitting a grant proposal.

Figure 8.4 includes excerpts from each of the primary chapters of a student's dissertation proposal: the introduction and problem statement, literature review, research questions, and methods and procedures. While many examples have been provided regarding how you should prepare these parts of your proposal, and this abridged example does not match every specification outlined, it still would be helpful for you to read the abbreviated portions from this proposal so that you can see how the parts might fit together.

Proposal Format

Though you should look elsewhere for a primer on good writing style, let's highlight two key concepts that can immensely enhance the quality of your proposal: organization and clarity. In other words, regardless of how good your idea or the content of your proposal is, you must be able to communicate it well.

Organization is the first key to a well-written proposal. Use headings and subheadings to help readers (particularly your proposal committee members) to understand how you have organized not only the chapters of your proposal but the content within the chapters as well. Be sure that the form of the headings is as consistent as possible (e.g., use of questions or statements, verb tense). Also, arrange the sections and subsections with headings that follow a logical sequence.

FIGURE 8.4   ●   Excerpts From a Dissertation Proposal

Educator Implementation of a Professional Development Program: Examining Level of Use in Relation to Program Participation, Professional Background, and Organizational Engagement

A Dissertation Proposal by Tamara A. Nimkoff

The problem statement:

Policy makers have begun articulating the role that ongoing professional development is expected to serve in preparing our nation's educators for an increasingly diverse student population. These expectations are being translated into legislation and federal mandates for states to follow. The assumption is that when educators participate in high-quality professional development, they will then effectively implement the strategies and techniques they have learned in their own classrooms.

Organization of the literature review:

The context for the study is set through a review of literature related to teacher quality and its impact on student learning. Next, select literature on professional development models is reviewed, including research related to defining high-quality professional development and the development of educators' abilities to meet students' diverse learning needs. Select research related to change in teacher practice is then examined, including the measurement of educator implementation following professional development experiences.

Research Questions:

The central research questions are (1) What levels of use do educators report two to four years following participation in a professional development program aligned with standards of high quality? (2) How are those levels of use associated with (a) educators' participation in varying phases of the professional development program, (b) educators' professional backgrounds working with students with learning difficulties, and (c) educators' perceptions of organizational engagement?

Method:

One-on-one telephone interviews are to be used to gather data in the full study. All interviews will be conducted by the investigator, using a [levels of use] interview protocol. It is estimated that the interview will take approximately 40 minutes to complete. Following consent of each interviewee, each telephone interview will be recorded and imported into qualitative data analysis software. In addition to the primary investigator, one additional individual will independently rate a sample of the interview transcripts.

Analysis:

In addition to qualitative analysis, statistical relationships among variables will be examined by calculating chi-square-based analyses, and measures of association will be calculated to examine the strength and direction of variable relationships.

Source: Nimkoff (2003, pp. 7–8, 11, 44, 52)

Clarity is the second key. Use advance organizers at the beginning of sections and even lengthy subsections so that your audience continues to follow your organization and can see the relationship of various parts. Relatedly, use transition statements between sections and subsections (e.g., *nevertheless, that said, furthermore*) to help your audience follow the logic of your proposal's organization.

For further guidance, referencing *The Elements of Style* by Strunk and White (1999) and the *Publication Manual of the American Psychological Association* (2010) will be helpful. The APA manual, typically recommended by graduate programs in education, includes hundreds of pages of guidance and excellent examples of editorial style.

A Research Proposal Versus a Grant Application

This chapter has been devoted to writing a research proposal under the presumption that most of you are preparing for a major project, thesis, or dissertation in your graduate program. Some of you may also write proposals in order to acquire money to conduct research. This is a wonderful experience, one that can greatly enhance any graduate program, provide you with resources to conduct your research (always helpful!), and perhaps prepare you for professional responsibilities beyond your graduate program. That said, writing for grant money can be both the same and different from writing a research proposal for a project, thesis, or dissertation.

Whether you are writing for a grant from public funds (local, state, or federal) or from a private foundation, the first thing you need to understand is *you must follow the directions*. Institutions that offer money may vary greatly in terms of what kinds of information they require from the grant writer.

For instance, a recent request for federal research grant applications included criteria for proposals in six areas: significance, project design, project personnel, adequacy of resources, management plan, and project evaluation. In the significance section, which was worth 15 of a possible 100 points, the application requested information about the potential contribution of the proposed project to increased knowledge or understanding of educational problems, issues, or effective strategies; the likely utility of the products (such as information, materials, processes, or techniques) that would result from the proposed project; and the potential replicability of the proposed project in a variety of settings.

In the project design section (worth 20 points), grant writers were asked to describe the goals, objectives, and outcomes to be achieved by the proposed project; the extent to which the design of the proposed project was appropriate to, and would successfully address, the needs of the target population or other identified needs; a conceptual framework underlying the proposed research or demonstration activities; a review of the relevant literature; a high-quality plan for project implementation and the use of appropriate methodological tools; the extent to which the proposed project would be coordinated with similar or related efforts and with other appropriate community, state, and federal resources; and the extent to which the proposed project would encourage parental and consumer involvement.

The project personnel section (also worth 20 points) was to address the extent to which the applicant encouraged applications for employment from persons who were members of groups that have traditionally been underrepresented and the qualifications, including relevant training and experience, of key project personnel and project consultants or subcontractors.

In the adequacy of resources portion of the proposal (10 points), the researcher was to discuss the adequacy of support, including facilities, equipment, supplies, and other resources from the applicant organization or the lead applicant organization, and the extent to which the costs were reasonable in relation to the objectives, design, and potential significance of the proposed project.

The management plan section (10 points) was to describe the adequacy of the plan to achieve the objectives of the proposed project on time and within budget, including clearly defined responsibilities, timelines, and milestones for accomplishing project tasks, and the adequacy of procedures for ensuring feedback and continuous improvement in the operation of the proposed project.

In the project evaluation portion (25 points), the researcher was asked to write about the extent to which the methods of evaluation were thorough, feasible, and appropriate to the goals, objectives, and outcomes of the proposed project; the extent to which the methods of evaluation included objective performance measures that were clearly related to the intended outcomes of the project and would produce quantitative and qualitative data to the extent possible; and the extent to which the evaluation would provide guidance about effective strategies suitable for replication or testing in other settings.

In addition to reading the instructions carefully, many times it is also helpful to talk by phone or in person with the appropriate people at the agency or foundation, or participate in a webinar, to get helpful information about what the agency or foundation is looking for in research proposals, including copies of previous winning proposals.

Summary

Writing a research proposal is an important task. You must create a document that clearly spells out what you are doing, as well as a rationale for why you are doing it. You will also need to document the details of how you will carry out your plan, when you intend to carry out the particulars of your plan, and who will be involved. Writing a research proposal requires you to synthesize many of the skills and much of the knowledge gained through engaging in the tasks outlined earlier in this book. Whether you are writing for a graduate committee or a panel of grant proposal reviewers, a great deal of work is involved. It's also important to remember that when you actually carry out the research and conduct the analysis, some of your proposed ideas may change. By communicating a written plan, you set an effective course for yourself.

Discussion Questions

1. What is a research proposal?

2. What are the three parts of a research proposal?

3. What are the differences among a participant, target group, and population? How are all three relevant in your research study?

4. What is the difference between a research proposal and a grant application?

5. Are consent/assent forms really necessary? Why or why not?

Your Research Project in Action

1. What is your research purpose?

   _____

   _____

2. What are the research questions associated with your purpose?

   A. _____

   B. _____

   C. _____

3. Did your literature review suggest that your purpose and questions have been heavily or little studied? How could this enhance the importance of your research study?

   _____

   _____

   _____

4. What variables are you investigating?

   Independent variables:

   _____

   _____

   Dependent variables:

   _____

   _____

5. To investigate these variables, will you have to create a measurement instrument or administer an instrument, or is an instrument not required?

   _____

   _____

6. What is your timeline for recruiting participants?

   _____

   _____

7. What is the expected outcome of your study?

   _____

   _____

8. How do your potential biases on the topic affect your hypothesis of the expected outcome?

_____

_____

9. How are you ensuring the protection of human participants?

_____

_____

Further Reading

American Psychological Association. (2010). *Publication manual of the American Psychological Association* (6th ed.). Washington, DC: Author.

For students and researchers alike, this is your handbook for addressing questions regarding formatting, references, headings, use of abbreviations, editorial style, use of figures and tables, and many other items essential to producing high-quality technical and professional writing. This book, now in its sixth edition, is the standard in the field of educational research.

References

American Psychological Association. (2010). *Publication manual of the American Psychological Association* (6th ed.). Washington, DC: Author.

Corbin, J., & Strauss, A. (2014). *Basics of qualitative research: Techniques and procedures for developing grounded theory* (4th ed.). Thousand Oaks, CA: Sage.

Gall, M. D., Gall, J. P., & Borg, W. R. (2006). *Educational research: An introduction* (8th ed.). Boston: Allyn & Bacon.

Lincoln, Y. S., & Guba, E. G. (1985). *Naturalistic inquiry.* Newbury Park, CA: Sage.

McMillan, J. H. (2015). *Educational research: Fundamentals for the consumer* (7th ed.). London: Pearson.

Patton, M. Q. (2015). *Qualitative research & evaluation methods* (4th ed.). Thousand Oaks, CA: Sage.

Salkind, N. J. (2016). *Exploring research* (7th ed.). London: Pearson.

Strunk, W., & White, E. B. (1999). *The elements of style* (4th ed.). London: Pearson.

Literature Examples

Datchuk, S. M. (2017). A direct instruction and precision teaching intervention to improve the sentence construction of middle school students with writing difficulties. *The Journal of Special Education, 51*(2), 62–71.

Nimkoff, T. A. (2003). *Educator implementation of a professional development program: Examining level of use in relation to program participation, professional background, and organizational engagement.* Unpublished Dissertation Proposal. University of North Carolina at Chapel Hill.

Analyzing and Interpreting Experimental Research

As discussed in Chapter 5, there are numerous designs for conducting experimental and quasi-experimental research, and it is important to understand the purposes and characteristics of various designs in order to determine the best fit for your research question, to address validity issues, and to select ways to measure your dependent variable. You learned that experiments that have treatments but do not use random assignment to make comparisons are called quasi-experiments. Quasi-experimental research, like experimental research, attempts to determine if an independent variable (e.g., a new writing technique) has a direct impact on a dependent variable (e.g., student performance on a state test). If done well, the results of quasi-experimental research can be generalized beyond the context in which it was conducted to similar situations. For our purposes, both experimental and quasi-experimental research will continue to be referred to simply as experimental research.

Without a good match between your research question and design, your analysis may raise questions from readers, at best, or be nonsensical to readers, at worst. In Chapter 5, several commonly used group research designs were highlighted, as well as single-subject designs. From there, you learned how each design might (and should) match with a research question and measurement. In this chapter, let's take the next step by thinking about how to analyze and interpret your experimental data. The purpose is not to provide you with the kind of thorough treatment of each type of analysis that you should receive in additional or previous graduate coursework and through other, more detailed resources but to provide you with some reasonable, worthwhile, and understandable examples of analyses. Let's start by briefly reviewing key concepts regarding experimental data.

Experimental Data

The data collected from experimental research are **quantitative**. That is, you collect numerical data on the variables studied in order to conduct your analysis. You might, for example, collect and analyze numbers from actual performances on a state test (e.g., 78, 95, 62). Then, rather than using descriptive statistics such as averages or range of scores to highlight general information about a sample or population, you would use **inferential statistics** to look at differences between conditions in an experimental intervention or across/between experimental groups. Therefore, you must understand the type of data you have collected in order to select the appropriate inferential statistic to analyze your data.

Types of Data

As described in Chapter 5, there are four basic types of data: nominal, ordinal, interval, and ratio. These are also referred to as scales of measurement or levels of data. Why is it important to review the types of data? In short, to make sure you collect the right type of data that will allow you to run analyses appropriate to your research design. This, in turn, will allow you to make valid inferences in response to your research questions.

Selecting a Statistic Consistent With Your Design and Appropriate to Your Data

Statistical tests rely on certain assumptions in order to provide accurate information. For example, Rumrill, Cook, and Wiley (2011) suggested that in order for a researcher to compare means between groups, each group must represent a separate sample from the population and, thus, must have similar variances. If this assumption is violated (or not tested), the results of the statistical analyses will be invalid. That said, the purpose of this section is not to detail the dozens of possible **statistical test assumptions** but, more practically, to help you pull together research questions and designs with measurement, possible data sources, and statistics, going one step further than in Chapter 5. In this way, you will continue to see the relatedness of parts of your research as consistent with the steps previously outlined for designing your study:

1. Create your research question(s).
2. Determine your variables and address validity.
3. Select your design.
4. Decide on your measurement and data to collect.
5. Determine how you will analyze the data.

First, though, it is important to highlight a few other things regarding inferential statistics to enhance your understanding of the material in this section as well as in the later section on interpreting analyses. Inferential statistics help you to determine the likelihood that a hypothesis is true. In addition, and more technically, inferential statistics help the researcher to discern the probability of being wrong in rejecting the null hypothesis. The probability is called the **level of significance**, and it is set by researchers in each experiment *prior* to the analysis. Researchers indicate probability with the small letter p or the Greek letter for alpha (α). For example, $p < .05$ would be literally interpreted as a 5% probability that the statistical differences in an analysis would be due to chance or measurement error. In other words, there is a 95% statistical probability that differences *are* due to the intervention. An alpha level set at .05 is very common in educational research.

In addition to satisfying the underlying assumptions of a statistical test, selecting or matching the right statistic depends on the type of data you have and whether you want to, for instance, analyze differences in mean scores for the dependent variable across groups or conditions. You also should consider the number of groups and independent variables you are analyzing, as well as the number of dependent variables in your analysis. This all goes back to your research questions and purpose, of course. See Gall, Gall, and Borg (2006) or Mills and Gay (2015) for detailed descriptions of statistical tests, both parametric and nonparametric. Table 9.1 gives a brief summary of commonly used statistics and their purposes.

To illustrate how to match inferential statistics with your research questions and design information, this chapter uses the same research examples from "Putting It All Together" in Chapter 5, extending the examples by noting the type or level of data that measurement might yield and statistics appropriate to each research example. To begin, take a look at Table 9.2. This table is similar to Table 5.1 in Chapter 5, but information has been added in the *Possible Data* column for each example and another column has been added to the far right for statistics appropriate to each example. Now let's highlight the information that has been added to each row.

In the first row, the research question is *Can students find main ideas after learning a new reading strategy?* This question is matched with a posttest-only design. The data simply consisted of correct or incorrect responses, which are nominal data. If the correct responses were converted to a percentage of the total number of responses or items, the data would be interval level. You can't use inferential statistics with the posttest-only design, however, because you have only one experimental condition

TABLE 9.1 ● Common Statistics and Their Purposes	
Statistic	**Purpose**
t test	To test differences between mean scores of only two groups, using interval or ratio data; typically, one independent variable and one dependent variable
Analysis of variance (ANOVA)	To test differences among multiple group scores, based on the variance in the groups, using interval or ratio data; typically, one independent variable (with multiple levels) and one dependent variable
Two-way ANOVA	To test differences between two independent variables, their interactions, and effect on dependent variable
Analysis of covariance (ANCOVA)	To account/control for differences among groups related to the dependent variable before making comparison on dependent variable (i.e., to make them equal prior to analysis)
Multivariate analysis of variance (MANOVA)	To analyze differences among groups on several dependent variables at once
Chi-square	Nonparametric test to compare frequencies occurring in different groups or categories, using nominal data; typically, one independent variable and one dependent variable (although may be multiple levels)

and one group. Thus, you can't measure any differences from other conditions. This is why some (e.g., Gall et al., 2006) hesitate to classify the posttest-only design as an experimental design. Still, you are left with an opportunity to communicate findings in terms of descriptive statistics, which might include frequencies, mean scores, or percentages.

In the second row, the research question *Can students more accurately find main ideas after learning a new reading strategy?* is matched with a pretest-posttest design. If the data consisted of correct or incorrect responses, they would be nominal data. If, as in the last example, the correct responses were converted to a percentage of the total number of responses or items, the data would be interval level. If you wanted to compare differences in the pretest and posttest data with *nominal* level data, you could use a **chi-square analysis** to compare differences in the number of correct responses in the two conditions. If you decided to compare differences in the percentage correct in each condition using *interval* level data, you would probably want to use **analysis of variance (ANOVA)** to compare the differences in the percentage correct on the pretest and posttest. The *t* test (noted in Figure 9.1 and discussed in more detail in Chapter 11) only tests means between two groups, whereas an ANOVA tests scores for multiple groups (typically three or more) at the same time. ANOVA tests the null hypothesis that the mean scores of multiple groups are equal.

TABLE 9.2 ● Putting It All Together

Research Question	Design	Measurement	Possible Data	Statistic
Can students find main ideas after learning a new reading strategy?	Posttest-only	Verbal prompt to identify main ideas from text passages	Correct or incorrect responses; percentage correct (nominal or interval level)	Descriptive statistics (e.g., frequencies, means, percentages)
Can students more accurately find main ideas after learning a new reading strategy?	Pretest-posttest	Prompts from a standardized test	Correct or incorrect responses; percentage correct (nominal or interval level)	Chi-square or analysis of variance (ANOVA)
Do students in Algebra I classes who engage in the XYZ curriculum perform significantly differently on state tests than students who do not?	Comparison group	Prompts from state tests	Correct or incorrect responses; scaled scores; percentage correct (nominal or interval level)	Chi-square or ANOVA
Does the performance of children from different racial backgrounds differ in response to a new writing technique?	Factorial	Writing prompt	Rating scores (e.g., based on organization of ideas, details, mechanics) (ordinal level)	Two-way ANOVA, analysis of covariance (ANCOVA), or multivariate analysis of variance (MANOVA)
Do gifts and other recognition affect the frequency with which middle school teachers refer students to the principal for behavioral issues?	Time-series	Discipline referrals over designated period of time	Frequency counts (nominal level, if statistically analyzed pretest-posttest intervention)	Visual display typically used; chi-square if statistically analyzed
Do students with disabilities engage in a greater number of positive classroom behaviors after positive notes and phone calls are regularly made to home?	Single-subject	Event recording protocol	Frequency count (nominal level)	None; visual display typically used

In the third row of Table 9.2, the research question is *Do students in Algebra I classes who engage in the XYZ curriculum perform significantly differently on state tests than students who do not?* The researcher elected to use a comparison group design. If the data consisted of correct or incorrect responses, they would be nominal data. If, as in the preceding two examples, the correct responses were converted to a percentage of the total number of responses or items, the data would be interval level. If you wanted to analyze the pretest and posttest data for the experimental group or the differences in posttest scores for the experimental and comparison groups on with nominal level data, you could use chi-square analysis to analyze the number of correct responses. If you decided to analyze the difference in the percentage correct between the pretest and posttest for the experimental group or the differences in posttest percentage scores for the experimental and comparison groups (interval data), you would probably want to run two separate analysis of variance (ANOVA) procedures. That would allow you to look at the differences in the percentage correct in each analysis.

In the fourth row of Table 9.2, the research question is *Does the performance of children from different racial backgrounds differ in response to a new writing technique?* This employed a factorial design. In this example, there were multiple factors; the new writing technique and racial background were the independent variables. The dependent measure yielded rating scores based on characteristics of organization of ideas, details, and mechanics. If the characteristics were holistically integrated into a single rating, you would have one dependent variable, whereas if they were separate ratings, you could look at multiple dependent variables. If you had but one rating to analyze, you would probably want to use a **two-way ANOVA** because there are two independent variables. That said, if you suspected that another variable, such as differences in the length of the written compositions during the pretest and posttest, might account for some of the difference in or covary with our dependent variable, you might want to try to account for that. To do so statistically, you would use **analysis of covariance (ANCOVA)**.

Furthermore, in a more complex analysis, if you did indeed have several ratings to analyze as separate dependent variables, you could use **multivariate analysis of variance (MANOVA)**, or if you wanted to account for any suspected covariance, you would use multivariate analysis of covariance (MANCOVA).

A significant point regarding more complex experimental analyses bears mentioning. When researchers statistically analyze multiple variables, independent or dependent, results yield what are called main effects. If the main effects are significant, this means that there is a statistical probability that some independent variable, or level of the variable, was related to an effect on some dependent variable, or level of the dependent variable. Interaction effects may exist also; these are the interaction of the effects of two or more independent variables on a dependent variable. If there are significant interaction effects, you may not know which pair or pairs of dependent means are different. For instance, subgroups of children may have responded differently to the intervention, accounting for some of the differences in scores on the dependent measure. Furthermore, if another one of the research questions addressed testing participating children from a particular racial or ethnic background (e.g., Latino) to see if they performed significantly different on a writing test than another group (i.e., independent variable with multiple levels), you would have to conduct an additional

post hoc statistical test such as the Bonforonni, Tukey, or Scheffe. Such analyses are follow-ups to the original statistical analysis. See, for example, Gall et al. (2006) for a thorough explanation of main effects, interaction effects, and post hoc tests.

Now then, the fifth row in Table 9.2 lists the question *Do gifts and other recognition affect the frequency in which middle school teachers refer students to the principal for behavioral issues?* A time-series design was selected. If you wanted to look at preintervention and postintervention differences in what would be equivalent to a pretest-posttest design using the frequency counts of principal referrals, you would have nominal level data that could analyze using a chi-square test. Typically, however, time-series designs are not analyzed with statistical tests but rather through visual displays that are similar to the display of single-subject design data.

The question in the last row of Table 9.2 is *Do students with disabilities engage in a greater number of positive classroom behaviors after positive notes and phone calls are regularly made to home?* The purpose is to investigate responses to the intervention by individual students using a single-subject design. The frequency count of the number of positive student responses in each of the experimental conditions would then be plotted in either a single visual display as in Figure 5.4 or, if desired, a multiple-baseline graph like that illustrated in Figure 5.5 (both those figures are found in Chapter 5).

Even after spending much time and effort implementing a research study, some researchers will find no pre-/posttest or between-group differences on their dependent measures. That can be good or bad. If the result is not what the researcher wanted to find, he may be tempted to "fish" for some evidence (any evidence) of change, using multiple or inappropriate statistical analyses. Each additional statistical test adds a potential level of error to the entire study, which may lead to false indications of change. As previously insisted, statistical tests should be consistent with your research question and hypothesis, as well as fit with your design, measurement, and data in order to increase validity in your study.

Interpreting the Results of Analyses

The goal of this portion of the chapter is to highlight ways of understanding and discussing the results of your analysis, provide you with some guidelines, identify and define some important values that appear in your results, and share a couple of examples of research results. To get from the selection of your statistical analysis to your results, however, you have to enter your data into a computer (assuming you're not going to do this by hand!) and run the actual statistical analysis. So let's first talk briefly about data entry.

Data Entry

Whether you are using Statistical Package for the Social Sciences (SPSS), Statistical Analysis Software (SAS), or some other statistical software, you'll obviously need to be familiar with how the software works in order to enter your data as well as run your analyses. The purpose here is not to provide you with a tutorial on using statistical software but merely to offer an example of the kinds of things you need to understand in order to complete your research project. See https://www.spss-tutorials.com/basics/ for

FIGURE 9.1 ● **Sample SPSS Data Set**

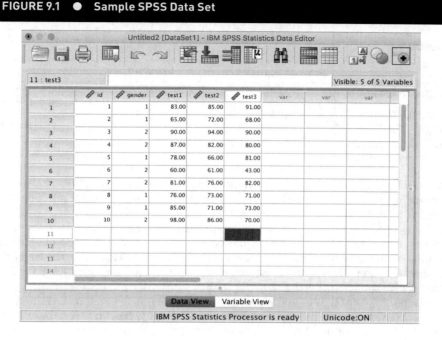

free with its helpful online tutorials for using SPSS software, or you can stream videos that will introduce you to the software and walk you through using it, for example, https://www.youtube.com/watch?v=ADDR3_Ng5CA.

In a new statistical program data file, you will not only need to enter the numbers from your data collection accurately, but more importantly, you will need to know how to use the software menus and commands in order to carry out critical tasks such as labeling your variables and defining the type of data and range of values entered in each column. These tasks are all part of the data entry process and, without them, knowing where to click on ANOVA or another analysis won't result in any output that you can use as results. Figure 9.1 is a sample SPSS data set.

Understanding Output From Statistical Analysis

Depending on what analysis you run, you will get different information in your output. Figure 9.2 shows a portion of output, including outcomes that you will need to report in the results section of your research report.

In this example, the output from an ANOVA yielded the *F* value and the level of significance. Earlier in the chapter, it was mentioned that the level of significance is the probability that statistical differences in an analysis would be due to chance or measurement error. In this case, the level of significance, noted in the far right top portion of the output table, is.003. This would mean that there is three-tenths of 1 percent chance that the results were due to chance or error. Alternatively, there is a

FIGURE 9.2 ● Sample Output From Statistical Analysis

ANOVA

	Sum of Squares	df	Mean Square	F	Sig
Between Groups	322.650	2	161.325	6.559	.003
Within Groups	4567.490	44	171.467		
Total	6001.765	46			

99.7% statistical probability that differences are due to the intervention. This sounds convincing, particularly if you had set a maximum alpha level of .05 for rejecting your null hypothesis and determining statistically significant results.

The second important value is the **F statistic** or F ratio. This statistical value, employed to obtain the level of significance of your analysis, is the ratio of between-groups variance to within-groups variance (Gall et al., 2006). Generally, the larger the F value, the more likely your significance level will be lower and your results will be statistically significant.

In reporting your results, you will need to report the F statistic, alpha level, and one other set of values from the output table, the **degrees of freedom** (df on the example output table). These numbers, used in the statistical calculation of the level of significance, are approximately equal to the number of participants for whom you have entered data (McMillan, 2015). Thus, in reporting the F statistic, your report of results should list the degrees of freedom between groups and within groups in the following way, followed by the level of significance: $[F(2, 44) = 6.559, p < .003]$.

Reporting Experimental Results

As discussed in Chapter 3, the results section of an experimental research article can be difficult for educators to navigate because it is where statistical outcomes are reported. The results section is meant to be simply a factual statement of data-based outcomes, whereas the discussion section is the researcher's interpretation of the outcomes. The results section should provide answers to the research questions and state the effects of the intervention rather than include extraneous data or opinions of the researcher. In Chapter 3, you learned what to look for in the results section of research reports; this is also your blueprint for what to include when you write your report. In this section, let's take a look at a couple of sample excerpts from research results with an eye toward some of the elements mentioned in Chapter 3 (i.e., explanation of outcomes or effects for different groups/populations, explanations of results with minimal jargon) and, of course, a clear understanding of what the results mean.

> For the entire group of students, there was a significant difference between the mean total raw scores on the GRADE pretest (M=37.39, SD=8.02) and posttest (M=47.40, SD=9.58); t(203)=16.47, p=.000. The effect size was 1.13 (Cohen's d),

a large effect size. There was a statistically significant difference between the mean raw scores on the TOSCRF pretest (M=76.05, SD=23.47) and posttest (M=103.87, SD=24.90); t(205)=19.30, p=.000. The effect size was 1.15 (Cohen's d), a large effect size. (Boudah, 2018, p. 154)

Let's say that this was your analysis using a t-test. There were some differences—but were they significant? Most likely they were, given the low probability values reported. In the next example of the results of a statistical analysis, a MANOVA was chosen for the analysis because of multiple factors. Note that there were main effects, but not interaction effects.

In order to compare the research groups' word-reading performances, two MANOVAs were conducted, computing the research group (students with poor and proficient syllable-awareness skills) as the between-subject factor, and the level of processing (LoP) (real and pseudo-words) as the within-subject factor.

The main effect of LoP was statistically significant for both reaction times [F(1,88)=29.74, p<.05, n²=.25] and error rates [F(1,88)=26.65, p<.05, n²=.22], suggesting that participants processed real word stimulus pairs significantly faster and more accurate than pseudo ones (Table 5). The main effect of groups was also statistically significant for both reaction times [F(1,88)=8.55, p<.05, n²=.08] and error rates [F(1,88)=16.22, p<.05, n²=.15), indicating that overall students with proficient syllable awareness skills processed written words significantly faster and more accurate than students with poor syllable awareness skills. The interaction between LoP and research groups was statistically not significant for both reaction times [F(1,88)=2.89, p>.05, n²=.03] and error rates [F(1,88)=.02, p>.05, n²=.00, suggesting that the error rates and reaction times differences between the two participant groups were similar for both real and pseudo word reading performances. (Guldenoglu, 2016, pp. 434–435)

One additional statistic that was noted in the first excerpt is effect size. You may see this reported in studies as well, and it may be necessary for you to compute and report, depending on the expectations of your advisor. **Effect size** is the degree of difference between groups or conditions or, perhaps, the magnitude of difference in outcomes among experimental groups or experimental conditions (McMillan, 2015). There are several different effect size calculations, but one that is commonly used is called Cohen's *d*. It can be computed either in your software as Cohen's *d* for two groups, in a stand-alone online calculator, or it can be computed fairly simply by hand by dividing the difference in the means of two groups by the pooled standard deviations for the two groups. The equation is *d* = M1 – M2 / SDpooled. A value of .02 is considered a small effect size, a value of .05 is considered a medium effect size, and a value of .08 or higher is considered a large effect size.

Data Displays

In addition to using inferential statistics, you can employ tools to extend and enhance your data analysis, as well as help you to clearly share the outcomes of your analysis with others. Particularly with group design research, data displays provide you with the advantage of visually analyzing data, as in single-subject designs, and literally "seeing" any differences that may be present in ways different from what *F* values or *p* values may (or may not) show you. Two useful displays include frequency tables (which are typically illustrated in bar graphs) and histograms.

Nominal or categorical data can be used to develop **frequency tables**, which provide you and your readers with information about how often a certain response occurred or the percentage of responses that the frequency indicates. For example, if you analyzed a data set regarding the pretest and posttest performance of students in response to a main idea strategy, you may get some nominal or categorical data that you want to illustrate with a frequency table. See Figure 9.3 for an example of a frequency table, in this case for student off-task behaviors over 5 days.

Frequency and percentage tables are relatively easy to create and can give you some interesting and helpful information in a format that is easy for you and your readers to interpret. In some cases, frequency counts or means placed in table format may be very helpful to illuminate patterns in data. Other visual data displays can help readers see the "big picture" and uncover relationships and patterns also. For example, another way to compare groups is through the use of bar graphs or bar charts referred to as **histograms**. Histograms illustrate the relationship between two variables whose measures yield continuous scores, such as SAT scores (Gall et al., 2006). See Figure 9.4 for an example histogram.

Many computer database or spreadsheet programs are fairly easy to use and enable even novice researchers to compile and display their numerical data in tables, graphs,

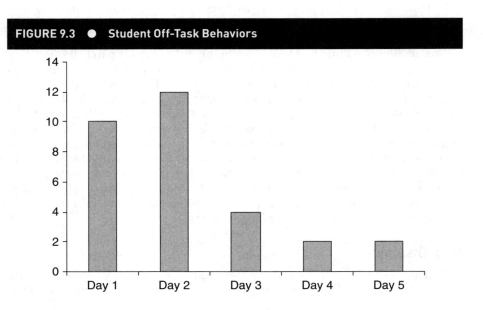

FIGURE 9.3 ● Student Off-Task Behaviors

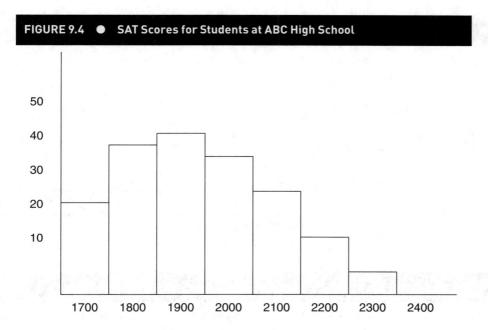

FIGURE 9.4 ● SAT Scores for Students at ABC High School

or charts. While data displays are primarily a way of illustrating descriptive data sets, they can also be valuable in enhancing your analyses and assisting in the presentation and discussion of the results of experimental research.

Single-Subject Designs

As described in Chapter 5, single-subject designs, also called *single-case designs*, are not group designs, and attempt to investigate the effects of an intervention on individuals rather than aggregating individual differences. The dependent variable receives repeated measurement before and after the intervention, and data are graphed for visual analysis rather than statistically analyzed.

As you recall from Chapter 5, the What Works Clearinghouse (2014) contended that without three demonstrations of an effect (i.e., use of an A-B-A-B design), there is no evidence of a causal relationship between the independent and dependent variables. That said, WWC standards also provide excellent guidance with regard to analyzing and interpreting effects in single-subject design data as displayed in graphs. Specifically, in order to assess the pattern of effect within each condition of a design and thereby assess internal validity, researchers should consider level, trend, and variability. **Level** is determined by computing the mean score for data points and drawing a straight horizontal line to represent the mean score within each condition. See Figure 9.5. **Trend** is determined by computing the slope of the best-fitting straight line for the data within each condition. See Figure 9.6. **Variability** is most easily determined by identifying the range of data points and drawing straight lines within each condition on the graph representing the upper and lower ends of the data range. See Figure 9.7.

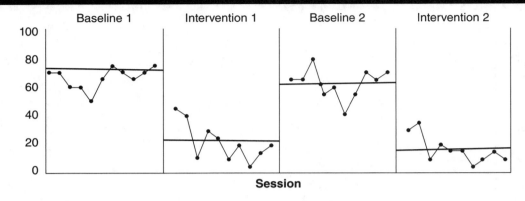

FIGURE 9.5 ● **An Example of Assessing Level with Four Phases of an ABAB Design**

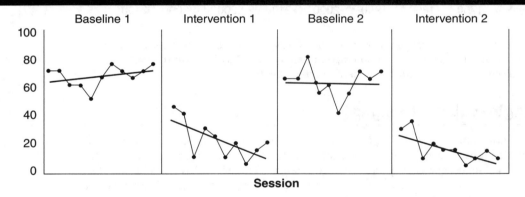

FIGURE 9.6 ● **An Example of Assessing Trend in Each Phase of an ABAB Design**

In short, by analyzing level, trend, and variability, the researcher can better ascertain the effect of the intervention. Similar to Figure 9.5, if the data levels are visibly different and consistent in baseline and intervention conditions, this suggests internal validity (i.e., causal determination). Likewise, if trend lines are similar in baseline and intervention conditions, and moving in the direction consistent with the objective of the intervention (e.g., downward in intervention conditions if the goal was to decrease behavior), then this suggests internal validity as well, similar to Figure 9.6. If variability within conditions is limited rather than dramatic, as in Figure 9.7, this also supports causal determination. To this point, some student or novice researchers often wonder how many data points are necessary within a condition. Three is a number

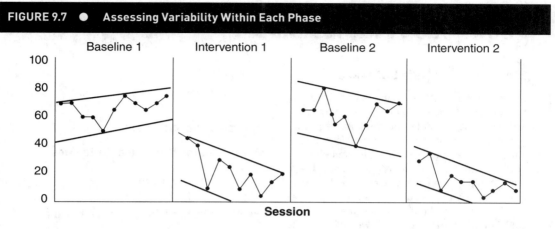

FIGURE 9.7 ● Assessing Variability Within Each Phase

often suggested, however, more than three data points may be necessary, especially in the initial baseline condition. More than three data points may be needed in the initial baseline condition in order to establish measurement stability (i.e., a consistent trend with limited variability) prior to proceeding to the intervention.

The WWC (2014) also suggests examining data patterns across conditions, including a) whether there are overlapping data points between baseline and intervention conditions, b) the immediacy of change between the last three data points in one condition and the first three data points of the following condition, and c) the general visual consistency of data within baseline conditions and intervention conditions.

Discussing Experimental Results

The discussion section of experimental research articles provides the researcher with an opportunity to interpret the results for readers. Of course, the researcher should not misinterpret the data or attempt to apply the results to people or settings that are dissimilar. This means that even though the methods of an experimental study may be chosen to promote generalizability across situations, a single study cannot have "the answer" for all teachers, students, classrooms, schools, or other educational environments. Therefore, the reader should consider the credibility of the interpretation, as well as commentary about the limitations of the study, implications for practice, and future research needs. In Chapter 3, you learned about what to look for in the discussion section of a research report. That same discussion and list applies when you are writing up your own conclusions.

The following is an example of part of the discussion of a study. Look for the elements described in Chapter 3 (i.e., interpretation does not infer beyond the results

TECHNOLOGY IN RESEARCH

Statistical Analysis Software

Statistical analysis is virtually impossible to do by hand with large data sets. Fortunately, there are a number of different computer software packages to manage and analyze experimental data. Most packages accomplish similar tasks, but may use different platforms, provide different outputs, or be easier/more difficult to use. One of the advantages of using a software package is that, in addition to doing the statistical calculations, most programs will also create charts, graphs, figures, and tables that can be dropped into your research report.

Statistical analysis software does require an understanding of both statistical concepts and the way in which the software requires you to organize your data at entry. In fact, there are many books, courses, and journals that are devoted to the topic of statistical analysis software. Therefore, the author provides an overview of the capabilities of two of the most widely used analysis packages, as well as where you can find more information.

One of the most widely used software packages is SPSS. There are multiple versions and add-ons for a base program in SPSS, and there are also professional and student versions. SPSS can generate the following:

Descriptive Statistics

- Cross-tabulations
- Frequencies
- Descriptives
- Descriptive ratio statistics

Bivariate Statistics

- Means
- *t* tests
- ANOVA
- Correlations

Nonparametric Tests
Prediction for Numerical Outcomes

- Linear regression

Prediction for Identifying Groups

- Factor analysis

Add-on modules and stand-alone software from SPSS offer much more for the data analysis stage, including these statistics:

- Inferential statistics (chi-square, pairwise comparisons of means and column proportions) in SPSS Tables™
- Categorical regression in SPSS Categories™
- Time-series analysis in SPSS Trends™

See spss.com for more information.

Another statistical software program that is widely used is SAS. It also has a base package with multiple add-ons and student and professional packages. The base package includes the following:

Analysis of Variance

- Balanced and unbalanced designs; multivariate analysis of variance and repeated measurements; linear and nonlinear mixed models

Regression

Categorical Data Analysis

Multivariate Analysis

Cluster Analysis

- Hierarchical clustering of multivariate data or distance data; disjoint clustering of large data sets; nonparametric clustering with hypothesis tests for the number of clusters

Nonparametric Analysis

- Nonparametric analysis of variance; exact probabilities computed for many nonparametric statistics
- Kruskal-Wallis, Wilcoxon-Mann-Whitney, and Friedman tests
- Other rank tests for balanced or unbalanced one-way or two-way designs

Survey Data Analysis

- Sample selection; descriptive statistics and *t* tests; linear and logistic regression; frequency table analysis

Study Planning

- Computation of sample sizes and characterization of power for *t* tests, confidence intervals, linear models, tests of proportions, and rank tests for survival analysis. PSS web application provides interface to this functionality.

Refer to the SAS website (sas.com) for more information.

When using inferential statistics, you may want to get support from a friendly, knowledgeable, and available statistician (unless you are one yourself). One of the hazards of using statistical software packages is that it is very easy to calculate statistics, but they may not be the "right" statistics. Also, the software does the calculating but not the interpreting. Therefore, the real work is still left to you.

previously presented, limitations or shortcomings are discussed, implications are noted), as well as a general sense of your understanding.

Results overall from the present study suggest a combined direct instruction and precision teaching approach is an effective and efficient way to improve the simple sentence construction of middle school students with disabilities and writing difficulties. The multi-component intervention featured targeted instruction on small instructional units (i.e., capitalization, punctuation, and simple sentences) to improve the accuracy of sentence construction and timed practice with picture-word prompts to promote fluency. Results extend research on direct instruction and precision teaching approaches to improve written expression (Datchuk, 2016; Datchuk et al., 2015; Viel-Ruma et al., 2010; Walker et al., 2005; White et al., 2014) . . .

The present study has several limitations. First, no data on the maintenance of experimental effects were collected. It is not known if gains in CIWS persisted following completion of intervention. Prior studies found gains maintained following completion of intervention (Datchuk, 2016; Datchuk et al., 2015), but maintenance has not been investigated with the altered procedures used in the present study. (Datchuk, 2017, pp. 69–70)

Note how the researchers discussed the results, in this example, without mentioning statistical values, instead focusing on what they think the values mean, particularly in reference to the research questions.

IN THEIR OWN WORDS

Howard DuBose, master's thesis writer

Analyzing data from research in your own classroom and with your own students is not always as easy as you might expect. For one thing, you know the data and the subjects so well that getting the proper detachment and distance can be difficult. Your students may be anonymous to your readers, but to you they are "your kids."

A related difficulty occurs when you sometimes need to throw away data that are incomplete or corrupted. The conflict is that since you worked so hard to get the data, you want to keep every bit. You have to get on with your analysis, however, just as you would with data regarding complete strangers.

Statistical Conclusion Validity

Before concluding this chapter, let's think again for a moment about the construct of statistical conclusion validity. This is important to consider with regard to analyzing and interpreting experimental research. **Statistical conclusion validity**, as described in Chapter 4, is closely related to internal validity. It is based on reliable implementation of an independent variable, as well as appropriate and correctly used measures and statistics, in order to draw conclusions regarding the effect of the independent variable on the dependent variable. If, for example, researchers do not evaluate the **fidelity of treatment implementation**, they will not be able to say that the treatment was implemented reliably enough to know that it was the reason for the effects. In addition, if researchers measure the dependent variable with a measurement tool that is not very reliable, then it is difficult to defend the conclusion that the intervention caused change.

As another example of poor statistical conclusion validity, let's say a researcher taught students a strategy for solving mathematics word problems and then used a test to measure the skills of three students in the experimental group and two in the comparison group. After completing a statistical analysis of the difference between the two groups' scores, the researcher determined that the experimental group showed no significant difference from the comparison group on the measure. The researcher concluded that the strategy did not result in better performance and, therefore, was not successful in improving the students' word problem solving. Is that a valid conclusion? Maybe. But such a small sample may have contributed to **low statistical power**, or less likelihood that a statistical test could find significant differences. In addition, conducting only a posttest may have violated the statistical test assumption that the sample was, in fact, a separate but equivalent sample of the population. Both occurrences would increase the chance of a **Type II error** by the researcher (i.e., the researcher concludes that there are no experimental differences when there actually are). For more discussion of calculating **statistical power**, as well as Type I and Type II error, see Gall et al., 2006.

Putting It All Together

Table 9.2 includes several research questions presented in previous chapters and a possible design for each question. Each question and design is matched with a measurement strategy, possible data yielded by such measurement, and potential statistics that might be used in the analysis. Therefore, in each row, you should see the relationship of the critical parts of each example research design and be able to extrapolate to your own study.

Summary

The information presented in this chapter should help guide you from selecting an experimental research design and conducting your research, to analyzing and interpreting your data. As noted up front, however, the purpose of this chapter was not to provide you with the kind of thorough treatment of each type of analysis that you should receive in specific graduate coursework and through other resources. Rather, it was to help you better understand concepts of measurement and validity as they apply to experimental research analyses and then walk you through the process of selecting an appropriate statistic, entering data and interpreting results, and enhancing your analysis through data displays. Please keep in mind that inferential analyses of experimental research lead to statistical levels of significance, not necessarily practical levels of significance (McMillan, 2015). It is up to researchers and educators to work together to translate results into materials or resources that can be of substantive value and thereby have the potential to impact educational endeavors in the larger population.

Discussion Questions

1. Why is it so important to have your research questions, design, measurement plan, and data type(s) match or be aligned?

2. Locate a student version of SPSS at your university (many universities have site licenses for free student versions) and familiarize yourself with how to input data and run some analysis. You may want to look at https://www.spss-tutorials .com/basics/ for free with its helpful online tutorials for using SPSS software, or stream videos that will introduce you to the software and walk you through using it, for example, https://www.youtube.com/watch?v=ADDR3_Ng5CA.

3. Return to the two sample research report excerpts in the chapter section "Reporting Experimental Results." Take a second look at those excerpts and see if you can find the key elements of result sections noted in Chapter 3.

Your Research Project in Action

Take a look at your own research thus far and fill in the appropriate information in the table below, just like the examples in Table 9.2.

Research Question	Design	Measurement	Possible Data	Statistic

Further Reading

Mills, G. E., & Gay, L. R. (2015). *Educational research: Competencies for analysis and applications* (11th ed.). London: Pearson.
This is an excellent resource book. Used by many students in introductory research classes, it provides a thorough introduction to all forms of common research in education, including experimental, descriptive, and qualitative research. There are helpful examples, summary points, and activities in each chapter.

References

Gall, M. D., Gall, J. P., & Borg, W. R. (2006). *Educational research* (8th ed.). Boston: Allyn & Bacon.

Kratochwill, T. R., Hitchcock, J. H., Horner, R. H., Levin, J. R., Odom, S. L., Rindskopf, D. M., & Shadish, W. R. (2013). Single-case intervention research design standards. *Remedial and Special Education, 34*, 26–38.

McMillan, J. H. (2015). *Educational research: Fundamentals for the consumer* (7th ed.). London: Pearson.

Mills, G. E., & Gay, L. R. (2015). *Educational research: Competencies for analysis and applications* (11th ed.). London: Pearson.

Rumrill, P. D., Cook, B. G., & Wiley, A. L. (2011). *Research in special education: Designs, methods, and applications* (2nd ed.). Springfield, IL: Charles C. Thomas.

What Works Clearinghouse. (2014). *Procedures and standards handbook. Version 3.0.* Princeton, NJ: What Works Clearinghouse. (ERIC Document Reproduction Service No. ED544775)

Literature Examples

Boudah, D. J. (2018). Evaluation of intensive reading strategies intervention for low-performing adolescents with and without learning disabilities. *Insights into Learning Disabilities*, 15(2), 149–159.

Datchuk, S. M. (2017). A direct instruction and precision teaching intervention to improve the sentence construction of middle school students with writing difficulties. *The Journal of Special Education, 51*(2), 62–71.

Guldenoglu, B. (2016). The effects of syllable-awareness skills on the word-reading performances of students reading in a transparent orthography. *International Electronic Journal of Elementary Education, 8*(3), 425–442.

Analyzing and Interpreting Qualitative Data

Chapter Objectives

In this chapter, the reader will

- understand how to manage data from a qualitative inquiry.

- understand how to code data collected in a qualitative inquiry.

- identify techniques to analyse and interpret qualitative data.

- review examples of analysis of qualitative data.

In Chapter 6, you learned how to plan and begin a descriptive study using qualitative methods. In a qualitative inquiry, unlike experimental research, data analysis begins as soon as data collection begins. Qualitative methods force a researcher constantly to evaluate the available data in order to plan how to continue data collection. In this chapter, you will learn how to manage and code the data that are collected, as well as how to work through the continuous data analysis and interpretation process.

Data Management

It is important to remember that the data in a qualitative inquiry most often consists of words. When people talk about topics of importance to them, as they do in interviews, they generally use many words to get their descriptions just right. When researchers observe situations, they must describe all aspects of the context by using a great number of words. Words become paragraphs, paragraphs become pages, and pages become reams of paper (or huge data files). A researcher can easily become overwhelmed and give up, or miss important concepts. Data management and focus are extremely important in descriptive research that uses qualitative methods.

Some qualitative researchers begin the process of data analysis in large rooms, surrounded by paper. These researchers then use detailed coding systems to indicate interview or observation information, as well as page number, on each page of data. Once each page is marked, the researcher reads everything several times. Then, he begins to sort pages, paragraphs, or even sentences by patterns into **concepts** by placing them into piles on the floor. Next, he may cut out key phrases and paste them onto index cards for further sorting, slowly whittling ideas down to manageable amounts. There is always the unwelcome possibility of someone coming into the room with good intentions to clean things up (or alternatively, to mess them up).

Using Technology

Some researchers still prefer a process similar to that just highlighted. However, with today's technology, virtually everything a qualitative researcher does can be done electronically with the right software. This includes managing everything from observation notes to transcription of interviews to retrieving documents from websites on a laptop computer. Once all data are put into an electronic format or retrieved from electronic sources, a researcher can manipulate them using analytic software that will do as much or as little analysis as the researcher desires. Some programs will help develop categories and descriptive terms, present concepts graphically, and even connect categories. Other programs will allow someone to highlight information and organize it, much as in the paper-sorting process described above. It is best to become familiar with a few software programs, because different programs may fit different analytic procedures better. Many software packages are available, including Ethnograph, Atlas.ti, NVivo, and HyperResearch. See the *Technology in Research* section later in this chapter for a more in-depth look at NVivo.

Organizing Documents

As said throughout this text, research purpose and questions drive design, analysis, and reporting. Answers to questions about the process for organizing data should always go back to "What is the purpose, and what is the research question?" Here are some related questions to consider:

- Is the purpose to describe a single case of a person, program, or situation? If so, organize data by individual case. If the purpose is to describe several people's experience within a single program, then organize the data by each individual first and then conduct a cross-individual analysis.

- Is the research purpose to describe change? In that case, organize interviews and observations chronologically.

- Is the purpose to describe similarities and differences in situations? Then, organize by situation descriptors, such as teacher, content area, school, district, time of day, or condition.

Thinking through how to organize data is important for both paper documents and for electronic documents. If using a computer program to help with analysis, a researcher would want to make sure to create files that make analysis straightforward. For example, if you create individual files for each interview and for each observation, will the program allow you to analyze an interview and observation of a particular individual at the same time? If not, it will be difficult to organize your analysis by individual case. If you cut and paste paragraphs, phrases, or other parts of data into a separate document (say, a document with examples of a certain topic), will you be able to find the original document for each example? In short, you need to decide how you want to proceed with your analysis and, therefore, how you want to organize your data for use.

In qualitative research, the organizational system may change as more data are collected or as the researcher becomes more familiar with the data. In fact, researchers have been known to scrap their initial strategy and begin anew several times during the process. Process notes are extremely important and, therefore, should be kept for every analytic decision made. There is no substitute for keeping good notes. It is virtually impossible to remember everything that has been done, and why, with the volume of material reviewed in a qualitative inquiry. There is little chance that you will actually remember the specifics of how things began when you sit down to write the report.

Above all else, since researchers manage and manipulate data in a myriad of ways throughout the analytic process, *keep multiple copies of data*. It is best to keep at least one clean copy or digital back up of the data in a very safe place, just in case. Unfortunately, computers may crash, puppies can eat paper, and small children sometimes like to draw on anything. Develop a routine for copying data as soon as it is collected and stick with it.

Data Analysis

As mentioned, in qualitative research, data analysis begins as soon as data collection begins. The researcher constantly reviews data for patterns, concepts, and looks for ways that categories fit into themes that lead to a theory about a phenomenon that responds to the research question. With regard to electronic and print data, your mantra should become *read, read, and read again*. The sections that follow describe general analytic techniques for both description and interpretation of data. Following the general guidelines, you will read specific examples using grounded theory techniques. Research analysis follows similar patterns across qualitative domains or traditions. However, the perspective or insight a researcher takes will vary according to that tradition. (To review qualitative research traditions, refer to Chapter 6.)

The most important point to remember when conducting analysis and interpretation of qualitative data is that you *must* keep track of your process and communicate that process to the audience in detail. Therefore, it is imperative to keep **memos** and notes about coding and analysis procedures throughout the study. Later in the chapter, you will read examples of analysis notes.

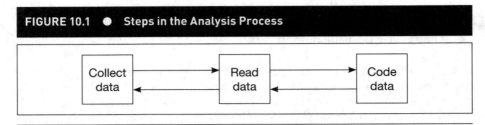

FIGURE 10.1 ● Steps in the Analysis Process

Source: Adapted from Weiss (1999).

General Techniques for Data Analysis

The general process for analysis in qualitative research is similar across traditions. Because it is a recursive process, it can be best explained with a simple illustration. Figure 10.1 shows the recurring steps in the process. You begin by collecting data and reading it. Next you code the data. Then collect more data, read it, and code it. Finally go back and read earlier data to clarify or elaborate on concepts that were coded. So, the process includes collecting, reading, and coding data until you arrive at the answers to the research questions. As researchers read and code, they make notes about thoughts, **codes**, and processes to be included in the final report.

Reading Data

Chances are, by the time you sit down to begin analyzing, you are already familiar with your data. Still, it is very important that you get to know your data further during analysis. Therefore, you begin analysis by reading your data—all of it. Then, you read it again. While you read, you jot down notes about the ideas that come to your mind, including answers to questions such as these:

What comments, observations, information are related to the research question?

Does an event occur or topic appear repeatedly?

Does an unexpected event occur?

Does someone use a provocative term in a response?

Does someone act in a way counter to their meaning in words?

Answers to these kinds of questions provide data points that will focus your coding.

Coding Data

Coding data takes place in a series of steps that may or may not be linear. Figure 10.2 shows steps in the process of **coding** with arrows to indicate that as you proceed to another step, you may find that subsequent data collection will cause you to return to a previous step. For example, you may read through your data, notice recurring or interesting items, create topical **categories**, and describe them. After another interview, you may notice new items and have to create and describe new categories. This may occur again and again as you collect more data.

FIGURE 10.2 ● The Process of Coding

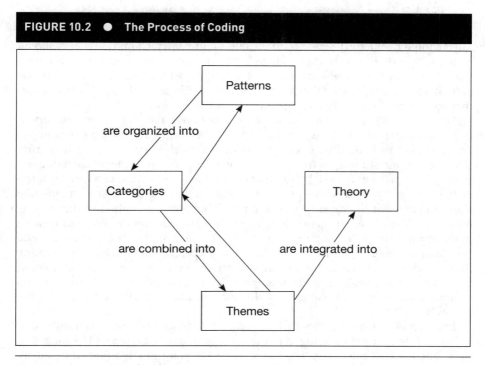

Source: Adapted from Weiss (1999).

Creating and Describing Patterns and Categories. When you begin to code your data, you search for **patterns**. These patterns, which should reflect something interesting and related to the research question, are made up of recurring concepts in the data (e.g., recurring comments, language, observed events). You collect similar concepts into categories. You then develop the category characteristics by describing what makes the included patterns similar to each other and different from patterns in other categories.

For example, if you were examining teacher and student interactions in a classroom, you might observe patterns of interactions that could be called *content-questioning interactions.* In these interactions, the teacher asks a question related to the content being taught, and a student responds with an answer or a further question. The exchange may be something like this:

> **Teacher:** Who can tell me one reason that the Southern states went to war in the American Civil War?
>
> **Student:** I know! The Southern states wanted to keep their slaves.

The next pattern of interaction may be called a *teaching interaction.*

> **Teacher:** That is partially correct, Jason. The Southern states wanted to keep their slaves, for sure, but they also wanted to be able to make choices by themselves, without the intervention of the federal government. They went to war to maintain a state's right to make its own decisions.

In this second interaction, the teacher was providing information related to the content of the lesson. She was not asking a question. Therefore, the content of this interaction is distinctly different from the questioning interaction. However, it should be similar to other interactions in which the teacher provides students with information. Thus, you may have a category of interactions with content questions as one pattern and teaching interaction as another pattern. These are the kinds of categories that you create as you collect and then further analyze the data.

Once categories are developed, you must get enough samples of that category to create a rich description of its characteristics and any **subcategories**. For example, let's say you identified the category of *content-questioning interactions*. Perhaps after ten observations of a teacher (or teachers), you have many examples of content questioning. You may have enough examples to develop a description of when the interaction is most likely to occur, its context, and its characteristics. After completing these observations, however, you may not have enough description of the *teaching interaction*. Therefore, you must go back to the classroom and attempt to observe more occurrences of the teaching interaction. This may mean a change in when and how long you observe or which classroom you observe. Whatever it is, if the teaching interaction is important to the research question, you must find more examples of this phenomenon to describe it thoroughly. Seeking further observations may lead to more refinement of the category or discovery of other categories. So you see, the process is iterative.

In addition, some categories that are initially developed will later be dismissed as inconsequential or not meaningful to the research question. Others will be subsumed into better-defined categories. You may create what you think is a fine group of categories, only to toss them out as more data are collected and you realize the data are unhelpful in addressing your research question(s). As you begin the data analysis process, you must be flexible because you cannot predict what future data will contain. Your goal is, however, to get to the point that your categories are so well developed and descriptive that when data comes in, it fits into your categorizing system.

Developing Themes. Once you have described your categories completely (or as you are getting close to a complete description), you can begin to integrate the categories into themes that respond directly to the research question. To do this, ask yourself the following questions:

Which categories belong together?

Why do they belong together?

What makes them similar in some way yet still unique?

In some cases, you will want to develop themes that are descriptive. In other words, you may ask: *How do categories fit together to make a descriptive picture of the phenomena under study?* In this case, the themes should create a picture for the reader of what you found in the data you examined.

In the previous example of teacher interaction, the research purpose may be to describe one teacher's classroom. So one theme may be that the teacher uses different types of student-teacher interaction throughout the school day. The researcher would then describe the different patterns of interactions. Another theme may be that this teacher provides a rich environment for student learning. The researcher may then describe the different patterns related to the environment in the classroom. Finally, the researcher may give an overview of how these themes fit together to make up this teacher's classroom. The themes are developed to be descriptive, although not verbatim, of the important recurring data that the researcher has collected from study of the phenomena of interest.

Developing Theory. If the researcher's intent is to develop a theory about the phenomena studied that addresses the research question(s), then the data analysis process must go one step beyond just describing the themes. In this case, the themes or categories must be integrated in some way, for example, to highlight the relationships between the themes.

   Let's say that one of the theory components in the previous example is that the teacher uses student-teacher interaction to increase student engagement in classroom activities. In this case, you should have examples of teacher-student interaction to show that each category is somehow related to this concept of increasing student engagement. You may say that the teacher uses directed content-questioning interactions (i.e., calls on a specific student when asking a question) when she notices that a student is not focused on the discussion. You would then provide examples of the questioning and how the questioning engaged the student in the discussion. Next, you may say that this is different from when the teacher notices that all students are attending. At that point, the teacher uses nondirected content questioning (i.e., asks generally to the class). In this short example, it should be clear that supporting the theory that "The teacher uses directed-content questioning interactions to focus students during discussion," is much different from merely describing the different types of teacher-student interactions. To develop a theory, you must integrate all themes into a concise statement of what phenomenon exists.

   As an extension of our example, here is a possible statement of the theory developed about the teacher's classroom.

> The goal of Ms. A's classroom is to engage students in active learning in order to meet her curriculum goals. She uses her verbal interactions with students to maintain focus and provide information. She uses physical proximity with selected students to redirect inattention and a program of tangible rewards and consequences with other students. Ms. A promotes student independence by increasing student responsibility for their learning as they show improvement in grades and class participation.

   From this statement, you can describe all aspects of the research study, including interactions, physical actions, tangible rewards, and changes in teacher level of direction, but you must also go beyond just describing these items to describing the relationships among them and what they mean in painting a picture of the teacher, the environment, and addressing the research question(s).

   This brief, general overview of the process of data analysis does not compare to nor account for the volume of data you will analyze or the length of the analysis process. The overview does suggest, however, that parts of the qualitative analysis process are related and built upon one another, much like as illustrated in Figure 10.3. Multiple

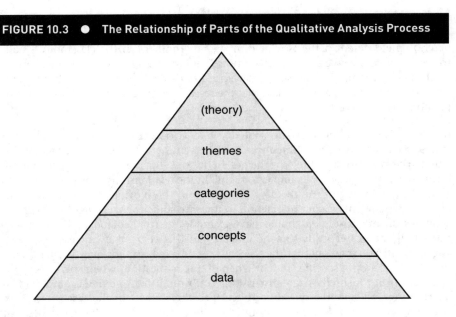

FIGURE 10.3 ● **The Relationship of Parts of the Qualitative Analysis Process**

forms of data are the foundation, with initial concepts built upon patterns in the data. Concepts are integrated into categories and categories into themes. Out of your themes come the theory and response to your research question(s).

As you can surmise, data analysis is a lengthy process that takes considerable thought and focus. Do not be afraid of it! Embrace it and be ready to make mistakes, scrap ideas, and begin again. That said, let's next examine the analytic process more deeply using grounded theory methodology. Grounded theory was chosen because it includes a reasonably clear set of procedures for the entire process of analysis, from developing categories to integrating themes into a theory in response to research questions.

Using Grounded Theory

The purpose of grounded theory as qualitative methodology is to develop a clear, descriptive theory in response to research questions using all of the data collected in the study. The grounded theory method employs systematic data collection and analysis until a theory is inductively understood about a phenomenon of study (Corbin & Strauss, 2015). There are three stages of coding in the grounded theory method, including **open coding**, **axial coding**, and **selective coding**.

As in all qualitative research, data analysis and data collection occur simultaneously and recursively. In each stage, coding continues until no new patterns appear in the data.

Open Coding. Analysis begins with open coding, breaking down the collected data by comparing each incident, comment, or artifact so that similar phenomena or patterns can be given the same name (Corbin & Strauss, 2015). These groups of similar data points are called concepts. Concepts are the unit of analysis for making comparisons and asking questions. Once you have identified several concepts, you must analyze them and group similar ones into categories and subcategories. Categories are given names that are more abstract than the original concepts. Using the concepts within the category, you develop dimensions and properties of the category. **Properties** are "characteristics that define and describe concepts," and **dimensions** are variations within properties along a continuum (Corbin & Strauss, 2015, p. 220). In other words, properties can have subproperties that exist under certain conditions.

To begin open coding, the researcher should read through observations, interviews, and look at other data line-by-line and item-by-item, highlighting information that indicates items of interest to the study focus. These highlights become concepts, which are labeled. Refer to Table 10.1 for examples of open coding labels organized by dates by Weiss (1999).

As Weiss (1999) compared observational incidents, interview comments, and other data artifacts, it became clear that some of the labels overlapped, occurred across settings, and did not allow for clear definition of categories. As observations continued across teachers, the researcher split the observations into separate teacher databases, and a more definitive categorization model developed. These categories included (a) tutor/aide, (b) team teacher, and (c) independent instructor. These categories did not only exist in isolation by teacher (e.g., Esther did not always appear as tutor/aide.) but, in some cases, varied by setting. As coding continued, the initial categories developed into (a) instructing within special education, (b) providing support in general education, (c) independent instructing outside of the general education classroom, (d) independent instructing within the general education classroom, and (e) team teaching. Interestingly, most of the categories

TABLE 10.1 ● Examples of Labels in Open Coding

10/12	11/8	12/21
instructing	adjusting	adjusting
questioning	questioning	questioning
reviewing	explaining	explaining
	clarifying	
	reading	
	talking to class	
encouraging	reinforcing	
giving answers	giving answers	giving help
	taking care of	
giving directives	giving directives	giving directives
giving feedback	giving feedback	giving feedback
	reprimanding	giving reprimands

Source: Adapted from Weiss (1999).

TABLE 10.2 ● One Property and Its Dimensions Across Categories

Category	Property	Dimensions	
Providing support	Explaining	Assisting students at their desk while general educator instructed	Helping general educator with content when he or she had a question
Same content in separate class	Explaining	Explaining answers to review guides sped teachers prepared	Explaining concepts to students after no response to a question
Separate content in co-taught class	Explaining	Explaining rules of game run by special educator	Explaining new concepts to students
Team teaching	Explaining	Explaining concepts at the board during review	Explaining steps and details of tasks the students would complete on their own
Instructing in special education	Explaining	Explaining grading of assignment	Explaining new concepts to students at board, overhead, or by reading text

Source: Adapted from Weiss (1999).

included similar properties. This was plausible because the phenomena studied existed across the same contexts.

As open coding continued, the dimensions and properties of the categories developed. These dimensions and properties distinguished categories from one another. Table 10.2 is an example of how Weiss (1999) organized one property and its dimensions across categories.

Axial Coding. As open coding concludes, the process of axial coding begins (Corbin & Strauss, 2015). With axial coding, the researcher identifies the causal conditions, contexts, **intervening conditions**, action and interactional strategies, and consequences of actions involved in each category. The intent is to discover and relate categories in terms of the model being developed. This stage of coding

> is a mix of induction and deduction—working back and forth from the emerging grounded theory to specific clusters of data, back to the emerging theory and modifications, and so on. (Marshall & Rossman, 2016, p. 223)

The concept of axial coding may be fairly abstract. To make it more concrete, here is an example of coding notes written by one researcher during the process.

> I coded the interview transcripts to conceptualize the data and move from lower level concepts (derived from open coding, including in vivo coding) to higher level concepts including categories and themes (derived from a combination of axial and selective coding). Axial coding involved combing multiple open codes from a single interview into a higher level concept as

described through memos. Selective coding included constant comparative analysis and combining open or axial codes across interviews and describing the increased theoretical sensitivity through memos. I also concurrently wrote code memos to describe the evolving description of the code, document memos to track my interpretations of codes or concepts within the transcriptions, and reflexive free memos to track my evolving interpretation of the data. The conceptualizing process described was not linear but was in constant flux as new raw data (interviews) were added and as new categories were developing. (Wronowski, 2018, p. 554)

It is at this point that many researchers stop because the purpose of their research is to describe. After axial coding, categories may be so well described that general ideas about a situation, context, or phenomenon can be expressed. If the question requires the development of a theory about how all of the categories fit together, however then the researcher must continue to the process of selective coding.

Selective Coding. The final coding step is called selective coding. In selective coding, the researcher integrates all of the data by choosing a core category and relating each category to it. The core category is developed in terms of properties and dimensions. The other categories are related to it using the systems developed during axial coding so that the core category has its own conditions, context, strategies, and consequences. This elaboration of the core category develops into a grounded theory.

The following example highlights some researcher notes about the process of selective coding. Reading these notes should give you a better idea of the decision-making involved during the continued review and analysis of data.

Once the primary coder concluded selective coding, each coder independently coded one randomly selected transcript using the core categories. Upon completion of the independent coding practice, the primary and secondary coders met to discuss codes and application of codes through Dedoose so as to ensure the appropriateness of the codes and their applications. Coders discussed coding discrepancies, clarified intent behind codes applied when there were differences, and added codes as needed. For example, coders used the "private/public facility impact" and "systemic/context issues of JC" codes in similar ways. In instances such as this, the coders agreed upon descriptions to distinguish nuance and added them to the codebook. Subsequently, the secondary coder reviewed and coded (with 85% agreement followed by discussion of discrepancies) the transcripts to ensure trustworthiness of coding and analysis. (McCray et al., 2017, p. 265)

Theoretical Sampling. After selective coding has been completed, the researcher may choose to engage in theoretical sampling. As described in Chapter 6, sampling of phenomena is very important to qualitative research. Sampling is based upon the theory developed with regard to the research questions and follows from the analysis that occurs as data is collected. The purpose of theoretical sampling is then to "collect data from places, people, and events that will maximize opportunities to develop concepts in terms of their properties and dimensions, uncover variations, and identify relationships between concepts" (Corbin & Strauss, 2015, p. 134). This may mean adjusting observation guides and interview questions to focus on relevant categories, modifying observations or interview times, or collecting additional documents. In short, after initial steps of data collection, any theoretical sampling should focus on the verification of hypotheses about how categories and subcategories are related.

The following example of researcher notes includes a description of changes in data collection based upon theoretical sampling. The changes included additional observations, observations in different settings, and additional interviews.

> As data collection and analysis progressed, the sampling process shifted to theoretical sampling to develop the conceptual categories and emerging theory (CHARMAZ & HENWOOD, 2008; STERN, 2007). Researchers can use theoretical sampling to seek out participants who have had particular experiences, or in whom particular concepts appear significant (MORSE, 2007), in order to gather data related to conceptual categories and their properties (CORBIN & STRAUSS, 2008). During data analysis, the emerging theory prompted me to pursue interviewing additional subjects to build the abstract concepts. The data analysis led to additional data collection, to seek out data from other sources that might be conceptually relevant. (Webster, 2016, p. 8)

Following open, axial, and selective coding, theoretical sampling of observations, interviews, and documents continues until **data saturation** is achieved. That is, at the point where all or most new data fits into existing categories and there is probably little to gain by continuing data collection, you have reached data saturation and can probably conclude data collection (Marshall & Rossman, 2016).

Trustworthiness

Once all data are collected and before discussing documenting and reporting results, it is important to reemphasize the importance of trustworthiness. Given the subjectivity that is evident in all forms of qualitative research, being forthright about theoretical sensitivity or biases is important. Building a case for credibility (i.e., *validity* in experimental and quantitative descriptive research) is essential too. In Chapter 6, you were first introduced to the concept of trustworthiness as simply the degree to which a researcher is able to persuade readers that the findings of a study are credible. You were encouraged to plan for trustworthiness in the design of your study. It was suggested that activities such as peer debriefing, member checking, and data auditing would enhance trustworthiness of the results. Certainly, showing the results of the analysis to research team members can lead to valuable feedback, however, showing preliminary or emerging findings to participants in the research (e.g., educators, clinicians, parents, other stakeholders) before and after stating the grounded theory may be more valuable in terms of enhancing trustworthiness. In addition, triangulation is always recommended, i.e., verifying conclusions through the use of multiple data sources (e.g., observation, interview, as well as other documents, photographs, video). If, for example, a category or theme can be backed up by data from multiple data sources, you enhance the trustworthiness or credibility of your findings. Here is a short excerpt from a study where a research, also noted how data were triangulated to enhance trustworthiness.

> Interview data were limited by their self-report nature, and observation data may represent altered behavior because an observer was in the room. Another limitation is the subjectivity of qualitative data analysis and interpretation, but trustworthiness of the findings was increased through triangulation of multiple data sources, member checks, and writing frequent memos documenting the research process (Denzin & Lincoln, 1994). (Baker, 2017, p. 674)

Documenting and Reporting Results

Once the researcher has developed core categories and themes, most grounded theories can be represented graphically to communicate ideas succinctly to readers. By depicting key categories and themes visually, the researcher makes the relationships clearer to herself and her readers, thereby enhancing the credibility of findings (Patton, 2015). A graphic, therefore, is an important addition to the discussion section of your research report. Figure 10.4 illustrated the relationships of the specific categories and themes from the study by Weiss (1999).

Conditional Matrix. A conditional matrix also helps to visually identify the range of conditions and consequences associated with the phenomenon and to illustrate the theory that emerged from the data. The following are some sample method notes to help you understand the decision-making process involved in creating a conditional matrix.

> The conditional matrix for this study begins with the actions/interactions of the special educator in the center. From this level, teachers' actions are affected by classroom setting and instructional conditions, the general education milieu, the school administration and structure, the district administration and structure, the community pressure, and, finally, the national/professional pressures. (Weiss, 1999, p. 91)

Figure 10.5 is the conditional matrix developed in the Weiss (1999) study on co-teaching. Whereas the graphic in Figure 10.4 illustrated the relationships of the specific concepts and themes from the study, the conditional matrix in Figure 10.5 highlighted how the actions of the teachers were nested within larger, related contexts. Like the grounded theory graphic, this too communicates to readers and enhances credibility of findings. Therefore, a conditional matrix may also be an important addition to the discussion section of your research report.

Stating the Theory. As outlined, analysis of qualitative data using grounded theory methodology requires that the researcher complete a series of coding steps and perhaps theoretical sampling as well. Illustrating emergent categories and themes in a graphic and/or matrix is also highly recommended. This process of analysis concludes with a concise statement of the theory developed in response to the research question(s). Once the theory is stated, the researcher must detail a rich description of the supporting categories, conditions, and themes so that the audience understands the entirety of the situation of

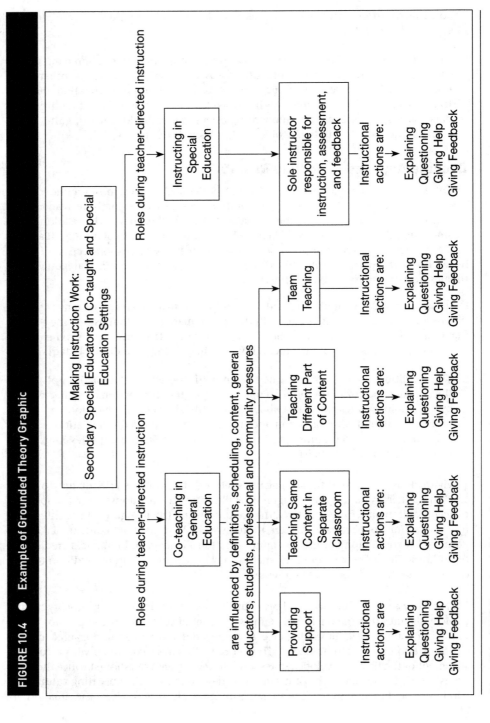

FIGURE 10.4 ● Example of Grounded Theory Graphic

Making Instruction Work:
Secondary Special Educators In Co-taught and Special
Education Settings

Roles during teacher-directed instruction

Co-teaching in
General
Education

are influenced by definitions, scheduling, content, general
educators, students, professional and community pressures

Providing
Support

Instructional
actions are

Explaining
Questioning
Giving Help
Giving Feedback

Teaching Same
Content in
Separate
Classroom

Instructional
actions are:

Explaining
Questioning
Giving Help
Giving Feedback

Teaching
Different Part
of Content

Instructional
actions are:

Explaining
Questioning
Giving Help
Giving Feedback

Team
Teaching

Instructional
actions are:

Explaining
Questioning
Giving Help
Giving Feedback

Roles during teacher-directed instruction

Instructing in
Special
Education

Sole instructor
responsible for
instruction, assessment,
and feedback

Instructional
actions are:

Explaining
Questioning
Giving Help
Giving Feedback

Source: Weiss (1999). Reproduced with permission.

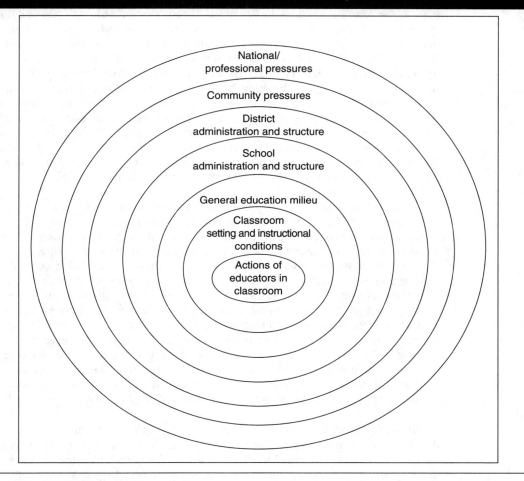

FIGURE 10.5 ● Example Conditional Matrix

National/
professional pressures

Community pressures

District
administration and structure

School
administration and structure

General education milieu

Classroom
setting and instructional
conditions

Actions of
educators in
classroom

Source: Weiss (1999). Reproduced with permission.

inquiry. Following is the statement of a theory from a study on reading intervention in a juvenile corrections school. Notice how key concepts and themes were summarized.

> The grounded theory model developed for implementing a READ 180 intervention in a juvenile corrections facility is presented . . . The context affected the faculty, staff, and students in different ways and influenced the commitment to and implementation of the intervention. Additionally, teachers' experience and background seemed to influence their perception of the program. Individual student characteristics affected their motivation for participation. In the following sections, the authors explain each category and illustrate how they interrelate, sharing the experience of teachers, students, and staff at the study site during implementation. (McCray et al., 2018, pp. 266–267)

Theoretical Sensitivity. So you've collected your qualitative data and completed your analysis. You've created a graphic and responded to your original research question, perhaps in the form of a theory (in Grounded Theory methodology). As one additional important part of reporting on a qualitative inquiry and the methods used, researchers need to be sure to state their point of view or biases, as well as make their case regarding the credibility of the findings. To do so, researchers must address theoretical sensitivity. **Theoretical sensitivity** is the insight and understanding of the topic of interest that the researcher brings to the study. It is the experience and/or philosophical disposition that he or she uses as a lens through which to analyze interview, observation, and document data. Conversely, perhaps, it is also the source of their biases. A researcher develops theoretical sensitivity to a topic in a variety of ways, including university study, personal experience, professional experience, and use of grounded theory procedures. Therefore, it is important to describe the sources of theoretical sensitivity to the audience. Following is an example of how Weiss described her theoretical sensitivity.

> I addressed theoretical sensitivity in a variety of ways throughout the course of this study. First, I used my professional experience and a preliminary review of the literature on co-teaching to guide my initial questions and open coding. Following the initial round of coding and throughout the study, I participated in weekly questioning sessions with a colleague. In these sessions, I described my categories, subcategories, and links. My colleague then questioned the foundation of these categories, what made them different, how I could verify these things were happening, and why I linked them in certain ways. These questioning sessions led to at least four instances when I scrapped my coding labels and category links and began anew. I also systematically compared concept to concept and category to category. For example, I compared the property of explaining across team teaching and providing support to verify differences that existed in the data, not just from models within the professional literature. This caused me to change the category labels and expand the subcategory properties and dimensions. (Weiss, 1999, p. 94)

Although the topic of theoretical sensitivity is addressed in this chapter after a description of the processes of data analysis and reporting, a description of theoretical sensitivity should be presented in the description of study methodology at the *beginning* of your report because, as in this example, it provides a helpful glimpse into how a researcher was the research instrument, a concept central to qualitative inquiry as noted in Chapter 6.

Putting It All Together

To pull together all the material from this chapter, focus your attention on addressing these important questions about *organizing your data*:

- Is the purpose of your qualitative study to describe a single case of a person, program, or situation?
- Is the research purpose to describe change?
- Is the purpose to describe similarities and differences in situations?

IN THEIR OWN WORDS

A Picture Is Worth 1,000 Words

Jean Crockett, University of Florida

Qualitative analysis is a process of reducing, selecting, and summarizing data to provide descriptions—"thick descriptions"—of the focus of our inquiry. Findings and conclusions are presented most often in carefully chosen words to communicate the meaning of our data and to engage readers through refined and polished prose. Words are the medium of qualitative research, but it helps to cut a swath through the verbal underbrush of "thick description" as we analyze and communicate our findings. One way to do this is to create visual displays that foster analysis and promote confidence in our findings by illustrating relationships and patterns within the data.

I learned the power of displaying data visually in a Chinese restaurant from my friend and mentor. As we talked at lunch, he asked about my current work. I eagerly showed him a list of five principles of practice I'd derived from an historical and conceptual analysis of previous research. Without saying a word, he began to draw the picture of a star on a paper napkin. He labeled each point of the star with one of the five principles. Starting from one point, he traced a line across the star to another point, asking me, "Does this principle link with this one?" He continued the process of tracing lines from one point of the star to another, systematically repeating his question each time as I caught on, exclaiming "Yes! That principle links with this one, and here's how it relates. . ."

As we made our way through lunch, we made our way across each line that shaped the star, analyzing the relationship between the principle at the starting point and the one at its conclusion. When we'd finished, my mentor had helped me see how the list of five principles I'd derived from my data could be reconceived and analyzed at a deeper level through a visual display. What he drew on the paper napkin illustrated the interactive nature of the five principles in a way I hadn't seen before, and in a way that was more convincing and more true to life, than the list of words in the original analysis. In short, his picture was worth 1,000 words.

TECHNOLOGY IN RESEARCH

NVivo: A Primer

NVivo is a data analysis software program, available for Mac or Windows operating systems. The software allows the researcher to analyze qualitative data as well as an array of descriptive quantitative data, making the software also viable for use in mixed method research. The software can accommodate data in the form of Word files, video files, audio files, email, PDFs, JPEG photos, Excel files, websites, online files from Survey Monkey, and other sources. As a result, NVivo allows the researcher to store and analyze interviews, focus group conversations, field notes, permanent records, photos, videos, as well as survey data, demographics, and other products.

NVivo allows the researcher to sort, categorize, and classify data by themes, as well

(Continued)

(Continued)

as organize results of queries, but does not take the place of analysis and reflection by the researcher. The software allows researchers to explore relationships among themes in addition to visualize results in matrices, word clouds, word/concept trees, comparison diagrams, and graphs that can be exported for presentations. NVivo data can be shared by researchers and easily coded for multiple analyses.

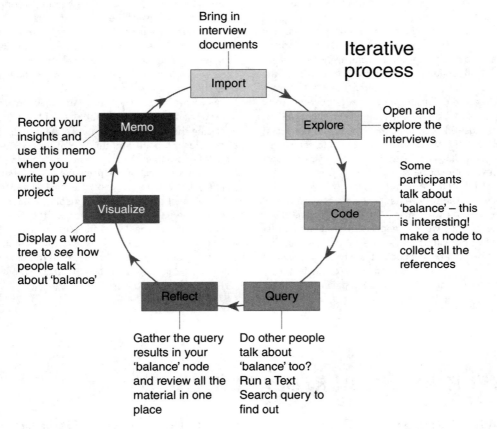

Republished with kind permission from QSR International. Source: NVivo 12 Help, February 2019.

NVivo is particularly useful for those methodological approaches including:

- Grounded theory
- Qualitative content analysis
- Ethnography

NVivo software has a free trial, and includes tutorials with sample data as well as product support from QSR. https://www.qsrinternational.com/nvivo/home

In addition, address these important guiding questions as you begin *reading your data*:

- Which data are related to the research question(s)?
- Does an event occur or topic appear repeatedly?
- Does an unexpected event occur?
- Does someone use a provocative term in a response?
- Does someone act in a way counter to their meaning in words?

Address these questions as you think about *developing themes*:

- Which categories belong together?
- Why do they belong together?
- What makes them similar in some way yet still unique?
- How do the characteristics of a category interact?

Summary

In this chapter, you learned ways to analyze and interpret qualitative descriptive data. Analyzing words requires a process of reading and re-reading all the data that are available. As you read, you begin to notice recurring patterns in the data. These patterns are grouped into concepts and then categories. You then identify the characteristics of each category and how they are different from characteristics of other categories. Next, categories are grouped into themes that describe major ideas within the data. Finally, themes can be integrated to develop a theory in response to the research question. Once the theory is stated, the researcher must detail a rich description of the supporting categories, conditions, and themes so that the audience understands the entirety of the situation of inquiry. Illustrating the related categories and themes in a graphic will help communicate the rich description to your audience.

In each of the examples of published research cited in this chapter, researchers employed multiple levels of coding to the development of a theory about the phenomena of study that addressed their research questions. As mentioned earlier, a researcher may use all levels of coding or only a few.

Grounded theory includes the following steps:

1. Open coding
2. Axial coding
3. Selective coding
4. Theoretical sampling
5. Creating a visual
6. Stating the theory

Throughout the entire process of data analysis, you must keep detailed notes about your coding process and decisions that you make regarding the progression of the study. Researchers must clearly explain their analysis in the methods section of the report.

Discussion Questions

1. Briefly describe the iterative process for qualitative data analysis.

2. Compare and contrast *patterns* and *categories* in the process of coding data.

3. Identify and describe the differences among the three types of coding used in grounded theory.

4. What is the purpose of theoretical sampling?

Your Research Project in Action

1. Is your research purpose to

    a. describe a single case of a person, program, or situation?   Yes   No

    If yes, how would you organize your data? _____

    b. describe change?   Yes   No

    If yes, how would you organize your data? _____

    c. describe similarities and differences in situations?   Yes   No

    If yes, how would you organize your data? _____

2. What key items are you looking for when reading your collected data?

    _____

    _____

    _____

3. After reading over some of your collected data, what key *patterns* do you notice?

    _____

    _____

4. How do those patterns relate back to your research question?

    _____

    _____

5. Why are those patterns significant for answering your research question?

    _____

    _____

6. Identify any potential *concepts* and *categories* you can begin creating from the patterns you have noted.

    _____

    _____

7. How do those categories relate to your research question?

    _____

    _____

8. How will you use the three types of coding in your research project?

    _____

    _____

9. Describe your theoretical sensitivity.

    _____

    _____

10. Make a first attempt at writing your statement of theory.

    _____

    _____

    _____

Further Reading

Patton, M. Q. (2015). *Qualitative research & evaluation methods* (4th ed.). Thousand Oaks, CA: Sage.

This text provides a comprehensive description of the process and priorities of qualitative research. The author addresses topics such as determining conceptual framework, using alternative data collection methods, and enhancing credibility. In addition, the author compares different techniques based on different theoretical and philosophical approaches to qualitative inquiry. Extensive examples are provided.

References

Corbin, J., & Strauss, A. (2015). *Basics of qualitative research: Techniques and procedures for developing grounded theory* (4th ed.). Thousand Oaks, CA: Sage.

Marshall, C., & Rossman, G. B. (2016). *Designing qualitative research* (6th ed.). Thousand Oaks, CA: Sage.

Patton, M. Q. (2015). *Qualitative research & evaluation methods* (4th ed.). Thousand Oaks, CA: Sage.

Literature Examples

Baker, L. L. (2017). What it takes to succeed: The importance of social support for academically successful middle school English learners. *Youth & Society, 49*(5), 658–678.

McCray, E. D., Ribuffo, C., Lane, H., Murphy, K. M., Gagnon, J. C., Houchins, D. E., & Lambert, R. G. (2018). "As real as it gets": A grounded theory study of a reading intervention in a juvenile correctional school. *Child Youth Care Forum, 47*, 259–281.

Webster, M. D. (2016). Examining philosophy of technology using grounded theory methods. *Qualitative Social Research, 17*(2), 202–229.

Weiss, M. P. (1999). The actions of secondary special educators in co-taught and special education settings (Doctoral dissertation, University of Virginia.) *Dissertation Abstracts International, 60*, 06A.

Wronowski, M. L. (2018). Filling the void: A grounded theory approach to addressing teacher recruitment and retention in urban schools. *Education and Urban Society, 50*(6), 548–574.

Analyzing and Interpreting Descriptive Research

Chapter Objectives

In this chapter, the reader will

- understand how to select a statistic appropriate to a descriptive design and data.
- understand how to interpret correlational and causal comparative analyses.
- understand how to discuss descriptive, correlational, and causal comparative results.
- understand how to display descriptive data visually.

As you recall from Chapter 7, quantitative descriptive research was categorized in terms of descriptive research, correlational, and causal comparative research. In descriptive research, the researchers attempt to describe features or provide a broad picture of a condition or phenomenon, such as teacher beliefs about inclusion or student perceptions of peer pressure. Descriptive research methods often rely on responses of participants to specific survey or interview questions, and they result in frequency counts, percentages, means, and standard deviations.

In correlational research, the broad objective is to explore relationships. The researcher looks at the magnitude or degree of relationship between two or more variables, or predicts the score on one variable based on participant scores on another variable.

In causal comparative research, sometimes called *ex post facto research*, the researcher investigates the cause of, reason for, or relationship among differences in participant groups in terms of a pre-existing condition. The condition might be a behavior, attitude, or performance. That is, the researcher compares the perceived cause of differences on a dependent variable after the behavior, attitude, or performance has already occurred without experimental manipulation (Mills & Gay, 2015). In causal comparative and correlational research, data may be gathered from a survey or an extant database that includes performance and other information, and then analyzed through various statistics as appropriate.

In this chapter, the goal is to enable you to learn how to analyze and interpret results of your descriptive, correlational, or causal comparative research. As in Chapters 9 and 10, various appropriate approaches will be discussed and guide you from implementation and data analysis through reporting results. You will learn about common concepts and techniques that coincide with descriptive, correlational, and causal comparative research. As with earlier chapters, the purpose is not to provide you with the kind of thorough treatment of each type of analysis that you should receive in specific graduate research methods coursework. Rather the intent is to provide you with some reasonable, worthwhile, and understandable examples of analyses. Let's start by looking at basic descriptive research.

Descriptive Data Analysis and Interpretation

In basic descriptive research, data analysis essentially refers to computing collected data and displaying it so that the researcher can more easily interpret and communicate it to others. For correlational and causal comparative research, computing descriptive statistics is the first step in data analysis. For each kind of descriptive research, the type of data you have collected will determine how you will analyze and display your results. (See Chapter 5 to review the various types of data.)

Data Displays

Data displays enable the researcher to visually analyze data by literally seeing any differences that may be present and to communicate results to audiences. There are various computer tools that you can use, including the chart-making feature of Microsoft Excel. A couple of useful displays include frequency tables (which are typically illustrated in bar graphs) and histograms. See Appendix B for more information about using Excel to analyze data.

Nominal or categorical data can be used to create frequency tables. Frequency tables provide information to you and the reader about how often a certain response occurred or the percentage of responses that a frequency indicates. For example, if you analyzed a data set regarding the number of teachers who used various literacy practices, you are likely to get nominal or categorical data to illustrate in a frequency table such as that in Figure 11.1.

Frequency and percentage tables are relatively easy to create and can give you meaningful information that is accessible to you and your readers. Other data displays can also help us see the "big picture" and uncover relationships and patterns. For example, another way to compare groups is through the use of bar graphs or bar charts referred to as histograms. Histograms illustrate the relationship between two variables whose measures yield interval or ratio data, or continuous scores (Gall, Gall, & Borg, 2006). See Figure 11.2 for an example histogram created in Microsoft Excel.

Many computer database or spreadsheet programs are easy to use and enable even novice researchers to compile and display their numerical data in tables, graphs, or charts. While data displays are primarily a way of illustrating descriptive data sets, they can also be valuable in enhancing your analyses and assisting in the discussion of the results of correlational, causal comparative, as well as experimental research.

FIGURE 11.1 ● Literacy Practices Used by Teachers

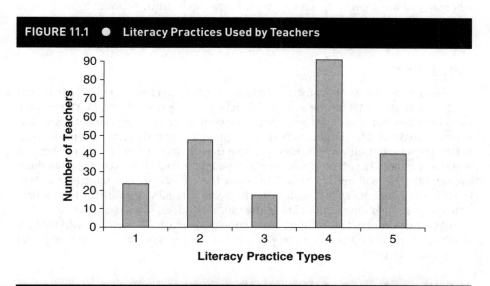

FIGURE 11.2 ● State Reading Test Scores for Students at ABC High School

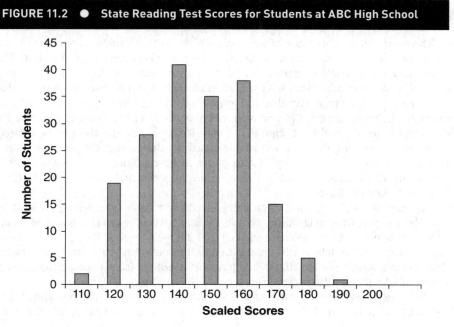

Correlational Research

In correlational research, as in causal comparative research, you will conduct statistical analysis, but in correlational research your objective is to analyze the strength of relationship between two or more variables. The choice of statistical test depends on whether you are comparing mean scores, frequency counts, or some other type of data. In this section of the chapter, let's take a look at choosing the appropriate statistic and then interpreting and discussing results of correlational analysis.

Data Entry

Whether you are using Statistical Package for the Social Sciences (SPSS), Statistical Analysis Software (SAS), or the statistical functions in Microsoft Excel, you'll certainly need to be familiar with how the software works in order to enter your data as well as run your analyses. The purpose here is not to provide you with a tutorial on using statistical software but simply to remind you that in each data file on your computer, you will not only need to enter the numbers from your data collection accurately, but more importantly, you will need to know how to use the software menus and commands in order to carry out critical tasks such as labeling your variables, defining the type of data entered in each column, and defining the range of values. These tasks are all part of the data entry process, and without them, knowing where to click on a certain analysis won't result in any output that you can use as results of your correlational or causal comparative research.

Selecting a Statistic Consistent With Your Design and Appropriate to Your Data

The most common measure of the degree or extent that variables are related is the correlation coefficient, an index expressed as a number between –1.00 and +1.00. The more variables are related, or the more variance that they share, the greater the number will be (positive or negative). A correlation coefficient can be direct or positive; that is, as one variable changes its value, the other changes value in the same direction. For example, the taller you get, the more you weigh; or the less a child interrupts a teacher, the fewer times she will be disciplined. A correlation coefficient also can be indirect or negative, meaning that as one variable changes value in one direction, the other changes in the opposite direction. For example, as we get older, our eyesight tends to deteriorate; or the more you study, the fewer mistakes you make on an exam (Mills & Gay, 2015; Salkind, 2016).

Correlation coefficients are often categorized on a scale from strong to weak in order to interpret their magnitude. That is, a 0.8 to 1.0 coefficient is considered strong or high, whereas a 0.5 is moderate and 0.0 to 0.2 is weak or low. Keep in mind, however, that strength of relationship is also tied to the coefficient's absolute value, rather than its sign (positive or negative). That is, a coefficient of –0.8 is stronger than a coefficient of +0.5; it's just that –0.8 shows a negative or indirect relationship.

There are several types of correlational techniques or statistics. The one you choose depends on the type of data or variables you want to correlate; that is, whether your data are nominal/dichotomous, ordinal, rank, or ratio (see Chapter 5). Perhaps the most commonly used correlational statistic is the **Pearson product-moment coefficient**, represented by r. In a printed analysis output, you would see the Pearson r written as $r = .xx$, followed by the level of significance. The Pearson r is used when examining relationships between variables that yield continuous scores (i.e., interval or ratio types of data). This statistic may be appropriate to answer the sample research question, *What is the relationship between the use of literacy practices of high school teachers and student performance on state reading tests?* Another correlational statistic is the **Spearman rho**, typically used for evaluating the relationship between variables that are rank or rating scores (i.e., ordinal data, such as you might find on a survey item with a scale of *strongly agree* to *strongly disagree*). Refer to Gall et al. (2006) for more detail on other correlational statistics such as **multiple regression**, which enables you to correlate multiple variables at one time.

You can compute the Pearson r fairly easily with a calculator. See Gall et al. (2006) or Mills & Gay, 2015) for details. You can also use Microsoft Excel functions or a dedicated statistics program such as SAS or SPSS. Here's an excerpt from recent research that described the purpose of the investigation. As suggested earlier in the chapter, for correlational and causal comparative research, computing descriptive statistics is commonly the first step in data analysis. Thus, you will note that the researchers did so in this study and then extended their examination of variables with correlational analysis:

> To address the first research aim, the investigators conducted descriptive analyses on the *ERAS* scores. A point value was assigned to each response on the *ERAS*. The points were added to yield a set of three scores: a recreational reading attitude score, an academic reading attitude score and a composite ERAS total score. To answer the second research question, analysis of variance was conducted with two between subjects effects (grade and gender) and within subjects effects (recreational and academic reading attitudes, and total composite ERAS score) to examine differences in CRA between recreational and academic reading and to examine CRA differentially between girls and boys and grade levels. To address the third research aim, Pearson correlation coefficients were examined to observe the strength of the relationship between reading attitudes and children's performance on the standardised language and literacy assessments. (Wood & Cabas, 2017, p. 417)

Interpreting Results of Analyses

Depending on what correlational analysis you run, you will get different information in your output. Depending on which computer software you use, you will also get different output information for an analysis (e.g., Microsoft Excel will only provide correlation coefficients, not significance levels). In Figure 11.3, let's take a look at a portion of some example output from a Pearson r correlational analysis using SPSS. You will report such outcomes in the results section of your research report.

The four variables are listed in rows and in the columns, creating a *matrix* of all possible correlations. Each cell of the matrix contains three rows. The first row contains the Pearson r coefficient for the comparison of each pair of variables. The second

FIGURE 11.3 ● Sample Output for Correlational Analysis

	Lit Prac 1	Lit Prac 2	Lit Prac 3	Rdg Score
Lit Prac 1 Pearson Correlation	1	.541	.123	.789**
Sig. (2-tailed)		.030	.077	.000
N	64	64	64	64
Lit Prac 2 Pearson Correlation	.541	1	.498	.090
Sig. (2-tailed)	.030		.068	.323
N	64	64	64	64
Lit Prac 3 Pearson Correlation	.123	.498	1	−.145
Sig.(2-tailed)	.077	.068		.088
N	64	64	64	64
Rdg score Pearson Correlation	.789**	090	−.145	1
Sig. (2-tailed)	.000	.323	.088	
N	64	64	64	64

** Correlation is significant at the .01 level (2-tailed).

contains the two-tailed probability, or level of significance for the coefficient. The third row shows the number of pairs of scores on which each *r* value was computed.

Note that the *r* value for the correlation between each variable and itself (e.g., Literacy Practice 1 and itself) equals 1. This is because the correlation of any variable with itself is perfect. Also note that the 1s form a diagonal from the upper left to the lower right of the matrix and that all of the correlations listed below the diagonal are the same as the correlations above the diagonal. You should also note that asterisks appear next to the *r* values for which the probability is less than or equal to .01, since these are statistically significant correlations.

From this output, you can first see that only one of the correlation coefficients was significant, the relationship between Literacy Practice 1 and Reading Scores. The *r* value was .789, which you can interpret in terms of direction and degree of relationship. Since it is a positive number, you know that as the level of use of Literacy Practice 1 increased, so did the Reading Scores. Secondly, you can say that the degree of relationship is strong on a scale of 0.00 to 1.00. Since this strong, positive relationship appears to exist between these two variables, and the significance level was .000, lower than the .01 level of significance, you would reject a null hypothesis stating that the variables are unrelated.

Here's an excerpt from recent research that illustrates how the results of a correlational analysis might be reported:

. . . there was a small positive significant relationship between CRA overall and children's performance on standardised receptive vocabulary tests in Spanish ($r = .17, p = .03$) particularly for the subtest of questions related to reading attitudes on academic items ($r = .16, p = .03$). In other words, high receptive vocabulary in Spanish was associated with high positive reading attitudes for ELs, although the magnitude of the relationship was very small. Recreational reading attitudes also demonstrated a small positive significant relationship with receptive Spanish vocabulary skills for first-grade participants ($r = .24, p = .02$) but was non-significant for children in kindergarten ($r = .07, p = .51$). (Wood & Cabas, 2017, p. 419)

Scatter Plot

One way to visually depict correlations is by using a **scatter plot**. A scatter plot, also called a scatter diagram, is a graph that includes plotted points representing correlational scores. For example, look at the example data points in Table 11.1.

You could easily create a graph to plot the scores in the left-hand column on the y-axis and the score on the x-axis, resulting in a scatter plot like the one created using Microsoft Excel in Figure 11.4.

TABLE 11.1 ● Sample Data Points for a Scatter Plot

Income Level	Rating
50	3
80	3
32	1
100	2
65	2
152	5
58	3
96	4
123	4
75	4
40	1
147	5
121	5
35	2

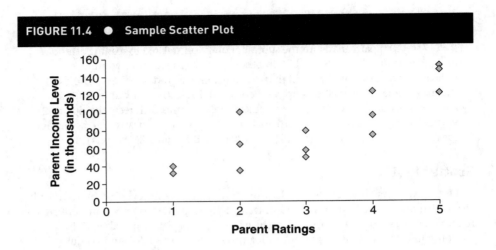

FIGURE 11.4 ● Sample Scatter Plot

Without computing a correlation coefficient for this data set, you might guess that the correlation is positive and strong.

Discussing Results

You know that in the discussion section of a research article, the researcher interprets the results but does not overgeneralize them to people or settings that are dissimilar. In correlational research, as in causal comparative research, this means all results are interpreted with caution. The researcher should discuss relationships among variables, direction of relationships, and strength or degree of relationships. The researcher should also provide honest commentary about the limitations of the study, implications for practice, and future research needs, including potential experimental study. The following is an example of part of the discussion of a correlational study. Look for some of the elements just noted and the language used to describe the relationships.

> . . . results indicated that higher Spanish receptive vocabulary skills were associated with higher or more positive reading attitudes. For kindergarten participants, positive academic reading attitudes were also associated with better phonological awareness skills. Students' overall reading attitude was not otherwise associated with their English receptive vocabulary, rapid automatic naming or other performance indicators tested. . . explaining the nature of the relationship between reading attitudes and language and literacy performance is beyond the scope of the current study. Results must be interpreted cautiously, as the ERAS was not originally normed for Spanish-speaking ELs nor students in kindergarten. Although the survey was administered in both English and Spanish to facilitate students' comprehension, students' level of understanding in either language may have affected their responses. (Wood & Cabas, 2017, pp. 420, 422)

Causal Comparative Research

In causal comparative research, after computing basic descriptive statistics, the second step of analysis is to test the statistical significance of the differences between groups in relation to the dependent variable. As in correlational research, your choice of statistic depends on the type of data. In this section of the chapter, let's look at entering data for causal comparative analysis, choosing the appropriate statistic, and then interpreting and discussing results.

Selecting a Statistic Consistent With Your Design and Appropriate to Your Data

Perhaps the most commonly used inferential statistic used in causal comparative research is the **t test**. The *t* test is used to test the null hypothesis that the mean scores of two groups are the same. This makes sense, since you know that in causal comparative research, you are often testing differences between two groups on a dependent variable. The *t* test fits one of our recurring research examples from Chapter 7 based on the question: *What is the relationship of gender and computer competency test scores of seventh graders?* The *t* test would then test the statistical difference between the mean test scores of males and females. If you were comparing the mean scores of a dependent variable between two or more groups at the same time, then analysis of variance (ANOVA) would be the better choice for your statistical analysis. The *t* test tests means only between two groups, whereas ANOVA tests scores for multiple groups (typically three or more) all at the same time. ANOVA tests the null hypothesis that the mean scores of multiple groups are equal. Here's an excerpt from recent research that describes the use of ANOVA:

> To answer the first research question, the means and standard deviations for all the scales were computed for the entire sample of students. To answer the second research question, the means and standard deviations of all the scales were computed for the sample obtained from teachers and guides. These means were compared with the student results from an ANOVA with respondent type (student vs. teacher vs. guide) as the explanatory variable. (Vennix, den Brok, & Toconis, 2017, p. 28)

In the case of the *t* test and ANOVA, the dependent variable data are mean scores (i.e., interval-level data). If your dependent variable data were frequency counts, for example, rather than means, and you had two or more group performances to compare, then the chi-square analysis would be more appropriate. The chi-square test compares the observed or actual frequency of observations or responses with an expected frequency of responses. That is, one would statistically compare the frequency of different responses to an equal distribution of responses (Mills & Gay, 2015). For example, think about our sample research question: *What is the relationship of teachers' experience and attitudes toward inclusion?* The attitudes (dependent variable) might be measured by a questionnaire with questions that prompt participants to choose among responses of never, sometimes, often, daily. After researchers tallied the number of respondents with various levels of experience that responded to each of the choices, they would analyze the nominal level data using the chi-square test. Here's an excerpt from recent research that describes the use of the chi-square test in a comparative research study using an existing database rather than data collected through a questionnaire:

> The purpose of this study was to compare the performance of Hispanic students from California, Texas, and Arizona on AP English exams. Data for the 16 years from 1997 through 2012 were analyzed. A series of 3 (state of residency) × 5 (AP exam score) chi-square procedures were conducted to examine the relationship between the variables. Specifically, Pearson chi-square tests were utilized to ascertain whether statistically significant differences in AP exam score distributions were present among the three states: California, Texas, and Arizona. (Koch, Slate & Moore, 2016, p. 690)

Interpreting Results of Analyses

Depending on what analysis you run, you will get different information in your output. As is the case throughout this book, the purpose is to focus on the key points you will need to understand in order to complete your project or thesis. In the next example, the focus is on interpreting and reporting results. For a far more detailed analysis of statistical output, see Gall et al. (2006).

In Figure 11.5, let's take a look at a portion of some example output from an ANOVA using the function command of Microsoft Excel. You will need to report such outcomes in the results section of your research report. From the output in Figure 11.3, you can see that the ANOVA yielded an F value and the level of significance. Chapter 9 mentioned that the level of significance is the probability that the statistical differences in an analysis would be due to chance or measurement error. In this example, the level of significance, noted in the far right top portion of the output table, is .298077, or .30 if rounded to the nearest hundredth. This would mean that there is about a 3 out of 10 chance that the results were due to chance or error, or in other words, there is about a 70% statistical probability that differences are due to a causal variable. This result does not sound overly convincing, particularly if you had set a maximum alpha level of .05 for rejecting your null hypothesis.

The second important value is the F statistic or F ratio. This statistical value, used in obtaining the level of significance of your analysis, is the ratio of between-groups variance to within-groups variance (Gall et al., 2006). Generally, the larger the F value, the more likely your significance level will be lower and you can reject your null hypothesis.

In reporting your results, you will need to report the F statistic, alpha level, and one other set of values from the output table, the degrees of freedom (df on the output table). These numbers, used in the statistical calculation of the level of significance, are approximately equal to the number of participants for which you have entered data (Mills & Gay, 2015). Thus, in reporting the F statistic, you list the degrees of freedom between groups and within groups in the following way, followed by the level of significance: $[F(3, 12) = 1.3732, p < .2981]$. Note that, by convention, the values are reported to the nearest 10,000th, or four decimal places.

FIGURE 11.5 ● Sample Output From ANOVA

ANOVA					
Source of variation	*SS*	*df*	*MS*	*F*	*p value*
Between groups	973.1875	3	324.3958	1.373225	0.298077
Within groups	2834.75	12	236.2292		
Total	3807.938	15			

Here's an excerpt from recent research that illustrates how the results of an ANOVA might be reported:

> Relative to teachers and guides, students had statistically significantly more positive perceptions of cohesiveness ($F(2, 760) = 8.50$; $p <.000$; $n^2=0.027$). Also, guides' and teachers' perceptions differed statistically significantly for personal relevance. Teachers thought that outreach was more personally relevant for students than either guides or students themselves thought ($F(1, 33) = 4.61$; $p <.01$; $n^2=0.12$). (Vennix, den Brok, & Toconis, 2017, pp. 35–36)

You will notice that the statistic n^2 was reported in this study. That is effect size. You may recall from Chapter 9 that effect size is the degree of difference between groups or conditions or, perhaps, the magnitude of difference in outcomes among experimental groups or experimental conditions. There are several different effect size calculations, and in Chapter 9 you read that one commonly used calculation is called Cohen's *d*. Another effect size calculation is **eta squared**, reported as n^2, and is commonly used in ANOVA calculations. For eta squared, a value of .02 is considered a small effect size, a value of .13 is considered a medium effect size, and a value of .26 or higher is considered a large effect size.

Now let's take a look at some example output from a chi-square analysis in Figure 11.6, followed by a discussion of the outcomes that you would need to report in a results section.

From this analysis output, you get a great deal of inferential as well as descriptive data. First of all, you get the chi-square value, as well as the degrees of freedom and level of significance. In this example, the chi-square, also written as X^2, gives an index of the comparison between the actual frequency of responses with an expected frequency of responses to a survey question about the postschool status of respondents across three categories of disabilities. Generally, the higher the X^2 value, the greater the level of significance. Certainly, a significance level of .00013 is statistically significant. Thus, in this case, one would write that there are comparative differences among the groups with regard to their postschool status ($X^2 = 27.3308$, $df = 6$, $p <.0001$).

The descriptive analysis gives a clue as to where some of the differences occur. For example, the percentage of individuals with learning disabilities (LD) who engaged in

FIGURE 11.6 ● Sample Output From Chi-square Analysis

Disabil Type	Count Row Pct Col Pct Tot Pct	Post school status				
		Second Ed 1	Employ 2	Voc Training 3	Unemploy & Unenroll 4	Row Total
LD	1	14	32	6	6	58
		24.1	55.2	10.3	10.3	40.3
		56	59.3	16.2	21.4	
		9.7	22.2	4.2	4.2	
BD	2	6	15	18	9	48
		12.5	31.3	37.5	18.8	33.3
		24	27.8	48.6	32.1	
		4.2	10.4	12.5	6.6	
ID	3	5	7	13	13	38
		13.2	18.4	34.2	34.2	26.4
		20	13	35.1	46.4	
		3.5	4.9	9	9	
	Column Total	25	54	37	28	144
		17.4	37.5	25.7	19.4	100

Chi-Square	Value	DF	Significance
Pearson	27.33083	6	.00013

Source: Green (1994)

postsecondary education is nearly twice as high (24.1) as for individuals with behavioral disabilities (BD) (12.5) and those with intellectual disabilities (ID; 13.2). The employment rate is much higher for individuals with LD (55.2) than that of the other groups also, and the percentage of individuals with ID who are neither employed nor enrolled in any additional education or training is quite a bit higher (34.2) than that of the other groups. These descriptive results might be communicated well in the form of a frequency chart.

Here's an excerpt from the research cited earlier comparing the performance of Hispanic students from three states on AP English exams, illustrating how the results of chi-square tests were reported:

> For the first research question, the focus was on comparing the performance of Hispanic students from California, Texas, and Arizona on the AP English Language and Composition exam for each test administration from 1997 through 2012. Frequencies and percentages of overall exam scores for Hispanic students from California, Texas, and Arizona for the 1997 through 2001 test administrations are included in Table 1. For the 1997 test administration, the result was statistically significant, X^2 (8, $N = 2,173$) = 22.49, $p = .004$, Cramer's $V = .07$, a trivial effect size (Cohen, 1992). In general, Arizona (50.00%) had a greater percentage of students who earned a score of 3 or higher than did California (42.15%) and Texas (34.44%). (Koch, Slate & Moore, 2016, p. 690)

As previously noted, there are different effect size calculations based on the statistic you use, and we have mentioned Cohen's d and most recently eta squared, commonly used in ANOVA calculations. The effect size calculation used is this study with chi-square was Cramer's V, where .1 is considered a small effect size, a value of .3 is considered a medium effect size, and a value of .5 or higher is considered a large effect size.

Discussing Results

As you recall, the discussion section of a research article provides the researcher with an opportunity to interpret the results. Of course, the researcher should not overstate or attempt to apply the results to people or settings that are dissimilar to the sample population studied. In the case of causal comparative research, this means all results are interpreted with caution. Since there is no manipulation of an independent variable or assigning of participants to groups prior to implementation of the study, causation can only be suggested. Moreover, minimal or no control is exercised over potentially unlimited extraneous independent variables. Other issues may complicate matters as well. For example, let's say one wanted to explore the relationship of attitudes toward computer use and computer competency test performance—could causality not occur in either direction? Therefore, the researcher should provide honest commentary about the limitations of the study, implications for practice, and future research needs. Chapter 3 detailed what to look for in the discussion section of a research report during your literature review. These criteria certainly can be applied to what you include when writing your own results too.

The following is part of the discussion from the AP exam research. Look for the elements described in Chapter 3 (i.e., interpretation does not infer beyond the results previously presented, limitations or shortcomings are discussed, and implications for classroom or other use are noted).

The comparison of Hispanic student performance on the two AP English exams over 16 years revealed 31 statistically significant results. Furthermore, Hispanic students from Arizona outperformed their peers in California and Texas in 20 of the statistically significant comparisons. Hispanic students from California were the highest achievers in 11 of the statistically significant cases, and Hispanic students from Texas earned the lowest scores in all comparisons. . . although statistically different distributions of exam scores were present between Arizona, California, and Texas, no attempt was made to determine why the distributions differed between the three states. Moreover, the results of Hispanic students were not compared with any other ethnic group. Determining specific reasons for these differences or comparing the achievement of Hispanic students with other ethnic groups are areas for future research. . . The mission to provide access to AP for all students is an admirable one. However, placing underprepared students in AP courses is problematic (Klopfenstein & Thomas, 2009). Simply stated, if a student does not have prerequisite skills to succeed in college-level coursework, then placement in a rigorous college preparatory course may be beneficial for students as a means of developing fundamental academic skills and non-cognitive college readiness skills (Klopfenstein & Thomas, 2009). Therefore, educators should begin to examine prerequisite curriculum to determine if proper alignment exists to develop skills and knowledge necessary for student success in the most rigorous placement (Moore & Slate, 2010). (Koch, Slate & Moore, 2016, pp. 707, 708, 710)

Mixed Methods Research

As you recall from Chapter 1, some research studies include questions that are best answered using mixed methods research. In Chapter 7, you read that mixed methods research typically either employs experimental and descriptive designs, or qualitative methods and at least one type of descriptive research design. Again, although it is not uncommon for researchers to use mixed methods, typically, one design will be the primary focus of the research. Once more, as you have learned throughout the book, it all depends on what questions you are asking.

For example, Boudah (2018) investigated the effects of an intensive reading intervention on the performance of low-achieving middle school students, primarily utilizing quasi-experimental methods and inferential statistics yet also utilizing descriptive analyses to address questions regarding student performance by school and by teacher. Frazier and Trekles (2018) employed qualitative and quantitative descriptive methods to investigate the use of 1:1 iPad implementation in elementary schools. Obviously, these are but two examples of many studies that are considered mixed methods research. Other investigations may include correlational or causal comparison analyses similar to what is highlighted in this chapter, along with qualitative analysis of observation and questionnaire data. While you may find mixed methods research published in numerous professional outlets, Sage publishes a journal exclusively devoted to mixed methods research across social, behavioral, health, and human sciences. It is appropriately titled the *Journal of Mixed Methods Research* (http://journals.sagepub.com/home/mmr).

IN THEIR OWN WORDS

Lora Lee Smith-Canter, upon completing her dissertation

Descriptive research should be approached judiciously and logically. For causal comparative and correlational research, in particular, you should be very thoughtful from the start, including with your variable selections. Your variable selections should be grounded in theory and experience, making sure that any relationships you examine make sense. Secondly, your approach to analysis should fall in line with your research question and/or your hypothesis about the relationships that might exist between the variables. You may opt to examine the relationship between two variables or examine the relationships among more than two. Still, the most important concept to remember about causal comparative and correlational research is that such research is about the relationships that exist between variables and the research does not address causation. Causation is a matter for experimental research.

Putting It All Together

As in previous chapters, in this section you are presented with several examples of research questions along with possible research designs, samples, instrument/data sources, and analyses. The purpose is to enable you to see examples of how your descriptive study design might be matched with the appropriate analysis. Table 11.2 includes the examples of descriptive, correlational, and causal comparative research first introduced in Chapter 7 and highlighted throughout this chapter, along with an additional column for analysis. Can you figure out which analysis might be appropriate for the study presented in each row? Explanations follow.

In row 2, this is a correlational study, and data for the independent variable are likely nominal level and data for the dependent variable are likely ordinal level. Therefore, the Pearson r would be appropriate.

Since the study in row 3 is causal comparative, the independent variable (gender) is nominal, and the test scores are likely to be interval level. Thus, a simple t test may be in order.

In row 4, this study is descriptive and likely yields nominal and ordinal data from personal and phone interviews. Therefore, the analysis would include frequencies, percentages, means, ranges, and standard deviations.

For the correlational study in row 5, which yields ordinal data from phone interviews and the school district database, a multiple regression might be in order to analyze the variety of possible relationships among the data.

In row 6, since the study is causal comparative and may yield ordinal data on levels of teacher experience and interval data on attitudes toward inclusion, a chi square would be appropriate.

TABLE 11.2 ● Putting Your Descriptive Study All Together

Research Question	Design	Sample	Possible Data Sources and Levels of Measurement	Analysis
What are the literacy practices among high school teachers in district X?	Descriptive	Stratified sample of 100 teachers across the district high schools	Mailed questionnaire; nominal and/or ordinal data	Frequencies, percentages
What is the relationship between the use of literacy practices of high school teachers and student performance on state reading tests?	Correlational	Stratified sample of 100 teachers across the district high schools	Mailed questionnaire and state test scores from district database; nominal and interval data	
What is the relationship of gender and computer competency test scores of 7th graders?	Causal comparative	Random sample of 7th graders at a middle school	District database; nominal and interval data	
What are the views of parents toward year-round schooling?	Descriptive	Convenience sample of parents in car pool lane and from school directory at two schools	Personal and phone interviews; nominal and ordinal data	
What is the relationship between parent demographics and views toward year-round schooling?	Correlational	Random sample of parents in directory at two schools	Phone interviews and school district database; ordinal data	
What is the relationship between teachers' experience and attitudes toward inclusion?	Causal comparative	Convenience sample of high school teachers	Mailed questionnaire; ordinal and interval data	

Summary

This chapter has provided you with direction on how to analyze and interpret the results of the descriptive study that you have created and implemented. As with other forms of research, it is critical that you have an appropriate match among your questions; research design; data collection methods and procedures; analysis; and reporting, interpretation, and discussion of results. This chapter has attempted to illustrate how you might do that with several examples of descriptive, correlational, and causal comparative research. This aspect of research may be mystifying and frustrating at first, but when you understand and implement appropriate analyses, your research will become far more meaningful for you and your intended audience.

Discussion Questions

1. What is the biggest difference between correlational and causal comparative research?

2. What would be the most appropriate descriptive analysis of data from frequency counts?

3. In causal comparative research, what would be the most appropriate statistic to use when comparing scores on a state test by gender?

4. How would you report the following chi-square value [$X^2 = 6.78$, $df = 44$, $p < .01$]?

5. Interpret the following scatter plot in terms of direction and strength:

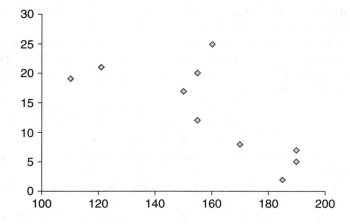

Your Research Project in Action

1. Were the instruments used in data collection valid and reliable?

2. How large were the group sample sizes to be used in the analysis?

3. If employing a correlational design, what statistic will you use in your analysis?

4. If employing a causal comparative design, what statistic will you use in your analysis?

5. After computing a correlation coefficient, did you accurately interpret the degree and magnitude of the result?

6. Would a scatter plot help your interpretation and communication of correlational results to others?

Further Reading

Loeb, S., Dynarski, S., McFarland, D., Morris, P., Reardon, S., & Reber, S. (2017). *Descriptive analysis in education: A guide for researchers.* (Report No. NCEE 2017-4023). Jessup, MD: National Center for Education Evaluation and Regional Assistance. (ERIC Document Reproduction Service No. ED ED573325)

This guide is written for educational researchers who conduct and publish descriptive and causal research as well as practitioners and other consumers of research. Chapters and sections address effective approaches to conducting and communicating findings from descriptive studies.

References

Gall, M. D., Gall, J. P., & Borg, W. R. (2006). *Educational research: An introduction* (8th ed.). Boston: Allyn & Bacon.

Green, S. (1994, April). *Crosstabulation* [Unpublished class materials]. Lawrence: University of Kansas.

Mills, G. E., & Gay, L. R. (2015). *Educational research: Competencies for analysis and applications* (11th ed.). London: Pearson.

Salkind, N. J. (2016). *Exploring research* (7th ed.). London: Pearson.

Literature Examples

Boudah, D. J. (2018). Evaluation of intensive reading strategies intervention for low-performing adolescents with and without learning disabilities. *Insights into Learning Disabilities*, 15(2), 149–159.

Frazier, D. K., & Trekles, A. M. (2018). Elementary 1:1 iPad implementation: Successes and struggles during the first year. *Journal of Educational Technology, 46*(4), 463–484.

Koch, B., Slate, J. R., & Moore, G. W. (2016). Advanced placement English exam scores: A comparison of scores for Hispanic students from California, Texas, and Arizona. *Education and Urban Society, 48*(7), 685–716.

Vennix, J., den Brok, P. & Taconis, R. (2017). Perceptions of STEM-based outreach learning activities in secondary education. *Learning Environments Research, 20*(1), 21–46.

Wood, C. L., & Gabas, C. M. (2017). Young Spanish-English speaking children's reading attitudes in relation to language skills. *Educational Research, 59*(4), 408–425. DOI: 10.1080/00131881.2017.1373028

Writing Research Reports

If you followed all of the steps outlined in this text, you likely have completed a quality research project and should now share your results. This is your opportunity to let others know what you investigated, what you found, and why it is relevant to education. There are several ways to do this, including making presentations, doing poster sessions, and writing articles for journals. This chapter focuses on preparing a final report of your research not only to meet the requirements of a college or university but also to submit to a journal or other professional outlet. In most cases, this basic written report structure can be adapted easily for oral presentations or poster sessions to professional audiences.

Writing for Publication

In education, researchers and practitioners most often use the style and conventions of the *Publication Manual of the American Psychological Association* (APA, 2010) for the writing of articles. This manual outlines how to do just about everything related to writing research reports, from headings to reference formats. It also includes a section on style and terminology use. As you prepare to write your research report, you should read

TABLE 12.1 ● Publication Style Resources	
American Psychological Association (APA) style	apastyle.org
Chicago style	chicagomanualofstyle.org
Modern Language Association (MLA) style	mla.org/style
Elements of Style (also called "Strunk and White" after the authors)	bartleby.com/141

through the manual for guidance. Although the *What Works Clearinghouse* has published a helpful reporting guide for study authors (WWC, 2012), to be published in the field of education, your article must adhere to the style used by the journal, which typically will be APA style. It is not a difficult task to make your writing conform to style guidelines, and it allows for some level of uniformity among articles and, therefore, greater ease in reading. Table 12.1 provides a list of several writing styles and websites for more information.

Again, if you are writing for educational or psychological publications, you should first review the *Publication Manual of the APA* for specifics about ethics of publication (Chapter 1), structure and content (Chapter 2), and organization of a manuscript and reducing bias in language (Chapter 3). Following are some major points to consider. First is a short description of the nuts and bolts of voice, tense, referents, and citations. Second is an outline of the requirements for each section of your report, where much of what you read in Chapters 3 and 8 (of this text) will be reviewed. To get a general idea about the style of writing necessary for publication, you should also read a variety of articles from the journal(s) in which you hope to publish. Due to space limitations, this chapter offers only a few short examples.

Nuts and Bolts

As far as a fair overview of the nuts and bolts of good writing, *Elements of Style* by William Strunk and E. B. White (2008) is recommended. If you have any questions about writing style, grammatical conventions, or misused words, this is a good reference.

Voice. The purpose of scientific writing is to convey information. It is not a venue for creative writing, but it should not be completely dull either. You should strive to use the active voice, be specific, and write clearly. For example,

The sample of 31 students included 20 boys and 11 girls.

is better than

In this study, the sample was made up of 31 students. The 31 students were divided as 20 boys and 11 girls.

Table 12.2 provides several more examples of voice.

TABLE 12.2 ● Examples of the Use of Voice	
Passive Voice	**Active Voice**
Participants were given three different assessments.	Graduate assistants administered three different assessments.
Teachers were given the opportunity to participate.	Teachers volunteered to participate.
Observations were conducted by trained observers.	Trained observers conducted 20 observations of classrooms.
Results of the reading assessment were evaluated.	Researchers evaluated reading assessment data.

Tense. In the introduction and literature review, use past tense (e.g., "Smith showed") or present perfect tense (e.g., "researchers have shown") because you are writing about research or other literature that was already published. In the description of the procedure (methods), be sure to use past tense also since you are writing about things that have already occurred. In the results section, also use past tense (e.g., "anxiety decreased significantly") to describe the results of experimental procedures or qualitative outcomes. In the discussion section, use present tense (e.g., "the results of Experiment 2 indicate") to present your conclusions (APA, 2010).

Therefore, in the introduction, "researchers *showed*" that something occurred, but in the discussion section, "this study *shows*" that something happened. Do not change tenses within paragraphs. Changing tenses can confuse the reader and make your writing style choppy. Here are two examples from one report showing the different tense uses.

Procedures

At each participating school, a daily class was created for target students who were several years behind their peers in reading performance, and at risk for continued failure and dropout. Seven teachers participated in *Xtreme Reading* professional development activities and received all necessary instructional and student materials. Teachers taught the *Xtreme Reading* class during regularly scheduled school hours on each school campus. Fidelity to instructional implementation was addressed by rigorous professional development, in-class instructional coaching by professional developers, and regularly scheduled principal walk throughs.

Discussion

Results from this evaluation, therefore, suggest that *Xtreme Reading* has promise for at-risk adolescent students, including students with learning disabilities, particularly given that one goal of *Xtreme Reading* is to close the reading performance gap for low-performing readers. This conclusion is consistent

with promising practice outcomes of *Xtreme Reading* recently recognized by
the *What Works Clearinghouse* (Boulay, Goodson, Frye, Blocklin, & Price, 2015).
(Boudah, 2018, p. 157)

Referents. In most cases, it is best to stick to the third person in professional writing,
even if it may seem silly to write "The researchers" instead of "we" or "I" if you are writing about research you have conducted. If you are referring to research done by others,
though, you should use the researchers' names (e.g., "Smith et al. proved . . .") or use
"the researchers." Try to avoid the pronouns *he* and *she*. Also, try to avoid using *he/she*
or *he or she* in your writing. If you are making a reference to a third person, choose a
pronoun and stick with it or rewrite the sentence to avoid its use. For example, in a
report about a writing strategy, the researchers would refer to the participants as "the
children" or "they" and never use a gender-specific pronoun.

Citations. You *must* give credit where credit is due in writing. If you borrow from
others, cite the source. You do not have to cite each sentence if you include a great
deal of information from the same source in the same paragraph, but you must give
credit for information borrowed as you use it. According to the *Publication Manual
of the APA* (2010), "Quotation marks should be used to indicate the exact words
of another. *Each time* you paraphrase another author (i.e., summarize a passage or

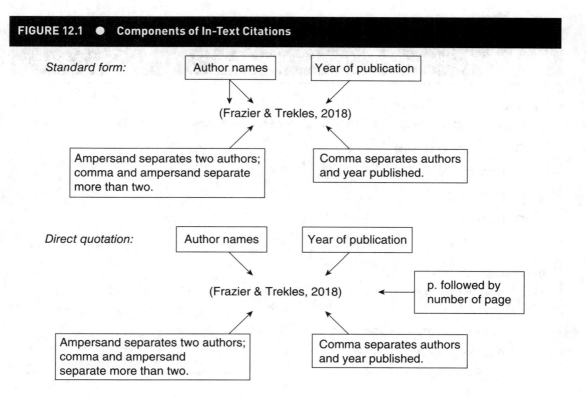

FIGURE 12.1 ● Components of In-Text Citations

Standard form: Author names   Year of publication

(Frazier & Trekles, 2018)

Ampersand separates two authors;
comma and ampersand separate
more than two.

Comma separates authors
and year published.

Direct quotation: Author names   Year of publication

(Frazier & Trekles, 2018)   p. followed by
number of page

Ampersand separates two authors;
comma and ampersand
separate more than two.

Comma separates authors
and year published.

rearrange the order of a sentence and change some of the words), you need to credit the source in the text" (p. 15). Citing others' work to support your ideas is very appropriate and necessary. However, the overuse of citations and references makes writing choppy and makes the reader wonder if you have any original thoughts. Examples of the standard APA form for in-text citations appear throughout this book; for example "(Frazier & Trekles, 2018)." See Figure 12.1 for an explanation of each component. If you use the authors' names in the text, only the year is included in the parentheses. If more than one source is cited in relation to an idea, then the sources are separated by a semicolon.

Sections of a Manuscript

In Chapter 3, you learned how to analyze the sections of research reports or articles for a literature review. Much of what was said there also applies to writing a manuscript. With all of the material you have from your study, you should not have difficulty with what to write about. Focus most of your energy on making decisions about what to include and the clearest, most specific way to express it. Following is a set of guidelines for the writing of each section of the manuscript. The sections are described in the order they are presented in the manuscript, although you may find it easier to write each section in a different order. That is up to you, as long as the final product fits together well. Figure 12.2 includes a sample checklist for each section of the manuscript.

FIGURE 12.2 ● Checklist for Writing Research Manuscript

Abstract

Brief summary of the study. Each item is a sentence or less. Usually limited to 50–100 words.

- ☐ Statement of problem/questions

- ☐ Participants

- ☐ Method

- ☐ Results

- ☐ Conclusions

Introduction

Places study in context of questions in the field. Use recent citations of relevant articles. Most articles should be research articles, not opinion papers.

- ☐ Relevance of research problem/question to the field in general

- ☐ Clear purpose of the research

Method

Describes the research process in detail. Include information about the major decisions you made and how you went about conducting the study. Use headings to help reader follow your organization. The list below is organized by topic area. You may include some of the information in a different section if it fits better there.

1. Participants (all that apply)

   ☐ Number

   ☐ Gender

   ☐ Age and grade level

   ☐ Ethnicity

   ☐ Socioeconomic status (SES)

   ☐ Standardized achievement and other test scores

   ☐ Behavioral characteristics linked to the research question

   ☐ Years of professional experience

   ☐ Degrees earned

   ☐ How chosen

2. Setting

   ☐ Urban, rural, or suburban

   ☐ Overall SES of students and families in the community

   ☐ Age of the school

   ☐ Extent of school resources and support

   ☐ Size of student population and average class size

   ☐ Classroom or school studied

   ☐ Description of classroom or school of study (e.g., content area, resources available, number of teachers, desks or tables, etc.)

3. Research Procedures (all that apply)

   ☐ Step-by-step description of experimental intervention implementation

   ☐ Necessary time and materials required for experimental intervention

   ☐ Training procedures and conditions for implementing intervention

(Continued)

(Continued)

- ☐ Who implemented the intervention, their responsibilities, and the extent of preparation for implementation
- ☐ How participants were selected and grouped
- ☐ Incentives to participants
- ☐ Monetary costs associated with implementing intervention
- ☐ Qualitative tradition of the study
- ☐ Role and perceptions or biases of researcher
4. Data Collection and Analysis
   - ☐ Description and/or examples of types of data collected
   - ☐ How data collectors were trained
   - ☐ How data were collected
   - ☐ How researcher made sure data collectors followed procedures (reliability)
   - ☐ How data were managed (e.g., transcribed, entered into statistics program)
   - ☐ If statistics were used in analyzing the data, an explanation of why each statistic was selected
   - ☐ If qualitative data were collected, a detailed description of data analysis procedures used (with examples)
   - ☐ Description of how validity and trustworthiness issues were addressed

Results

Details the results of the data you collected. Give only the facts and address each measure and question included in your methods section. Use minimal jargon. Display results in graphs or other visuals when possible.

- ☐ Explanation of outcomes or effects for different groups/populations
- ☐ Explanation of patterns or theories developed

Discussion

Interpret how the results are important to the field, how they fit into previous research, and what future research is necessary. Make sure the interpretation does not infer beyond the results presented.

- ☐ Limitations or shortcomings discussed
- ☐ Implications for classroom or other use noted
- ☐ Description given regarding where to get more information
- ☐ Future directions for research described

Source: Adapted from APA (2010, pp. 27–37)

Abstract. The abstract provides the reader with the vital information about the research, including a brief statement of purpose, a mention of sample and methods, and a short description of results. In many cases, editors restrict abstracts to 50–100 words.

Introduction. The introduction gives the reader a glimpse of your research question. In this section, you must describe your research purpose and show how it is relevant to the field. You can do this by developing an argument for the question by using previous research, noting theoretical or opinion papers calling for research on the topic, or identifying a gap in the research base related to your topic. Use citations of recent articles or related writings. Try to get across that you have reviewed the literature on your topic and found your research necessary to help complete it. Finish the introduction with a statement of your research question and purpose.

Methods. Once you have stated the purpose of your research, you must tell the reader how you went about conducting it. The methods section may be the longest section of your manuscript. You must report the following:

1. Participants

2. Setting

3. Research procedures

4. Data collection procedures

5. Data analysis procedures

See Figure 12.2 for specifics about what to include in each of these subsections. It is best to set up your methods section with subsection headings. Use the list above to start with and then choose more appropriate subheadings as you write. Headings and levels of heading are described in the *Publication Manual of the APA*. Using headings helps your readers tremendously and may alleviate the need to add extra sentences that cue them as to what you are going to write about next.

Results. The results section of your manuscript should describe how the study turned out. It is important to organize this section well and describe results for each measure you identified in the methods section. For example, organizing results by research question, if appropriate, makes for a readable research paper. In that way, you can then group your measures by overarching concept. If you conducted a study about the performance of students on reading comprehension tasks and their attitudes toward reading comprehension after learning a reading comprehension strategy, you might want to organize your results section into two subsections: one that gives results on measures of reading comprehension performance, and the other that gives results on measures of attitudes toward reading comprehension.

In addition, the purpose of the results section is to present results, not interpret them. That is for the discussion section. The results section is for "just the facts." Be sure always to refer to and use the word *data* in the plural form (e.g., "the data *were*," not "the data *was*").

Discussion. Writing the discussion section allows you to interpret the results of your study in terms of its relevance to the field. Here is where you should describe whether or not what you found means anything and, if it does, what that meaning is. In other words, let's say you found statistically significant differences between the group that received your intervention and the group that did not. Great. But is this statistical significance also of practical significance? How do your results fit in with previous research? Have you miraculously found significant results where others have not? Do you have an explanation for this? In addition, you should include a section noting the limitations of the study and a section about the research still necessary in this area.

References. Your reference page should begin on a separate page from the text of your manuscript. It should include *only* sources that were referenced in the manuscript. The list should be alphabetized by first author. The standard APA form (APA, 2010, p. 202) for a nonperiodical (e.g., book) reference is

Author, A. A. (1994). *Title of work.* Location: Publisher.

For a periodical (i.e., journal) reference, the standard APA form (APA, 2010, p. 198) is

Author, A. A., Author, B. B., & Author, C. C. (2018). Title of article. *Title of Periodical, xx*, ###–###. [where *xx* is the journal volume number and ### is the page number]

Many people today cite a variety of online references. If you are citing an online journal, you will want to add the phrase *Retrieved from http://xxxxxxxxx* following the page numbers of the journal. If you are citing other online sources such as websites, e-books, or even YouTube, please refer to the APA Style page at https://www.apastyle .org/learn/quick-guide-on-references for specific instructions and examples.

Figures and Tables. In writing manuscripts, it is always prudent to include information in tables and figures that will help the reader understand your study. Not every manuscript will have figures and tables, but a figure showing how concepts are related or a table including statistical results is often helpful. The point of figures and tables is to put information into a concise form and not to repeat everything in words. Therefore, if you include figures and tables, make sure they are relevant to the report and convey important information. If you repeat everything in the text, do not bother with figures and tables. The *Publication Manual of the APA* provides guidance for figures and tables.

Getting Your Writing Published

Having your manuscript published in a professional journal is a satisfying accomplishment. Not only do you get to see your name in print, but others in the profession see your name and associate it with your work. Most importantly, you are able to share the results of your hard work with others. How does this happen?

Instructions for Authors

Getting manuscripts published in professional journals can be a long process, so you must be patient. In every print journal or on the journal website, there is a section called "Instructions for Authors." In this section, the editors outline the purpose of the journal, the types of manuscripts they are interested in publishing, and the steps necessary to submit a manuscript for consideration. Typically, there will also be information on how to prepare figures and tables, whether the journal expects APA format or another style, and its policy on use of copyrighted material. There will usually be an explanation of the review process also—if there isn't, you might want to inquire about this.

In short, it is best that you read these instructions carefully before you begin to write your research report. If you hope to target certain journals, you may have to alter your format to fit their standards. For example, you may write a different manuscript for a journal published for practitioners than one published for researchers. The information that you share may be similar, but you will focus and expand on different aspects of the research as appropriate to the audience.

Submission and Review Process

Journal editors make the decisions about the publication of articles. Once you have written your manuscript and submitted electronic or hard copies, the editor reviews it for relevancy and appropriateness for the journal. If the editor decides that the manuscript fits the purpose of the journal, she typically sends it to several review board members. The review board membership is usually printed on the back of the front cover of a print journal or available on the journal website. The editor may have a policy of an open review (the reviewers know the names and affiliations of the authors) or of a blind review (the reviewers do not know the names and affiliations of the authors). The review policy is generally included in the author instructions. Editors choose reviewers based on their standing in the field (i.e., the quality of their research), their writing skills (i.e., their track record of publication), and their area of expertise (i.e., their knowledge of the journal's area of focus). There may be other considerations as well, but these are the major ones.

Once the reviewers receive the manuscript, they read it and provide feedback on its appropriateness, quality of the design, and character of writing. The reviewers also make a recommendation about publication: publish as is, publish with revision, revise and resubmit, or do not publish. The reviewers send their comments and recommendation to the editor. The editor compiles comments and recommendations, and then makes a final decision to send to the writer. If the editor decides to accept the manuscript outright or accept with revisions, you will receive notification with recommendations from the editor. Sometimes, after a manuscript has been revised and resubmitted, the editor will send the revised manuscript back to the same reviewers. Other times, the editor will determine if your revisions are sufficient. If the editor rejects your manuscript, you will receive notification of that decision also.

Once your manuscript has been accepted, the editor or assistant will remain in contact with you and will ask you to proof final copies for publication. It is very important that you try to make the deadlines given by the editor to ensure that your manuscript is published in a timely manner. If you do not meet the deadlines given, your manuscript may be assigned to later editions of the journal. Depending upon the backlog of articles for a journal and the number of times you are asked to revise your manuscript, it can take upwards of a year or more before you see it in print. Do not be discouraged. It is a professional honor to have your manuscript published in education, and it usually only costs you time! In other professions, it costs researchers big money to publish in certain journals.

The Ethics

Most journals require that you sign over the copyright of the article to the publisher of the journal. Though this seems a bit odd, it is common practice. This protects the publisher from unauthorized use of the material you submit. The publisher will also ask you to sign that you have given credit to sources you have used in the writing of the article and that you have not plagiarized others' work.

In addition, in the "Instructions for Authors" section, most journals will require that the manuscript not be submitted or published in its entirety in other journals. This does not mean that you must submit all of your research in one article to one journal. On the contrary, perhaps several aspects of your study can be included in separate articles. For example, if your mixed methods study included both quantitative and qualitative methods, it may be appropriate to divide these two pieces between separate articles. The introduction and methods sections may be similar, but the majority of the articles will differ. Also, if a journal editor rejects your work, it is okay to send it to another journal.

You may be saying, "This sounds like too much work. I've already spent so much time doing the research. Why would I want to spend more time writing it up (unless

TECHNOLOGY IN RESEARCH

APA-Style Helper

Most educational journals have adopted the style guidelines of the American Psychological Association. These guidelines provide details about how every aspect of a research report or journal article submission should look, including references, headings, charts, tables, citations, etc.

There are many ways to learn how to write in APA style: read the manual, take a course, or participate in a graduate program that requires you to submit all of your written work in APA style. Online tutorials may be helpful also. APA offers its own tutorial for the sixth edition at apastyle.org/learn/tutorials/brief-guide.aspx. Many universities have helpful online guides, tips, or tutorials as well. The Purdue Online Writing Lab (OWL) is one recommended resource; it is available at http://owl.english .purdue.edu/owl/resource/560/01/.

I have to)?" The simple answer is: *Because you must*. The professional knowledge base in education expands only by the participation of professionals in the field. If you followed the steps in this book, you designed a quality study. You worked hard to find answers to your research question. Share the results with others—even if the results are not necessarily what you had hoped for.

Putting It All Together

Once you have completed writing your research report, and even before you submit it to your professor, committee, or to a journal editor, give it to someone else to read. Choose someone who has some general knowledge in the area of inquiry, but who has not been intimately involved in the research project. Ask your reader to provide you with feedback both on the report's content and its writing style. You may want to ask more than one person to do this. When you get the report back, take some time to review the comments, think about them, and then decide what feedback you will use and what you will disregard.

Finally, after you have written the manuscript and submitted it for a grade or for publication, be sure to back up your copy electronically in more than one place. In addition, keep all of your research materials for at least 5 years. You may be ready to rid your office of clutter, but it is important to keep your files long enough to address any questions from reviewers or professors, or to reconsider results if needed.

Summary

The writing process is often long and arduous, but it is very important to share your research with the professional community. You can do this in a variety of ways, including giving presentations, writing research reports, and publishing journal articles. Professionals in education use several writing and style conventions, and you should adhere to these in your reports.

One way to communicate your findings to others in the field is by publishing in journals. Journal editors handle the process of choosing articles to publish and making sure they are revised to fit the standards of the journal. Many journals require that submitted articles be reviewed by other professionals in the field before publication. The "Instructions for Authors" section of journals outlines the process for article submission.

Articles about studies and research reports generally include the following sections: abstract, introduction, methods, results, discussion, as well as references. Most education journals require that an author use the guidelines of the American Psychological Association found in the *Publication Manual of the APA*.

When writing a journal article or research report, it is imperative that you give credit to the work of others that you use. This chapter outlined the necessary components of research reports and journal articles and described the basics of writing style for professional publications.

References

American Psychological Association (APA). (2010). *Publication manual of the American Psychological Association* (6th ed.). Washington, DC: Author.

Strunk, W., & White, E. B. (2008). *The Elements of Style* (50th anniversary ed.). New York: Longman.

What Works Clearinghouse. (2012). *What Works Clearinghouse reporting guide for study authors.* Princeton, NJ: What Works Clearinghouse. (ERIC Document Reproduction Service No. ED534326)

Literature Examples

Boudah, D. J. (2018). Evaluation of intensive reading strategies intervention for low-performing adolescents with and without learning disabilities. *Insights into Learning Disabilities*, 15(2), 149–159.

• Appendix A •

Organizations That Support Educational Research

There are many professional organizations and groups in education. The organizations that focus on research in education can provide valuable support and resources to beginning researchers. Some of these groups have members from all areas of education, and others serve smaller subsections of education professionals. This appendix contains information about some of these organizations, including each organization's mission statement and goals, its sources of support, how it supports researchers, where to find more information, and any type of funding these groups may provide. It was impossible to highlight all the groups that support educational research, so groups are highlighted based upon their commitment to research, the ease with which they are accessible, and the reputation they have attained in education.

Alliance for International Educational and Cultural Exchange

The Alliance for International Educational and Cultural Exchange was established in 1992 to promote federal policies that support and advance international exchange in all its dimensions. Representing 79 U.S.-based exchange organizations, the Alliance has established itself as the leading policy voice of the American exchange community. The Alliance formed through a merger of two predecessor organizations: the Liaison Group, which represented higher education associations, and the International Exchange Association (IEA), a coalition of citizen and youth exchange groups. (alliance-exchange.org)

1828 L Street, NW, Suite 1150
Washington, DC 20036
Phone: 202-293-6141
Fax: 202-293-6144

American Educational Research Association (AERA)

The American Educational Research Association (AERA), founded in 1916, is concerned with improving the educational process by encouraging scholarly inquiry related to education and by promoting the dissemination and practical application of research results. AERA is the most prominent international professional organization with the primary goal of advancing educational research and its practical application. Its 22,000 members are educators, administrators, directors of research, counselors, evaluators, graduate students, behavioral scientists, and persons working with testing or evaluation in federal, state, and local agencies. The broad range of disciplines represented by the membership includes education, psychology, statistics, sociology, history, economics, philosophy, anthropology, and political science. (aera.net)

1430 K Street, NW
Suite 1200
Washington, DC 20005
Phone (202) 238-3200
Fax (202) 238-3250
www.aera.net

American Psychological Association (APA)

Based in Washington, D.C., the American Psychological Association (APA) is a scientific and professional organization that represents psychology in the United States. With 150,000 members, APA is the largest association of psychologists worldwide. The goals of the American Psychological Association are to advance psychology as a science and profession and as a means of promoting health, education, and human welfare by

- the encouragement of psychology in all its branches in the broadest and most liberal manner;

- the promotion of research in psychology and the improvement of research methods and conditions;

- the improvement of the qualifications and usefulness of psychologists through high standards of ethics, conduct, education, and achievement;

- the establishment and maintenance of the highest standards of professional ethics and conduct of the members of the Association; and

- the increase and diffusion of psychological knowledge through meetings, professional contacts, reports, papers, discussions, and publications, thereby to advance scientific interests and inquiry, and the application of research findings to the promotion of health, education, and the public welfare. (apa.org)

750 First Street, NE
Washington, DC 20002-4242
(800) 374-2721 or (202) 336-5500

American Speech-Language-Hearing Association (ASHA)

ASHA is the professional, scientific, and credentialing association for more than 123,000 members and affiliates who are speech-language pathologists, audiologists, and speech, language, and hearing scientists in the United States and internationally. The mission of the American Speech-Language-Hearing Association is to promote the interests of and provide the highest-quality services for professionals in audiology, speech-language pathology, and speech and hearing science and to advocate for people with communication disabilities. (asha.org)

Members: 800-498-2071
Non-Members: 800-638-8255

Council for Exceptional Children–Division for Research (CEC-DR)

The CEC Division for Research (CEC-DR) is the official division of the Council for Exceptional Children devoted to the advancement of research related to the education of individuals with disabilities and/or who are gifted. The goals of CEC-DR include the promotion of equal partnership with practitioners in designing, conducting, and interpreting research in special education. The Division for Research of the Council for Exceptional Children supports and encourages useful and sound research about children, youth, and adults with disabilities, their families, and the people who work with them. (cecdr.org)

2900 Crystal Drive, Suite 100
Arlington, VA 22202-3557
P: 888-232-7733 TTY: 866-915-5000

International Literacy Association (ILA)

The International Literacy Association (ILA) is a professional organization for those involved in teaching reading to students of all ages. According to its website, ILA's "focus has expanded to address a broad range of issues in literacy education worldwide." One of the major areas of involvement for ILA is in supporting research and research dissemination. ILA has played an increasingly important role in advocating for research-based instruction in schools, most notably in promoting research-based instruction in reading during the development of the No Child Left Behind Act.

ILA promotes research and publication of research on literacy and literacy issues "through a series of dedicated research awards, grants, and fellowships." The following awards and grants might be of interest:

The *Teacher as Researcher Grant* supports classroom teachers in their inquiries about literacy and instruction. Grants will be awarded up to $5,000, although priority will be given to smaller grants (e.g., $1,000 to $2,000) in order to provide support for as many teacher researchers as possible.

The *Elva Knight Research Grant* provides up to $10,000 for research in reading and literacy. Contingent upon available funds in any given year, as many as four grants may be awarded. Projects should be completed within two years and may be carried out using any research method or approach as long as the focus of the project is on research in reading or literacy.

The *Jeanne S. Chall Research Fellowship* is a $6,000 grant established to encourage and support reading research by promising scholars. The special emphasis of the fellowship is to support research efforts in the following areas: beginning reading (theory, research, and practice that improves the effectiveness of learning to read); readability (methods of predicting the difficulty of texts); reading difficulty (diagnosis, treatment, and prevention); stages of reading development; the relationship of vocabulary to reading; and diagnosing and teaching adults with limited reading ability.

The Research and Studies Committee of ILA is dedicated to advancing research, as described in the following charges:

a. Determine issues that merit intensive study and make recommendations to the board.

b. Offer leadership in research activities in cooperation with other committees.

c. Encourage the submittal of proposals for ILA conferences and publications to disseminate research findings, subject to the regular review process.

(https://www.literacyworldwide.org/)
PO Box 8139
Newark, DE 19714-8139
800.336.7323 (U.S. and Canada)
302.731.1600 (all other countries)

National Association of School Psychologists (NASP)

The National Association of School Psychologists (NASP) is a nonprofit association representing over 22,000 school psychologists from across the United States and other countries. The mission of NASP is to represent and support school psychology with leadership to enhance the mental health and educational competence of all children. Partnering with all who share our commitment to children and youth is critical to our mission. The website is a resource for members, parents, educators, and others interested in helping children and their families. (nasponline.org)

4340 East West Highway
Suite 402
Bethesda, MD 20814
Main: 301-657-0270 or 866-331-6277 (toll free)
Fax: 301-657-0275

National Council for the Social Studies (NCSS)

The National Council for the Social Studies (NCSS) is an organization for all professionals involved in teaching social studies. NCSS defines *social studies* as "the integrated study of the social sciences and humanities to promote civic competence." On its website, NCSS describes social studies as being a coordinated, systematic study drawing upon such disciplines as anthropology, archaeology, economics, geography, history, law, philosophy, political science, psychology, religion, and sociology, as well as appropriate content from the humanities, mathematics, and natural sciences. In essence, social studies promotes knowledge of and involvement in civic affairs. And because civic issues—such as health care, crime, and foreign policy—are multidisciplinary in nature, understanding these issues and developing resolutions to them require multidisciplinary education. These characteristics are the key defining aspects of social studies.

With this in mind, NCSS provides support for educators in their quest to be better educators in many ways, including providing grants and awards for research. The NCSS and the Research Committee sponsor annual research awards for scholarly inquiry in the social studies. These awards are granted to inquiry in any area of social studies, and "research is broadly defined to include experimental, qualitative, historical, and philosophical work."

Two of the research awards of interest are these:

Larry Metcalf Exemplary Dissertation Award

Frequency: Biennial, odd-numbered years

Award: $250 commemorative gift, annual conference session for research presentation

Purpose: The Larry Metcalf Exemplary Dissertation Award recognizes outstanding research completed in pursuit of the doctoral degree.

Exemplary Research Award

Award: Commemorative gift, annual conference session for research presentation

Purpose: The Exemplary Research in Social Studies Award acknowledges and encourages scholarly inquiry in significant issues and possibilities for social studies education.

The NCSS also participates in numerous professional development activities, provides multiple publication outlets, and hosts an annual conference with many opportunities for presenting. (socialstudies.org)

8555 Sixteenth Street
Suite 500
Silver Spring, Maryland 20910
Telephone: (301) 588-1800
Fax: (301) 588-2049

The National Council of Teachers of English (NCTE)

The National Council of Teachers of English (NCTE) is an organization dedicated to improving the teaching and learning of English. The group boasts membership of over 60,000 in both the United States and other countries. The Council promotes the development of literacy and the use of language to construct personal and public worlds and to achieve full participation in society through the learning and teaching of English and the related arts and sciences of language.

NCTE includes a Research Foundation that sponsors several grants and encourages the conduct and dissemination of high-quality research:

The *Cultivating New Voices Among Scholars of Color (CNV) program* is intended to provide support, mentoring, and networking opportunities for early career scholars of color. The program aims to work with graduate students of color to cultivate their ability to draw from their own cultural/linguistic perspectives as they conceptualize, plan, conduct, and write their research. The program provides socialization into the research community and interaction with established scholars whose own work can be enriched by their engagement with new ideas and perspectives.

NCTE provides many opportunities for publication and professional development at its website. (ncte.org)

Urbana, IL, Office
1111 W. Kenyon Road
Urbana, IL 61801-1096
Phone: 217-328-3870 or 877-369-6283
Fax: 217-328-9645

National Council of Teachers of Mathematics (NCTM)

The National Council of Teachers of Mathematics (NCTM) is "a public voice of mathematics education, providing vision, leadership, and professional development to support teachers in ensuring mathematics learning of the highest quality for all students." In addition to providing leadership in mathematics research, NCTM provides numerous grants and awards through the Mathematics Education Trust. (nctm.org)

1906 Association Drive
Reston, VA 20191-1502
Phone: (800) 235-7566 | (703) 620-9840
Fax: (703) 476-2970

National Institute of Child Health and Human Development (NICHD), Child Development and Behavior (CDB) Branch

The National Institute of Child Health and Human Development (NICHD), created by Congress in 1962, supports and conducts research on topics related to the health of children, adults, families, and populations. These health topics include the following:

- Reducing infant deaths
- Improving the health of women and men

- Understanding reproductive health

- Learning about growth and development

- Examining problems of birth defects and mental retardation

- Enhancing function and involvement across the life span through medical rehabilitation research

The NICHD is part of the National Institutes of Health (NIH), the federal government's major medical research agency. NICHD research focuses on these ideas:

- Events that happen prior to and throughout pregnancy as well as during childhood have a great impact on the health and well-being of adults.

- Human growth and development is a lifelong process that has many phases and functions.

- Learning about the reproductive health of men and women and educating people about reproductive practices is important to both individuals and societies.

- Developing medical rehabilitation interventions can improve the health and well-being of people with disabilities.

Within the NICHD is the Child Development and Behavior Branch (CDB). This branch is most well known for its recent reading research. However, CDB also supports research on psychological, psychobiological, and educational development from conception to maturity, focusing on the following program areas:

- Social and affective development; child maltreatment and violence

- Developmental cognitive psychology, behavioral neuroscience, and psychobiology

- Behavioral pediatrics and health promotion research

- Human learning and learning disabilities

- Language, bilingual, and biliteracy development and disorders; adult, family, and adolescent literacy

- Early learning and school readiness

- Mathematics and science cognition and learning—development and disorders

The Child Development and Behavior Branch also provides information on these programs and makes funding opportunities available through NICHD. (nichd.nih.gov/about/org/crmc/cdb/)

Phone: 1-800-370-2943
TTY: 1-888-320-6942
Email: NICHDInformationResourceCenter@mail.nih.gov
Fax: 1-866-760-5947
Mail: P.O. Box 3006, Rockville, MD 20847

National Science Teachers Association

The National Science Teachers Association (NSTA) supports and encourages teaching, learning, and innovation in the sciences. The mission of NSTA is "to promote excellence and innovation in science teaching and learning for all." The NSTA supports research in several ways, including awards and grants to students, teachers, and principals. Many of these awards are specific to certain areas of science, such as rocketry or space. Following are examples of general awards. For more information about NSTA awards and recognition, see nsta.org/about/awards.aspx.

The *Vernier Technology Awards* recognize and reward the innovative use of data collection technology using a computer, graphing calculator, or other handheld device in the science classroom. A total of seven awards will be presented:

- One award at the elementary level (Grades K–5)
- Two awards at the middle level (Grades 6–8)
- Three awards at the high school level (Grades 9–12)
- One award at the college level

Each award will consist of $1,000 toward expenses to attend the NSTA National Convention, $1,000 in cash for the teacher, and $1,000 in Vernier products.

The *Delta Education/CPO Science Awards for Excellence in Inquiry-based Science Teaching* recognize and honor three full-time PreK–12 teachers of science who successfully use inquiry-based science to enhance teaching and learning in their classroom.

(nsta.org)
1840 Wilson Blvd.
Arlington VA 22201
Main number: 703.243.7100
Fax: 703.243.7177

National Association of Secondary School Principals

The National Association of Secondary School Principals is the leading association for principals and other school leaders across the United States. National Association of Secondary School Principals aims to transform education through school leadership, recognizing that the fulfillment of each student's potential relies on great leaders in every school committed to the success of each student.

School Leaders

Through award-winning publications, professional development opportunities, ready access to relevant research, and persistence in advocating on behalf of school leaders, NASSP helps to advance education by:

- Promoting high professional standards
- Focusing attention on school leaders' challenges
- Providing a "national voice" for school leaders
- Building public confidence in education
- Strengthening the role of the principal as instructional leader
- Publicizing the issues and interests of our members in the news media

Student Leaders

National Association of Secondary School Principals founded and administer the following student leadership programs:

- National Honor Society and National Junior Honor Society
- National Student Council
- National Elementary Honor Society

(www.nassp.org/?SSO=true)
1904 Association Drive
Reston, VA 20191-1537
Main: (703) 860-0200, (800) 253-7746
Sales: (866) 647-7253
Travel: (703) 860-7201, (800) 974-9393

American Counseling Association

The American Counseling Association is a non-profit, professional, and educational organization. The American Counseling Association is dedicated to the growth and enhancement of the counseling profession. It was founded in 1952 and is the world's largest association that exclusively represents professional counselors in a variety of settings. The American Counseling Association's mission statement is to enhance the quality of life in society by promoting the development of professional counselors, advancing the counseling profession, and using the profession and practice of counseling to promote respect for human dignity and diversity. The website has a variety of resources such as membership, which includes how to join and the benefits of becoming a member of American Counseling Associations, information about continuing education/licensure requirements, publications, and career tips and resources.

https://www.counseling.org
6101 Stevenson Ave.
Alexandria, VA 22304
Local Numbers:
ACA: (703) 823-9800
FAX: (703) 823-0252

Toll-Free Numbers:
ACA: (800) 347-6647
FAX: (800) 473-2329

The American Occupational Therapy Association

The American Occupational Therapy Association was established in 1917 to represent the interests and concerns of occupational therapy practitioners and students of occupational therapy to help improve the quality of occupational therapy services. The American Occupational Therapy has over 60,000 members, including occupational therapists, occupational therapy assistants, and occupational therapy students and represents 213,000 occupational therapy practitioners and students in the United States. The American Occupational Therapy Association helps educate the public and helps advance the professions by providing resources, setting standards, and serving as an advocate to improve health care. The American Occupational Therapy Association has several major programs and activities that are directed toward assuring the quality of occupational therapy services. The American Occupational Therapy Association educates the public and advances the profession by providing resources, setting standards, and serving as an advocate to improve health care. The American Occupational Therapy Association's Mission statement is to "advance occupational therapy practice, education, and research through standard setting and advocacy on behalf of its members, the profession, and the public."

https://www.aota.org
1-800-SAY-AOTA (729-2682)
Non-Members Phone Number
301-652-6611
4720 Montgomery Lane, Suite 200
Bethesda, MD 20814

American Physical Therapy Association

The American Physical Therapy Association is an individual membership and professional organization that represents over 100,000 members of physical therapists, physical therapist assistants, and students of physical therapy. American Physical Therapy Association aims to improve the health and quality of life of individuals. They do so by physical therapist practice, education, research, and by increasing the awareness of the roles of physical therapy in the nation's health care system.

https://www.apta.org
1111 North Fairfax Street
Alexandria, VA 22314-1488
Phone: 800/999-APTA (2782), or 703/684-APTA (2782)
Fax: 703/684-7343

• Appendix B •

Using Microsoft® Excel to Analyze Data

Microsoft Excel has numerous add-in features that support some statistical analyses. To access these features, you must load the Analysis ToolPak. Following are directions for using Excel 2015. More recent versions of Excel may have different menu starting points for accessing the commands, but the process of using the statistical functions and their results are very similar.

Loading the Analysis ToolPak

Open the *Tools* menu in Excel. If *Data Analysis* appears near the bottom of the menu, the Analysis ToolPak is already loaded. If the menu is not visible, choose *Add-Ins* from the *Tools* menu.

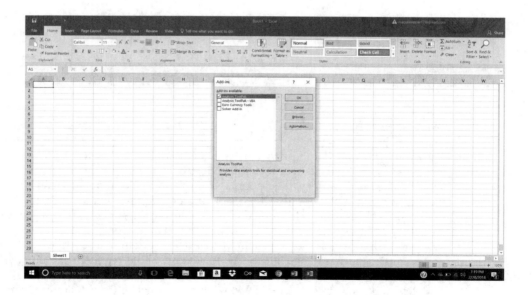

In the Add-Ins box, click the box next to Analysis ToolPak and click OK. The *Data Analysis* menu then should appear on the *Tools* menu. Depending on your Microsoft Office installation, you may be prompted to download this component.

Descriptive Statistics

The Descriptive Statistics tool generates simple descriptive statistics, including mean, median, and standard deviation for a data set. To compute these statistics, choose the *Tools* tab and *Data Analysis*. In the *Data Analysis* box, select *Descriptive Statistics* and specify the cells that contain your data in the Input Range box. Click the Summary Statistics checkbox in the lower left corner. By default, Excel generates the statistics on a new worksheet.

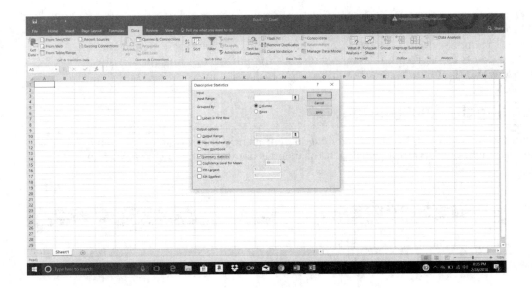

Histograms

The Excel Histogram tool allows you to represent descriptive data as noted in Chapter 11. The data may be from sources that you collected, or the data may be extant from a school database, an agency, the National Assessment of Educational Progress (NAEP) online, or other public records. The Histogram tool requires that a Bin Range or list of categories be specified. The Bin Range represents the categories for which you want frequency accounts. For example, Bin Range 1 in a column on your Excel worksheet might represent the number of people who earned a certain score such as 61, 72, 93, and so forth. and Bin Range 2 in a second column would represent the number of people who scored in the ranges from 0–20, 21–40, 41–60, 61–80, 81–100.

After you have your data in an Excel worksheet, generate the actual histogram. In older versions of Excel, choose *Tools* and *Data Analysis* and select Histogram in the Data Analysis box. In the Histogram box, the Input Range is the actual data you want to summarize; for example, the list of all test scores from your Excel spreadsheet. The Bin Range is the range you created with the different categories. Click the Chart Output box in the bottom of the dialog box and click OK. Excel produces a frequency distribution chart like the figures in Chapter 11. In newer versions of Excel, the task is even simpler. In fact, some online tutorials easily walk you through the process, including **https://www.excel-easy.com/examples/histogram.html** as well as YouTube videos such as **https://www.youtube.com/watch?v=is14ehdy7jo.**

ANOVA

The Excel ANOVA analysis tools provide several options. You must first determine the number of factors and the number of samples you have from the populations you want to test. To access ANOVA, click on the *Tools* tab, *Data Analysis,* and then in the box select one of the ANOVA options.

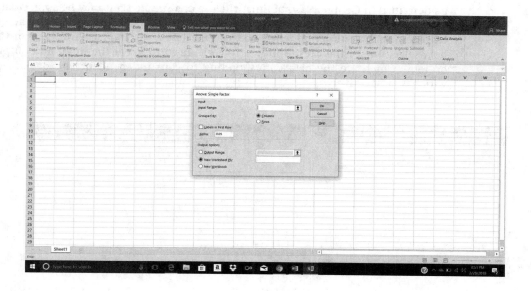

You will need to select the input and output options, which are the data corresponding to your independent and dependent variables, respectively. The following explanations are excerpted from the Microsoft Excel help function description:

ANOVA: Single Factor. This tool performs a simple analysis of variance on data from two or more samples. The analysis provides a test of the hypothesis that each sample is drawn from the same underlying probability distribution against the alternative hypothesis that underlying probability distributions are not the same for all samples. If there are only two samples, the worksheet function, TTEST, can equally well be used. With more than two samples, there is no convenient generalization of TTEST, and the Single Factor ANOVA model should be called upon instead.

ANOVA: Two-Factor With Replication. This analysis tool is useful when data can be classified along two dimensions. For example, in an experiment to measure the height of plants, the plants may be given different brands of fertilizer (for example, A, B, C) and might also be kept at different temperatures (for example, low and high). For each of the six possible pairs of fertilizer and temperature, one has an equal number of observations of plant height.

ANOVA: Two-Factor Without Replication. This analysis tool is useful when data are classified on two dimensions as in ANOVA: Two-Factor With Replication. However, for this tool, one assumes that there is only a single observation for each pair; for example, for each (fertilizer, temperature) pair. Using this tool, one can apply the tests in steps 1 and 2 of the ANOVA: Two-Factor With Replication case, but one does not have enough data to apply the test in step 3.

t Tests

As described in Chapter 9, sometimes the use of a simple *t* test may be appropriate. Microsoft Excel can quickly and easily help you with this analysis also. To access the *t* test analysis function, click on the *Tools* tab, *Data Analysis*, and then in the box, select one of the *t* test options. You will need to select the input and output options, which are the data corresponding to your independent and dependent variables, respectively.

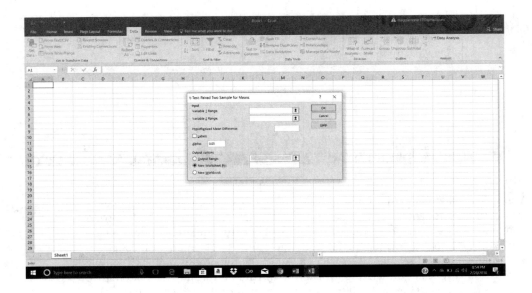

The following *t* test explanations are excerpted from the Microsoft Excel help function description:

The Two-Sample *t* Test analysis tools test for equality of the population means underlying each sample. The three tools employ different assumptions: (a) the population variances are equal, (b) the population variances are not equal, and (c) the two samples represent before-treatment and after-treatment observations on the same subjects.

For all three tools below, *t* is computed and shown as "t Stat" in the output tables. Depending on the data, *t* can be negative or nonnegative. Under the assumption of equal underlying population means, if $t < 0$, "P(T <= t) one-tail" gives the probability that a value of the *t* statistic would be observed that is more negative than *t*. If $t \geq 0$, "P(T <= t) one-tail" gives the probability that a value of the *t* statistic would be observed that is more positive than *t*. "t Critical one-tail" gives the cutoff value so that the probability of observing a value of the *t* statistic greater than or equal to "t Critical one-tail" is alpha. "P(T <= t) two-tail" gives the probability that a value of the *t* statistic would be observed that is larger in absolute value than *t*. "t Critical two-tail" gives the cutoff value such that the probability of an observed *t* statistic larger in absolute value than "P Critical two-tail" is alpha.

t-Test: Two-Sample Assuming Equal Variances. This analysis tool performs a two-sample *t* test. This *t* test form, referred to as a homoscedastic *t* test, assumes that the two data sets come from distributions with the same variances. You can use this *t* test to determine whether the two samples are likely to have come from distributions with equal population means.

t-Test: Two-Sample Assuming Unequal Variances. This analysis tool performs a two-sample *t* test. This *t* test form, referred to as a heteroscedastic *t* test, assumes that the two data sets came from distributions with unequal variances. As with the equal variances *t* test above, you can use this *t* test to determine whether the two samples are likely to have come from distributions with equal population means. Use this test when there are distinct subjects in the two samples. Use the paired test, described below, when there is a single set of subjects and the two samples represent measurements for each subject before and after a treatment.

The Excel worksheet function, TTEST, uses the calculated *df* value without rounding since it is possible to compute a value for TTEST with a noninteger *df*. Because of these different approaches to determining degrees of freedom, results of TTEST and this *t* test tool will differ in the unequal variances case.

t-Test: Paired Two Sample for Means. You can use a paired test when there is a natural pairing of observations in the samples, such as when a sample group is tested twice—before and after an experiment. This analysis tool and its formula perform a paired two-sample *t* test to determine whether observations taken before a treatment and observations taken after a treatment are likely to have come from distributions with equal population means. This *t* test form does not assume that the variances of both populations are equal.

Correlation

When you conduct correlational studies, Microsoft Excel statistical functions also may help you with less complex analyses. To access this analysis function, click on the *Tools* tab, *Data Analysis*, and then in the box select *Correlation*. You will need to select the input and output options, which are the data corresponding to your variables.

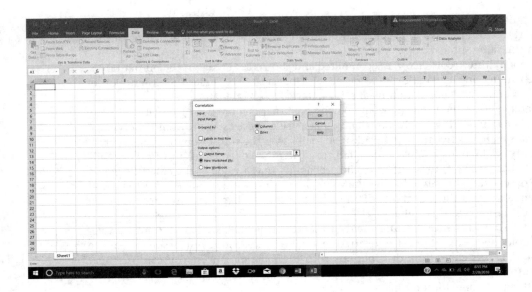

The following explanation is excerpted from the Microsoft Excel help function description:

> The CORREL and PEARSON worksheet functions both calculate the correlation coefficient between two measurement variables when measurements on each variable are observed for each of N subjects. (Any missing observation for any subject causes that subject to be ignored in the analysis.) The correlation analysis tool is particularly useful when there are more than two measurement variables for each of N subjects. It provides an output table, a correlation matrix, showing the value of CORREL (or PEARSON) applied to each possible pair of measurement variables.

See Microsoft Excel Help for further explanations of Excel's statistical analysis capabilities. There are a number of helpful websites also, such as **https://www.excel-easy .com/data-analysis/analysis-toolpak.html** in addition to various tutorial videos available on YouTube.

• Glossary •

A-B-A single subject design—a design in which there are three conditions: baseline, intervention, and return to baseline.

A-B-A-B design—a design (also called reversal design) in which there are four conditions: baseline, intervention, return to baseline, and return to intervention.

Abstract—a brief summary of the study.

Alternative causes—a threat to internal validity involving reasons for change in the dependent variable not due to effects of the independent variable.

Analysis of covariance (ANCOVA)—tests whether a variable other than the independent variable under study might account for some of the difference in, or covary with, the dependent variable.

Analysis of variance (ANOVA)—tests the null hypothesis that the means of more than two groups are equal.

Axial coding—making connections between a category and its subcategories.

Baseline—preliminary data regarding dependent variables that establishes current performance prior to the introduction of an independent variable or intervention.

Case sampling—determining who or what will be part of a research study.

Case study—a qualitative inquiry.

Categorical questions—require respondents to supply an answer from predetermined categories.

Categories—classification of similar data and/or patterns.

Causal comparative research—identifies potential cause-and-effect relationships between an independent variable (i.e., causal factor) and a dependent variable (i.e., effect factor) in targeted groups of individuals based on preexisting or extant data.

Chi-square analysis—compares the observed or actual frequency of observations or responses with an expected frequency of responses.

Closed, fixed-response interview—interview in which researcher has developed the questions and the alternative responses for the participant and the participant chooses the most suitable response.

Clustered sampling—sampling in which researcher chooses certain physical or geographical areas and identifies a certain number of units to be chosen from each area.

Code—a word, letter, number, or other symbol used in a code system to mark, represent, or identify something.

Coding—the transforming of a single data item into a more convenient alternative number or abbreviation.

Comparison group—the group in the study that does not receive the independent variable; also *control group*.

Comparison group design—a research design in which two groups matched by similar characteristics are pretested and posttested; however, only the experimental group receives the intervention.

Concept—the unit of analysis for making comparisons and asking questions.

Conceptual frameworks—the lens through which researchers view their study's purpose and outcomes.

Confirmability—whether a study's conclusions can be confirmed by outside observers or researchers.

Construct validity—the validity with which a study's results can make generalizations about constructs (i.e., data-based concepts or variables).

Control group—part of a sample in experimental research that does not receive the intervention or treatment.

Convenience sampling—sampling in which the researcher chooses the most efficient and convenient sample available.

Correlation coefficient—an index of the strength of relationships among variables.

Correlational research—describes or analyses relationships between variables, conditions, or events, any of which may be reported attitudes, beliefs, or behaviors.

Credibility—the truth value of a descriptive study that uses qualitative methods.

Criterion-referenced measurement—performance of study participants on a measure is compared to an objective standard.

Critical case sampling—sampling in which the researcher chooses the situations or participants because of their uniqueness or how important they are to the issue.

Cronbach's alpha—a statistical formula used to determine reliability based on at least two parts of a test; requires only one administration of the measure.

Curriculum-based measurement—a set of standard simple, short-duration fluency measures of reading, spelling, written expression, and mathematics computation; developed to serve as general outcome indicators measuring "vital signs" of student achievement in important areas of basic skills of literacy.

Data saturation—the point where all or most new data fits into existing categories and there is probably little to gain by continuing data collection, you have reached data saturation and can probably conclude data collection.

Degrees of freedom—numbers used in the statistical calculation of the level of significance that are approximately equal to the number of participants for which one has entered data.

Dependent variable—the variable that may change because of the independent variable; outcome, effect, or result of an intervention, measured in some way.

Descriptive research—research with the goal of describing a population or phenomenon without determining causality.

Dimensions—the locations of a property along a continuum.

Directional hypothesis—a hypothesis that implies a difference in a particular direction when two groups are compared or when a group is compared at two different points of time.

Discussion—interpretation of how a study's results are important to the field, how they fit into previous research, and what future research is necessary.

Effect size—the degree of difference between groups or conditions or the magnitude of difference in outcomes among experimental groups or experimental conditions.

Eta squared—an effect size calculation, reported as n^2, and commonly used in ANOVA calculations.

Ethnography—a branch of anthropology dealing with the scientific description of individual cultures.

Event-based observations—involve identifying a behavior, counting the number of times it occurs, and keeping a tally.

Event-sampling observation—helpful for determining the exact number of times a behavior occurs during a predetermined period of time.

Experimental designs—typically include these key characteristics: (a) selection of experimental participants, (b) direct manipulation of an independent variable, (c) control of extraneous variables, and (d) measurement of outcomes.

Experimental group—the group in a study that receives the independent variable.

Experimental research—research with the goal of identifying cause-and-effect relationships.

Extant database—an existing database that includes data collected by others.

External reliability—the extent to which a researcher could replicate the study in other settings.

External validity—the extent to which an observed relationship among variables can be generalized beyond the conditions of the investigation to other populations, settings, and conditions.

Extreme case sampling—researcher chooses cases that are extreme or dramatically different from the norm in some way; also called *deviant sampling*.

Factorial group design—a design in which more than one independent variable is analyzed in experimental research.

Fidelity—other researchers can do the same study similarly and to the same extent.

Fidelity of treatment implementation—ensuring that the treatment or independent variable is put into place adequately and equally by all involved in the study.

Field notes—include information about what a researcher has observed in the field.

Focus group—a group of individuals with characteristics similar to those under study who give ideas about concepts important to a study.

Formal observations—researchers identify and record (quantitatively) a discrete target behavior.

Frequency tables—provide researcher and the reader with information about how often a certain response occurred or the percentage of responses that this frequency indicates.

***F* statistic**—statistical value, used in obtaining the level of significance of an analysis, is the ratio of between-groups variance to within-groups variance.

Generalizable—a study is generalizable if its results can be applied to the population.

Going native—the possibility that the researcher gets too close to the situation or becomes biased in presentation because of the relationships developed. A study thus loses its credibility and becomes a statement of opinion that is not valued in the research community.

Grounded theory—over time, a grounded theory study works through the following, mostly overlapping phases: data collection, note taking, coding, and memoing.

Group differences—a threat to internal validity that occurs when the experimental and control groups are not equivalent in terms of important variables or characteristics.

Histograms—illustrate the relationship between two variables whose measures yield interval or ratio data or continuous scores.

History—a threat to internal validity that occurs when something unrelated to the independent variable impacts the dependent variable during the study.

Hypothesis—a brief statement expressing a possible answer to a research question.

Independent variable—the variable that is manipulated and controlled by the researcher in the hope of causing an effect; sometimes referred to as *intervention* or *treatment*.

Inferential statistics—used to reach conclusions that extend beyond the immediate data.

Informal conversational interview—interview that often occurs within the setting being observed; researcher engages participant in conversation about the situation and asks questions about specific events, interactions, or perceptions relevant to the situation.

Informal observations—researchers typically utilize anecdotal records and field notes that provide loosely structured, informal ways of recording observations.

Intensity sampling—researcher chooses settings or participants where the unit of study occurs most often.

Interaction effects—the interrelated effects of the two independent variables on the dependent variable.

Internal reliability—the degree to which the study would be carried out the same way if conducted under the same conditions.

Internal validity—the approximate validity with which we infer that a relationship between two variables is causal or absence of a relationship implies absence of cause.

Interobserver agreement—the degree to which two independent observers record observational data of the same situation similarly.

Interval data—are numeric and have equal intervals between values but do not have to contain a zero value.

Intervening conditions—contextual variables that that may affect conditions in the study.

Interview guide approach—interview in which researcher has a general guide outlining types of questions to ask but specifics about wording and elaboration are not included.

Intraobserver agreement—the degree to which an observer records similar data about the same observation or test on two occasions.

Introduction—section of research report that places study in the context of questions in the field.

Level—determined by computing the mean score for data points and drawing a straight horizontal line to represent the mean score within each condition.

Levels—different types of a variable, such as differing grade levels, when grade level is an independent variable.

Level of significance—the probability that the statistical differences in an analysis are due to chance or measurement error.

Likert scale—participants respond to statements with varying degrees of agreement or disagreement.

Linear numeric scale—items are judged on a single dimension and arrayed on a scale with equal intervals.

Literature search—the process of searching existing research on a topic to understand the state of current research and determine one's own research focus.

Low statistical power—a low likelihood that a statistical test will find significant differences due, for example, to small sample size.

Main effects—the effects of each independent variable on or its relationship to the dependent variable.

Maturation—a threat to internal validity that occurs when participants' knowledge, as measured by a dependent variable, changes due to getting older and gaining greater experience.

Measurement issues—a threat to internal validity that occurs when the frequency and practice of assessment and/or the assessment devices used affect the dependent variable.

Member checking—the participants in the study review the hypotheses, patterns, characteristics, analysis, interpretations, and conclusions of the researcher.

Memos—the most basic way to annotate data; as though working with small electronic sticky notes, the researcher can attach memos to all sorts of data bits.

Meta-analysis—literature review that includes statistical analysis of results in reviewed research reports.

Method—section of a research report that describes the research process in detail.

Method notes—notes that identify and help defend methodological choices in a research study.

Mixed methods research—employs experimental and descriptive designs, or more than one type of descriptive research design.

Multicase study—more than one case study occurs at the same time.

Multisite study—more than one site is used for the case study.

Multiple-baseline design—a design in which the intervention begins at different points in time for two or more participants.

Multiple regression—a statistical procedure that enables one to correlate multiple variables at a time.

Multivariate analysis of variance (MANOVA)—analysis of variance used when a study involves more than one dependent variable.

Negative case analysis—analysis of cases that show nonoccurrence of a phenomenon.

Nominal data—are arranged by unordered, categorical groups.

Nonresponse—occurs for at least three reasons: (a) participants are not given a chance to respond (i.e., not chosen), (b) participants are given a chance and refuse to participate, and (c) participants are given a chance to respond and cannot.

Norm-referenced measurement—performance of study participants on a measure is compared to the average performance of others.

Null hypothesis—a statement signifying that one expects no differences in outcomes or no relationships between the given variables in one's hypothesis.

Open coding—comparing one incident with another as research goes along so that similar phenomena can be given the same name.

Ordinal data—place responses in a certain order or rank, but this order does not have equal intervals between items.

Parallel forms reliability—the degree to which a person's score is similar when the person is given two forms of the same test.

Participant—a person from whom a researcher collects data.

Patterns—recurring items in the data.

Pearson product-moment coefficient—the Pearson r is used when examining relationships between variables that yield continuous scores (i.e., interval or ratio types of data).

Peer debriefing—reviewing data, data analysis, and interpretations with a peer who can provide feedback and question one's methods.

Persistent observation—conducting observations of phenomena until categories or patterns are saturated or complete; observing until new occurrences of phenomena are infrequent or nonexistent.

Phenomenon—the term for *research problem* in qualitative research; the topic one would like to address, investigate, or study.

Population—a group with identifying characteristics; the larger group of people to whom researchers wish to generalize, apply, or relate the results of their research.

Post hoc statistical test—analysis of data for patterns not defined before the research took place.

Posttest-only group design—a design in which participants are selected, introduced to the intervention, and then observed for some behavior or have their performance measured in some way of interest.

Pretest-posttest group design—a design in which participants are identified, pretested, given an intervention, and posttested through observation or some other measurement; the posttest performance can be compared to that measured by the pretest.

Primary sources—original literature pieces written by other authors that one cites in a research paper.

Prolonged engagement—conducting a study until evidence of the phenomenon studied is saturated or complete.

Properties—the characteristics or attributes of a category.

Qualitative methods—methods often used in descriptive research; researchers analyse language, written or oral, and actions to determine patterns, themes, or theories in order to provide insight into what is happening in certain situations.

Quantitative—research in which the researcher assigns numbers to variables or levels of variables being studied for purposes of statistical analysis.

Quantitative methods—methods often used in both experimental and quasi-experimental as well as descriptive research; involve assigning numbers to sequential levels of variables being studied for purposes of statistical analysis.

Quasi-experimental research—research in which random assignment is problematic or impossible but, like experimental research, attempts to determine if an independent variable has a direct impact on a dependent variable.

Random assignment of participants—participants in study have an equal chance of being selected.

Random sampling—researcher obtains a sample from a population in which every possible sample has the same chance of being selected for the study.

Ratio data—have the characteristics of interval data, but the equal intervals are also related by ratios.

Recruiting—process by which a researcher targets, informs, and secures the commitment of participants to be included in a research study.

Reliability—study occurs similarly across students and time.

Reliability coefficient—statistic indicating the relationship between multiple administrations, multiple items, or other analyses of evaluation measures.

Replication—the repetition of a study design with similar results.

Representative sample—a sample group that has characteristics similar to those of the population so that results of the experiment can be considered generalizable to the population.

Research—a broad term that usually means the systematic and rigorous process of posing a focused question, developing a hypothesis or focus, testing the hypothesis or focus by collecting and analyzing relevant data, and drawing conclusions.

Research hypothesis—a declarative statement of how one expects the research to turn out.

Research problem—the topic one would like to address, investigate, or study, whether descriptively or experimentally.

Research proposal—a written rationale and plan for conducting research, usually created by a researcher prior to conducting formal research.

Research question—a way of expressing one's interest in a problem or phenomenon.

Results—section of the research report that details the discoveries found in data collected.

Return rate—proportion of surveyed sample who returns responses.

Sample—participants included in the study.

Sample characteristics—a threat to external validity that involves a sample with characteristics different than those of the population to which the researcher wishes to generalize.

Sampling—the selection of participants for a study.

Scales—allow the researcher to organize and analyze data using statistics in order to compare responses across questions.

Scatter plot—a graph that includes plotted points representing correlation scores.

Science—an approach to the development of a consistent, documented system of knowledge, based on rigorous, systematic observations that lead to hypotheses or theories that are then tested and refined in an iterative process.

Secondary sources—sources that one cites that have already been cited by another author.

Selective coding—integration of all data by choosing a core category and relating each category to it.

Setting characteristics—a threat to external validity that includes resources and situations used by the researcher that are not present in the situation to which the research wishes to generalize.

Significance—the notion that differences between two groups or conditions are not due simply to chance.

Single-subject design—attempts to capture the effects of an intervention on individuals rather than pooling individual differences as in group designs; also known as *single-case design*.

Soloman four-group design—a design that controls for possible pretest sensitization and looks at possible interactions of pretest and experimental conditions by adding two additional groups that do not receive the pretest.

Spearman rho—statistic typically used to evaluate the relationship between variables that are rank or rating scores (i.e., ordinal data) such as one might find on a survey item with a scale of *strongly agree* to *strongly disagree*.

Split-half reliability—the degree to which a study participant receives a similar score on one half of the test items as compared to the other half; requires only one administration of the measure.

Standardized, open-ended interview—interview in which researcher has predetermined the questions but the responses can vary by participant.

Statistical conclusion validity—the validity with which a study's conclusions about covariation are appropriate, given the statistical tests used.

Statistical power—the odds one will observe a treatment effect when one occurs.

Statistical test assumption—basic situations that must be in place for a statistical test to be appropriate.

Statistically significant—the change in a variable is greater than the predicted change due to chance.

Stratified sampling—sampling in which the researcher creates subgroups in order to guarantee their representation in a sample.

Structured responses—include options for answers to questions.

Subcategories—smaller divisions of data that share common characteristics within a larger category.

Survey methods—the use of interviews or completion of questionnaires that yield data from respondents.

Survey research—research in which a researcher asks a sample group questions.

Symbolic interactionism—a conceptual framework consisting of three main premises: (1) human beings act toward things on the basis of the meanings that the things have for them, and such things include everything that the human being may note in this world; (2) the meaning of such things is derived from, or arises out of, the social interaction that one has with one's fellows; and (3) these meanings are handled in, and modified through, an interpretative process one uses in dealing with the things one encounters.

Test-retest reliability—the degree to which a study participant achieves a similar score on an assessment measure when the entire measure is administered once and then is administered again.

Themes—common concepts in qualitative research that emerge from several categories of multiple data sources over the life of a qualitative study.

Theoretical sampling—sampling on the basis of concepts that have proven theoretical relevance to the evolving theory.

Theoretical sensitivity—the insight and understanding of the topic of interest that the researcher brings to the study; the experience, philosophical disposition, and conceptual framework that a researcher uses as a lens through which to analyze interview, observation, and document data.

Threats to validity—variables that could reduce the validity of a study.

Time-based observations—involve keeping track of the duration of a particular behavior.

Time-sampling observation—helpful for determining the extent or duration of a behavior during a predetermined period of time.

Time-series group design—a design in which (1) a group of participants is observed or administered some form of measurement at multiple given intervals to establish a valid baseline effect, (2) an intervention is introduced, and (3) participants are observed or administered the same form of measurement at multiple given intervals to see if there has been a change in behavior or performance.

Tradition—scholarly approach whose conceptual underpinnings inform qualitative research; also called *domain*.

Treatment—the intervention; the conditions created by the researcher to produce a result.

Treatment characteristics—a threat to external validity that occurs when a treatment method or condition cannot be replicated with the population to which the researcher wishes to generalize.

Treatment fidelity—fidelity with which the treatment or intervention is implemented throughout the study; also called *fidelity to implementation, implementation fidelity*, and *intervention fidelity*.

Trend—determined by computing the slope of the best-fitting straight line for the data within each condition.

Triangulate—verify conclusions through the use of multiple methods (e.g., observation and interview).

Trustworthiness—how a researcher can persuade readers that the study is worthwhile and credible.

t **test.** The *t* test is used to test the null hypothesis that the mean scores of two groups are the same.

Two-way ANOVA—an analysis of variance used when a study involves two independent variables.

Type II error—researcher fails to reject the null hypothesis even when it is false.

Typical case sampling—researcher examines the most often occurring situation or participant to give a representative description.

Unit of analysis—the focus of the data analysis in a research study, for example, whether it is on individual performance, class performance, or school performance in a study.

Unstructured responses—responses that are open-ended and require respondents to give the answers that they feel are appropriate.

Validity—the best available approximation to the truth or falsity of propositions in a study.

Variability—most easily determined by identifying the range of data points and drawing straight lines within each condition on the graph representing the upper and lower ends of the data range.

Variables—the changeable parts of studies that researchers may want to manipulate; sometimes called *factors*.

Verbal frequency scale—the respondent is asked to rate how often something occurs along a continuum.

Working plan—a guide with which a researcher begins an inquiry that is relatively general in nature and is not prescriptive; also called *working design* or *emergent design*.

• Index •

• About the Author •

Daniel J. Boudah is a Professor in the Department of Special Education, Research & Foundations, and a former departmental Director of Graduate Studies at East Carolina University. Dr. Boudah previously taught general education and special education in public schools. He has been awarded federal and other grants and carried out school-based research in the areas of teacher planning and inquiry, learning strategies, content enhancement, systems change, and collaborative instruction. He has published work in professional journals, textbooks, newsletters, and teacher-training materials. Dr. Boudah has spoken at numerous national, international, and state conferences. He has received awards for excellence from several organizations in the field of education. Dr. Boudah has conducted many professional development, curriculum design, program evaluation, grant and foundation proposal development, and system change activities with public and private schools, as well as public and private agencies, to develop and support services to low-performing and at-risk students. He is a past president of the Council for Learning Disabilities. Dr. Boudah's continuing professional interests include programs and services for low-performing students and students with disabilities, learning and instructional strategies, dropout prevention, and systems change. Dr. Boudah can be reached at boudahd@ecu.edu